LF

The Paper House

Other books by Françoise Mallet-Joris

The Illusionist/The Red Room

House of Lies/Café Celeste

The Favourite/A Letter to Myself

Cordelia/The Uncompromising Heart

Signs and Wonders/The Witches

Françoise Mallet-Joris

The Paper House

Translated by Derek Coltman

Farrar, Straus & Giroux

NEW YORK

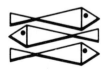

ALBRIGHT COLLEGE LIBRARY

Copyright © 1971 by Françoise Mallet-Joris

Published in French under the title La Maison de Papier

Copyright © 1970 by Editions Bernard Grasset

Library of Congress catalog card number: 70–148707

SBN 374.2.2978.3

All rights reserved

Published simultaneously in Canada

by Doubleday Canada Ltd., Toronto

Printed in the United States of America

First printing, 1971

Designed by Cynthia Krupat

843.91
M 253 p

165646

6.95

"It doesn't matter about being sensible

as long as you're serious," my father once said.

And to him

I tenderly dedicate this book.

Vincent and Me

Vincent (eleven): You know, Mother, for the world to be perfect . . .

Me: Yes?

Vincent: First you'd have to get rid of all the mosquitoes.

Me: Goodness!

Vincent: And all the adders too.

Me: Why?

Vincent: Because they make it difficult for the grass snakes. People get them confused, so that when they see a grass snake they say: Oh, look at that nasty, poisonous thing! It's very irritating. But if we had no snakes at all except grass snakes, then when people came across them they would know they don't bite, so they'd say: Oh, look at that beautiful snake, and it would be very happy. If I could make the world over . . .

Me: Do you think it was so badly made, then?

Vincent: No. But then I'm very easy to please.

Me: What else would you get rid of?

Vincent: As far as animals are concerned, not very much. I mean, I'd keep the lions, and the crocodiles . . .

Me: Would you? Really?

Vincent: Oh, yes. For the sake of the explorers. They wouldn't be very happy if exploring was made too easy. It wouldn't be an adventure any more.

Me: No, of course not.

Vincent: No, it's more when it comes to people, you know, that you'd have to . . . *[a mowing-down gesture].* Those, yes.

Me: What kind of people?

Vincent: Well, you'd have to put them into categories first. The ones who start wars, and revolutions, and the wicked ones too . . .

Me: Aren't they the same?

Vincent: Not necessarily. And then the gobblers . . .

Me: Who are they? The gobblers?

Vincent: The ones who want to gobble everything up even when they're not really hungry. But especially the ones that start wars, of course. Outside and inside. I mean inside families.

Me: Do you think we can stop them altogether?

Vincent: We can try. There'd have to be an eye.

Me: An eye?

Vincent: Yes. An eye in every house. When it saw that someone was beginning to quarrel, then the eye would put on some music, to tell them they must stop.

Me: And what if they didn't stop?

Vincent: There would have to be a Master of the Eyes. He would be warned by electronic signals, then he'd send them very kind policemen who would reason with them.

Me: Do you think they exist?

Vincent: What?

Me: Very kind policemen?

Vincent: They'd be trained to be. Scientifically.

Me: But don't you think all that would be contrary to freedom of conscience?

Vincent: Being free to argue, you mean?

Me: Yes.

Vincent: Maybe. But there could be an eye all the same. Blue. *[Pause.]* You know the game: "If I had the money to buy everything I wanted . . ."

Me: Yes, what would you buy?

Vincent: Everything! But actually I can make it so that I almost can, anyhow.

Me: Oh? How?

Vincent: I say to myself: I can buy everything. But I'm not in a hurry. So I won't buy anything just yet. Which comes to the same thing.

Me: Well, almost.

Vincent: I'd like to be there for the Resurrection, too.

Me: Oh, would you?

Vincent: There are some questions I'd like to ask certain people.

Me: For example?

Vincent: Gérard de Nerval. I could ask him what he meant exactly in that poem of his you couldn't explain to me: *Am I Love or Phoebus* . . . But perhaps he'd rather not be resurrected, in case people do start asking him questions like that.

Me: Perhaps.

Vincent: Perhaps he'd like to be resurrected so that he can be a greengrocer, something different.

I'd like to ask a prehistoric man some things too. I'd like to ask him if they were really magic, those drawings of bisons, the ones in the caves . . . I'd like to make him appear here and then ask him. No, perhaps not here, because he'd be afraid of the cars. Out in a field, so he'd feel more at home. And I'd have him interviewed by men dressed in animal skins, just like him. Only we'd have to be careful not to pick weedy ones.

I wonder whether a prehistoric man, once he'd seen the world of today—you know, the cars, the television, all those things—whether he'd rather live in our times or go back to his caves. The diplodocus and the plesiosaurus weren't funny, I know. But cars, and nighttime, and cancer, they're not funny, either.

Me: What would you advise him to do?

Vincent: Ultimately, you know, I think I'd advise him to go back to the diplodocus. Only I'd slip him a box of matches, just in case he hadn't discovered fire yet, and perhaps a flute too.

Me: But that would upset the whole history of the world.

Vincent: Do you think so?

Me: If he hasn't discovered fire yet, and you go and give him a box of matches, then you're making him jump years and years of thinking, do you see? It might be better to let him discover it on his own.

Vincent: Yes, but he'd be very cold all that time till it was discovered.

Me: Yes, I'm afraid so.

Vincent: Perhaps if he was really cold, he wouldn't give a damn whether it was him that discovered it or not.

Me: Perhaps.

Vincent: Perhaps—well, I don't want to criticize, but perhaps God could have given it to him from the start. Fire, I mean. The flute—well, that's different, though in the evening, living like that, with no electricity, it would be nice to have a little music. But fire! When you think that there were men who *never* knew it. Do you realize what that means? It makes me cold all over just thinking about it.

Me: There are still a lot of people who don't have any of the things we have, you know.

Vincent: Yes, but they know they exist.

Me: Do you think that's any consolation?

Vincent: I don't know. It does mean they could have said to themselves, those prehistoric men, they could have said: One day there will be fire . . .

Me: But then they wouldn't have had to invent it.

Vincent: Are we put on earth to invent things?

Me: In a way, yes.

Vincent: Let's talk about it again another time.

Two Remarks I'm Always Hearing

Who is Vincent? He is fourteen now, but to me he is still a little boy. My little boy. My second son. The first is Daniel, twenty this year. Then there's Alberte, who's eleven, and Pauline, nine. My children.

I think the remark I hear most often is: "I do admire you, the way you manage to write with four children," or "How ever do you find time to write?" And the people who ask me that question are generally the people who in the next breath ask me to lecture in Angoulême, to read a book one of their cousins has written, or to write an article about Mme de La Fayette or Flaubert's life that will "only take a moment."

How do I find time to write? I never know what to answer. I just say flatly: "It's a question of organization." What do they expect me to say?

The second most frequent comment, tinged sometimes with a certain sporting admiration, sometimes with a note of ironic indulgence, is: "It must be so convenient having a faith," or "I do so admire you for . . ." or "You're so lucky to have . . ."

Again, I never know what to answer. I say flatly: "Not so convenient as all that." Then I am filled with remorse and add: "Well, yes, convenient in a sense, of course."

I don't know how to answer questions. Or rather, the only way I can answer questions is with pictures. I look at my children, my work, my faith. I say to myself: "There they are," the way one stands in front of a looking glass and says: "There's my face." Let others do the defining. Definitions are just not my cup of tea.

The day Vincent and I had that conversation (I noted it down at the time because it amused me), we had gone out for tea in the English Pub near Saint-Sévérin, which has such good lemon tarts. It wasn't a reward for Vincent: he certainly hadn't done anything to earn such a treat. It was quite simply that we felt we wanted to talk. Vincent at the age of eleven: lazy at school, obstreperous, disobedient, always risking his neck on the scaffoldings of buildings, so sensitive he would dissolve in tears at the slightest reproach, an impenitent handyman eternally covered in glue and paint, a voracious consumer of natural-history books and Arsène Lupin; sometimes a little pedantic, filthy as anything, the most beautiful eyes in the world, and a smattering of theology. I can't define him, either.

The moment when he informed me that he wanted to talk to me, when he suggested that "we go for a cup of something somewhere so that we can talk in peace," was one of the red-letter points in my life, one of that sequence of moments that form the current of our lives, running in counterpoint through all the manuscripts gone over, all the dishes washed, the thread of what really counts, even though it does not always seem the most important thing at the time. The day when Alberte played the piano for the first time in public, and the day she picked up a little boy on the way home from nursery school; the day when Pauline said for the first time: "I'm dining out tonight" (she was five) and the day she won a prize for spelling—she was wearing a new pinafore that day, and with such an air of the well-brought-up child! Daniel's first poem and the first time he went out drinking, and the day he bought his saxophone and we all stood there frozen with wonder, gazing at the glittering instrument in its crushed-velvet bed, and the day he said to me, as he lay in his bath, a cigarette balanced on one rim, a half-eaten piece of cake in the soap dish: "Last night I had the most fabulous dream. I had just been on a very important, very dangerous mission, and everyone was cheering as I came home, and the most fantastic girl was waiting to marry me." And shining in his eyes, which are big and green, was all the simple youth of the world, the youth of songs and poems, the youth that has always plunged in with such joy right from the days of the Crusades.

All those moments undoubtedly were linked with the joy of writing. With the joy of faith. Others are linked with the pain of faith, the pain of writing. They are all part of a whole. But is that "whole" the answer to the two remarks I mentioned?

That evening I said to Jacques: "You ought to paint us. Do a big picture with the whole family in it. Us, and the children, and the animals, and Dolores. All painters do it. *Selbs-bildnis.* Artist and family."

"Yes," he mumbled, chewing his pipe. "The trouble is, I'm not doing anything figurative at the moment."

"All right, all right, I might have known. I always end up doing all the chores . . ."

"What hypocrisy!"

So I'm going to paint a picture. Are pictures a good answer to questions?

Pauline

Pauline: Do you love Papa?
Me: Yes.
Pauline: For always?
Me: Of course.
Pauline: How can you be sure?
Me: . . .
Pauline: Perhaps you'll suddenly say to yourself: His nose is too big!
Me: But I don't love your father because of his nose!
Pauline: I do. I'm crazy about his nose. But perhaps I'll go off it one day.
Me: And what will you do then?
Pauline: Oh, poor Papa! I shall pretend.

Dolores

Dolores has been with us for four years. Four years punctuated by storms and interregnums with various other maids.
Dolores: You mustn't say Dolorès, the way they do in France.

You must say Dolores. It means "griefs"; it's the most beautiful name of all.

Me: Ah!

Dolores: But it's too sad, so everyone calls me Lolo. That's more with it, more show-biz, sort of.

Me: Dolores, I'm having a bath.

Dolores: Oh, that's all right. It doesn't bother me.

[She settles down on a stool, turning her back to me as a concession to civilized values and my modesty.]

Dolores: Cigarette?

Me: Yes, please.

[She lights two cigarettes and hands me one. The chaos in the bathroom is epic in scale. Through the faded "stained glass" of the window, the entire building opposite can observe me without let or hindrance. The panes were painted twelve years ago, before our marriage, in the days when Jacques was nursing our budding love with fine promises. Those were the days when I still cherished the illusion that Jacques, a champion do-it-yourselfer, was going to build me a world worthy of *House & Garden.*]

Dolores: While you have your bath, I'll rest for five minutes.

[I don't like to tell her that my reason for taking a bath was precisely to get five minutes' rest for myself.]

Dolores: Yesterday I did a pile of washing as tall as a man. One thing all children know without being told is how to get dirty! Then in the evening I went out to a java! Today I have nothing to do, so I feel depressed. In my family we don't like to stop.

Me: All the same, it's nice to stop now and then.

Dolores: Ah? So, and when do you stop?

Me: Well . . . I try to.

Dolores: Pah! Even in your bath you read!

Me: It's not the same.

Dolores: It's exactly the same! When I'm rushing around, that's as if I was thinking. Now last night I didn't even get to bed, and it did me good. We went from café to café, we talked and talked with other Spaniards.

Me: Do you never go out with anyone but Spaniards?

Dolores: Spaniards or Moroccans. We understand one another, so why change just to change? Now Cristina, she goes out only with Portuguese. That way at least she knows what nationality her son is, even if she doesn't know who the father is.

Meanwhile, the bathroom has been filling up with a crowd of circumspect visitors. Juanito, Dolores's three-year-old son, is playing on the floor with the dog's leash, for which we'll soon be hunting everywhere in vain. Pauline is exploring my toilette things and dusting herself all over with talcum powder. Alberte is listening avidly to our conversation. The dog and Taxi the cat are sparring affectionately.

Alberte (with lively interest): She doesn't know who is whose father?

[Dolores switches without warning from a low-pitched, restrained tone to a stratospherically high bellow—a typically Spanish noise. She is shrieking at the top of her voice, yet no trace of animation disturbs that noble Roman face.]

Dolores: Will you let your mother have some peace, you little monkeys!

[The marketplace empties abruptly. The dog hurtles toward the door, bumps into Pauline, and leaves her sprawled under a scented cloud of talc. Tears. Alberte retreats outside the door, ears pricked. Juanito grabs the cat.]

Dolores (lighting another cigarette): Oh, those children! But they must at least be taught how to behave, mustn't they? Was Juan good last night?

[When Dolores wants to "go to a java," I am entrusted with her Juan, a beautiful, serious, somewhat glum baby, possessor of a wholly Spanish dignity, who curls up resignedly between Pauline and Alberte in a hollow of their mattress, and there without complaint accepts their passionate embraces.]

Me: Oh, very good!

Pauline (in a shrill voice; having by some miracle reappeared, albeit white from head to toe): No, he wasn't. He wasn't good at all. I said to him, "Go to sleep, my precious," and I sang him a lullaby, and he just yelled all the louder, and then Alberte pinched me.

Alberte (from outside the door): She was singing right in his ear!

Pauline (sobbing with rage): No! No! That's not true, that's not true!

Me (feebly conciliatory): Perhaps he doesn't like music.

Dolores (outraged): Juanito? My Juanito not like music? You shall see for yourselves!

[With a deft backhand she removes the cat from her off-spring's arms—interrupting his patient attempts to stuff it inside a plastic bag—plants Juanito on his feet in front of her, emits an abrupt "Olé!", then begins chanting a wild Spanish melody at him. Obediently the child snaps his fingers and jumps up and down, without for a moment forfeiting one jot of its inborn gravity. Dolores contemplates him for a moment with deep delight, snatches him up, covers him with kisses, sucks his cheek, and then, realizing that he is very wet, drops him back where he came from without missing a beat.]

Dolores: Oh, my little love, oh, what a horror!

[Juanito hits the floor like a cushion, snatches at the cat while still on the rebound, and resumes his attempts to push it into the plastic bag, which I recognize that instant as the one I keep my sponge in.]

Me: Dolores! That's my sponge bag!

Dolores (firmly): Your sponge is lost anyway. Now, what were we saying? Ah, yes, Cristina. She's a disgrace to Spain.

Me: Because of all the Portuguese?

Dolores: Oh, no. I don't mind that so much . . . She's a bit simple, you know, so she doesn't really notice any difference. She can't read or write.

Me: I suppose that is an explanation.

Dolores: But it doesn't excuse everything. Honesty, that's something you can't learn. It's in the blood, like dancing. And Cristina isn't honest.

Me: Really?

Dolores: No. She even steals her boyfriends. And she doesn't know how to accept things. Give her a present and she gets terribly upset. But stealing, oh yes. It leaves her free. I laughed so much the day she discovered she was pregnant. I said to her: "Well, this is one present you can't refuse, isn't it?"

[A silvery laugh from Alberte outside the door. Dolores leaps over and yanks the door open.]

Dolores: You horrid little beast! You were spying on us! Listening at keyholes! I'll cut off your ears for you! I won't give you any lunch! I . . .

Alberte (icy, scornful, a little pale, but determined to face out the storm): You have no choice in the matter *[knowing perfectly well what she's letting herself in for]*.

Dolores (exploding with fury): What do you mean, I have no choice? Do you know what Spanish girls earn these days in Marseilles? Do you? One hundred thousand francs, and more, *and* they have their weekends free, *and* they have television! If I stay here, it's only for your poor mother's sake!

Alberte (refusing to budge an inch): All the same, you have no choice but to feed me.

Dolores (beside herself with rage): I have every choice! I can do whatever I like! Tell me then, just tell me why I have no choice!

Alberte (with great dignity): Because I am a child.

[Stunned for a moment by this argument, the cogency of which has quite pulled the carpet out from under her, Dolores suddenly drops her anger as though it were a mask and bursts out laughing.]

Dolores (taking me as her witness): What a little love she is, isn't she?

[She hugs Alberte and covers her with kisses. Alberte lets her have her way, unmoved, like a boxer accepting the tiresome but inevitable ovation of the crowd after he's won by a knockout. The cat is suffocating inside the plastic bag. Juan is now attempting to sit on it.]

Dolores (with a fond look): Look at them. Don't they look sweet together?

Me: I think the cat is going to suffocate.

Dolores: Of course it's not, don't be silly . . . There, I'll let it out. Always the same, always getting worked up about everyone and everything! *[Then, on a sudden impulse]* Next month, when you pay me, I'll buy you a new sponge out of my wages!

Me: Thank you, Dolores.

[I emerge from my bath before the now-reassembled mob, having given up all idea of finding shelter against life's vicissitudes in the depths of a tub.]

In Frankfurt once, during her wanderings in the wilderness, Dolores bought two pantie girdles—purely out of love of beauty, since she loathes wearing a corset of any kind. These pantie girdles are black with fluttering pink butterflies all over them. In a moment of generosity she cried: "Here, you can have them; I've never worn them. They'll look even prettier on a blonde." So I wear them.

Marseilles

"The Spanish maids in Marseilles," Dolores informs me, "have television and hot water in their rooms. They can have people in, they can entertain."

"But you entertain, Dolores . . ."

"Yes, but who? Two or three very close friends two or three times a week. And I have to borrow the silver dish from you every time. If I were in Marseilles I'd have my own silver. I'd have a folding table, I'd have napkins with flowers on them, I'd have a studio couch in red-and-black leather with a doll on it. And I'd have a real picture on the wall."

"What's a real picture, Dolores?"

"A picture like the one I brought back from Mont-Saint-Michel," Dolores replies. "It's not that I want to criticize what your husband does. When I don't understand, I don't judge. What your husband does may be painting, but they're not pictures."

Anita, Cristina, Concha . . . There are several Spanish girls I run into in my apartment, though I don't know them well, and in a flat with only three rooms it can sometimes be embarrassing (though they are very polite and do everything they can to make me feel at home when I walk through one of the rooms in my slip).

I go looking for my sweater and find four or five of the girls in the bathroom; when I walk through the kitchen I trip over them having their tea with babies bouncing on their knees. They offer me petit-beurres. Anita, Cristina, Conchita, they all cherish the same myth, the same dream: the Spanish maids in Marseilles. The Spanish maids in Marseilles are free from five in the afternoon on and can spend the early evening out window shopping in their satin dresses. Beside their beds they have electric kettles, so they can have coffee in bed in the morning. (One of Lola's cousins even had a machine that could be set to any hour and woke her up with the coffee already made and piping hot. Lola, always honest, though, admits that the family she worked for was American. The American families in Marseilles represent the summit, the pinnacle, the supreme recompense of a girl's career, the Spanish maid's Nobel Prize.) The Spanish maids in Marseilles also have post-office savings accounts, for the simple reason that they earn more than they can spend. They go swimming in summer, they go on picnics, they go to dances that are much more fun than anything in Paris because the band plays paso dobles. And, what's more, they are the belles of the ball, because in Marseilles the men like beautiful women, not like Paris with its miniskirts. Lola, Anita, and Teresa are unanimous in their condemnation of the miniskirt. They are sticklers about that sort of thing. The miniskirt is indecent and, moreover, not at all becoming. What finer sight than a beautiful, springy-waisted Spanish girl, her haunches molded in fine satin above tiers of ruffled flounces? Dolores, more modern in outlook, has bought a polka-dot dress that ends halfway down her thighs. One of her Moroccan boyfriends, a house painter, called her a whore when he saw her in it. "Isn't that just like a man?" was her comment. "As soon as a woman takes a bit of interest in progress . . . He's a reactionary!" Ah, what can the Spanish maids in Marseilles not do! They have the best cinema programs, really beautiful Spanish or Mexican films; the ladies they work for take them to the bullfights in Bayonne; the pork butchers sell paella ready-made. Is it surprising, then, with all these conveniences at their disposal, with all the friends they are bound to make, that they have so little difficulty finding fathers for their children?

"Ah! So they do . . ."

In Paris, of course, such accidents are not infrequent, but I had assumed that in Marseilles . . .

"Oh, really!" Dolores exclaims. "After all, they are only women, aren't they, just like you and me?"

What must life be like for writers down there in Marseilles? I can't help musing on it. Dolores would be only too glad to let me have a share in the dream, too, but the fact is that neither of us knows what it would be like for writers.

Daniel and Poetry

Every year, in early July, we arrive in Normandy to the sound of many clanging saucepans, since our hope of seeing those utensils duplicate themselves by the well-known (scientifically observed) mystic phenomenon termed "bilocation" still remains unrealized—see further under CURTAINS. We have brought our favorite books, our musical instruments, the cat, the dog, twelve dolls without a stitch of clothing, and some paprika, but we have somehow managed to forget the forks and the raincoats. Never mind. When Jacques and I are tired of eating everything with spoons, we'll make a dash for home, abandoning our children in the green meadows, and return with sensual pleasure to the city's asphalt, rush into the first cinema we see, then into the first restaurant (suffering from intense guilt feelings, meanwhile), and finally get back to Gué-de-la-Chaîne late at night with both forks and raincoats— all except for Pauline's, which was, Dolores then informs us, in the coat closet, an eventuality we could scarcely have foreseen. Daniel is waiting for us, and the sight of his satisfied albeit grave expression tells us that the happy event has taken place: he has written his annual poem about the country. This poem is a sacred and ritual act that Daniel is spurred on to perform once a year by the sharp wind of the Perche hills. Once and once only, however: the rite is never repeated until the following year.

"Shall I read it to you?"

"Yes, please do."

Cheeks a little red, hands a little shaky, Daniel reads out his poem. So as to emphasize its ritual character, he always begins the poem with the same words: "In the morning when I wake . . ." and goes on to describe the beauties of nature and the wonder they inspire after a year spent at school. It praises the purity of the air, the curve and volume of the hills, the charms of solitude, the song of the birds. Occasionally a more realistic stroke (an allusion to the regular, recurring sound of cow pats splattering) or a more practical note (a denunciation of the crimes being perpetrated by crows in a newly sown field; a parenthesis on the art of milking) betrays a stirring of the writer's Flemish ancestry.

The verse is irregular in form, with assonances rather than true rhymes. Daniel was very uneasy about this for a long while.

"You're sure it's still a real poem?"

"Absolutely sure."

"But are there other people who've written poems like that?"

I provide him with references: Apollinaire, O. de Lubicz-Milosz. Daniel is satisfied. He perceives that he has indeed written a "real" poem, a poem corresponding to a given set of rules. He likes the idea that his act, over and beyond its lyric content, should also have social reverberations. He is not merely writing a poem, he is also *laying* a poem. And I too like this concept of poetry very much, as well as the lack of literary pretension indicated by the fact that Daniel will write nothing else all year long. Echoing Talleyrand, he says: "I don't see the need for it." I see in his attitude a sense of the sacred, a complete disinterestedness, an idea of the true importance and weight of poetry; a taste for contemplation, and a noble scorn for the exploitation of a gift. And thinking how I myself spent every day seeking and turning and patching with words, I even would feel a little humble when faced with Daniel's annual poem. He stopped writing it the year he was fifteen. The same year he stopped going to Mass. The one caused me almost as much distress as the other.

Alberte, too, had her season of poetry, much more intense and far more short-lived. It lasted two months, when she was five. Since she couldn't write, she used to compose orally and then ask me to take down the results. I would be upstairs in my room. I would hear a cry and lean out the window, and there below me I would see her small face turned up toward me, alight with wonder at her own discovery.

"Maman! I've *caught* another!"

When we bought this little farm ("ideal for modernization": a state in which it remains to this day) in Normandy, I was touched to see that above the front door, tiny and low, an unknown hand had painted a cross. It was like a welcome, a greeting from the stranger, perhaps dead now, who had put it there. That little whitewash cross was so faded as to be almost invisible when I repainted it this year, following the original outline exactly, with what was left of a tin of paint that had been used to touch up the bathroom. I did it without thinking. Then afterwards I thought: Isn't it a little bit unsuitable? Ostentatious? There are so few houses with a cross over the door these days. It looks as though we're trying to say: Here's a church, an example of what a Christian house should be, a beautiful picture to be admired, when all we really want to say is quite simply: "Come on in."

Oh, well. It's done now.

Mass

"Do you pray for me at Mass, Françoise?" Dolores asks me.

"Of course I do. Without fail."

"That's very sweet of you. I think of you too, you know.

When I go out in the evening for a 'little java,' I think: poor Françoise, alone in bed there with a book!"

The Feather-Duster Merchant

His name was Roger and he was about fifty, with a nice round head and very blue eyes brimming with a knowing stupidity. He first appeared one evening, at about five o'clock, trying to sell me some feather dusters, a type of equipment we don't go in for much. When I began making a feeble show of resistance, he cried lyrically: "But I'm an orphan!"

"Who isn't, at your age?" I said. (It was one of my hard-hearted days.)

"Yes, but I'm sensitive about it!"

So I bought a feather duster. Fatal seduction. All that year the house was full of vividly colored feather dusters. Sometimes bought ("I have only three left"), sometimes presented as gifts ("Don't refuse, it will hurt me so! Your turn will come." And it always did—very quickly). Sometimes merely deposited ("I'm just leaving my stuff with you, I'll be back soon" —the "soon" sometimes turning out to be after three or four days, sometimes after ten minutes). Whatever the reason, the feather dusters were always there, providing playthings for the children, decorating our hall in multicolored bunches, cluttering up cupboards already full to bursting. "Don't forget to spray them with moth killer now and then," Roger warned me. And resignedly I sprayed away.

"You're like a mother to me," my protégé informed me one day. I was twenty-five at the time and found this new maternal role as unexpected as it was inconvenient. Soon Roger's visitations began to increase in frequency. We started to feel haunted. The hall, which adjoined our bedroom, had struck him as a pleasant place to rest, clean and warm, and he fell into the habit of coming, uninvited, for a few hours' sleep and repose, whenever he found himself without shelter for the night. The first time this happened, as he stood there rambling on about his hotel being raided, about his shoes being stolen, about the license "they" were asking for and he couldn't produce, all in his gentle, not terribly sober, slurry voice, I failed for a long time to grasp his purpose. On and on he talked, as though time had long since come to a stop, the way one talks when one must at all costs win someone's favor, the way one talks to the cops, to the executioner, to God—with a mixture of familiarity, awe, cunning, childish trust, and scorn. And his eyes stayed covetously fixed on those four or five square meters of wooden flour that served as our hall, those four or five cubic meters of warmth, of security, of sleep. "That's a nice little room you have there," he informed me with a sort of shy impudence. Or: "It's nice and warm in your house." I thought for an instant that I could get out of the inevitable by telling him I hadn't any mattress or blankets to lend him. "Oh, that doesn't matter!" "Not even a pillow." "Oh, I don't want a pillow," he said. "I might get into the habit." There was nothing more to be said. He lay down where he was, on the bare floor, his bottle of red wine beside him, knees drawn up so as to take up less room—his overcoat, stiff with dirt, as a blanket. "Like this, if any burglars come, they'll have to climb over me," he said, beaming up at us.

"There's not much here to steal," Jacques put in.

"Oh, they can always find something to take."

It was very embarrassing having to step around him in my pajamas when I had to go to the bathroom at night.

His visits followed no pattern. Sometimes he would stay with us three nights in succession, only to disappear for several weeks. His life was spent in a kind of mist, its progress punctuated by a series of inexplicable disasters or pieces of good luck. Policemen would beat him up, confiscate his feather dusters, deport him to unidentifiable forests from which he would have to trudge back on foot; he would be thrown out of one flophouse, only to be welcomed in another; he was once given an unbelievable quantity of old jackets—so many that he could have gone into business with them—but then some tramps stole them all from him. He once gave Jacques a cap that was too new for him to wear himself. We kept it for ages, simply because we had to show it to him at least once in the course of every visit.

His presence on the other side of the thin partition wall between our bedroom and the hall eventually became a source of great anxiety to me. I lay in bed unable to sleep, while he lay there on the floor, under his coat, snoring away with his arm crooked under his head, as happy as if he were under a bridge somewhere. Every time he disappeared, I told myself that I wouldn't let him in next time, that I would force him to understand my position. I gave myself lectures. Was my house a flophouse? Would any of my friends ever put up with such a situation? It might even be bad for the children, seeing that human wreck asleep there, reeking of sweat and wine, blocking the hallway . . . In fact, of course, the children couldn't have cared less. If I had offered to put an elephant up, they would just have said: Oh, isn't he sweet, and that would have been that.

What prevented me from throwing him out was neither kindness nor any mistaken sense of duty or fellow feeling. It was quite simply the knowledge that he would accept my action with total resignation, just as he now accepted our hospitality completely without gratitude. He was surprised by nothing and he could take anything. Beaten up by the police, set upon by a gang of tramps, he would reappear black and blue, one eye closed, but not a bit downcast. "They've give me another going over!" he would say with an air of triumph. Merely surviving was in his eyes a proof of cleverness.

All these misfortunes stemmed from his not having a "license." "Ah, if only I had my license!" was his refrain, just as someone else might say: "Ah, if only I believed in God."

"But, Roger, is there no way of getting you one of these licenses?"

"To have a license, you have to have a domicile, and to have a domicile, you have to have money, and if you haven't got your license . . ."

"But if I lent you . . ."

He drank the money away, in the little cafés around Les Halles, drank it away very quietly, eyes half closed in his monstrous babe-in-arms face, drank as a baby sucks, gently, ingenuously. I saw him there one morning when I was out buying vegetables. He had attacks of delirium tremens, and then his money and his feather dusters would be stolen. Once an Arab raped him behind Les Halles. He displayed a certain detached pride in that incident. One evening when I was entertaining Denise Bourdet, hoping to make a good impression on her, he erupted into the dining room during the pudding, caparisoned in feather dusters, beaming with merriment. He was the evening's fireworks display.

He would spend eight, ten days in the hospital. I took him oranges. He was clean, pink, fresh as a well-washed baby, neatly tucked in his bed, very pleased with himself. This was his holiday, his Riviera. He liked discussing the respective merits of all the big hospitals, the Cochin, the Trousseau, the Salpêtrière . . . "But, Roger, what about giving up drinking?" "Ah, but what would I have left in life if I did, can you tell me that?" No, I couldn't tell him that. From the cafés around Les Halles, from the barred cages of police stations, from the kindness of some, the brutality of others, the blows, the hot soup, the alms, the hospitals, he had built up his own notion of what life is. How could I send that delicate structure crashing to the ground?

"But they must be very unpleasant, these attacks of yours?"

"They're horrible. And in the end you don't come out of it, the doctor tells me . . ." He beamed as he said it.

"And aren't you afraid that that will happen?"

"Oh, it's just a nasty moment you have to go through . . ."

That was really how he saw his whole life: a nasty moment to be gone through. And in the end I imagine he must have gone through it: suddenly we just never saw him any more. I wondered for a long time afterwards whether I felt anything for him or not.

Franca

Suzanne, Maria, Consolación with your gentlest of Christian names, Marie-Lou from Flanders, Ghislaine, Franca, Louisette, Marie-Ange, you were all, one after the other, over a period of fifteen years, my friends. Afterwards came Cathie and Dolores, even dearer to my heart. But after you have got up early, gone out at dawn (on dark winter mornings the first noises are pleasant, the pale lights of the buses are beautiful, the cafés where a North African with rolled-up sleeves is sprinkling eau de Javel or sawdust are so quiet; then later it all turns sour), with the feeling that you're going off to work in a chain gang, when you stagger back exhausted to read some manuscript or other, to answer the telephone, to rock the baby crying with a chill in its stomach, when you ask nothing more in the evening than to lie down and find yourself as quickly as possible back in those early-morning hours that will bring you a fresh store of energy, then the presence of another woman in your household must, inevitably, be a friendly presence. And in fact we always chose one another, those women and myself, on the basis of a mutual liking rather than for reasons of often debatable domestic abilities on their part or of the modest salary offered on mine.

A system of selection open to criticism. But how can you live in three rooms, and three rooms with doors that don't shut very well, with a person you don't like? Suzanne became engaged several times, Consolación wore my dresses to go out in, Maria was expecting a baby; Marie-Lou got married and I was forced to take her husband in; Ghislaine had attacks of hysteria; Louisette left me at a few minutes' notice one August 15; Marie-Ange disappeared with part of my library; Franca would drink. But all of them were goodhearted, loved my children, and taught me a great deal. All of them shared in my work, interested themselves in it in their own way. That is why I name them as my friends before all the others. "How many pages?" Suzanne would ask. And Marie-Ange: "Will it have a happy ending?" And Louisette, so clean and neat: "What beautiful handwriting you have!" But Dolores could probe my inner life with a glance, measure the absence of joy and excitement, the work accomplished grudgingly, the "why?" that rises to the lips at such moments, and "Me neither, today," she would say, and assimilate my writing into the fabric of life itself, hand me back my unity with a single phrase.

Suzanne is in Africa with her husband, Ghislaine and Geneviève are hairdressers. Maria has stopped working. I don't hear from Marie-Ange any more. Franca has gone back to the factory she left when she came to us.

I was very fond of Franca, despite her shrewish ways. She was forty-five, ravaged in appearance, thin, with a delicate, withered face, sparse hair, lovely eyes, a beautiful deep voice, and that sort of inner vacancy that poverty inflicts on all those who have really known it and can never forget it. Her coming to work for us was an attempt to escape from the nervous tension of factory life, with which she was no longer able to cope. Her account of that life, its slavery, its petty tyrannies, the cruelties, the inner void, was told with restraint and talent. She began the oilcloth era in our house: she laid it everywhere, even on the top of my desk. She was a North Italian, from a mining family, and our coffee was mixed with chicory and

ALBRIGHT COLLEGE LIBRARY 165646

simmered for ages on the stove. Franca had "been in the army" and run a little canteen for the Americans in Germany. How had she got there? Wholly unable to answer that question, she simply gazed at us with a measure of pity, as though we were children who still imagined that we had the power to direct our own lives, who had never heard of the all-powerful currents of history. Like Roger, she had very little belief in free choice; circumstances molded her, and she made no attempt to fight back. She lacked any specialized skills, any specific tastes, any will power; but there is a certain degree of poverty at which such a tenuousness of the ego is the only hope of survival.

It was not long before we noticed that though she was so calm, indolent even, in the morning, as she sat dreamily drinking her coffee with Vincent seated on her lap, Franca would become charged with extraordinary nervous tension as the evening drew on. She herself attributed this slight lightheadedness to violent migraines. And ingenuously we continued to believe this explanation—for several months in fact—until the day I asked her to bring three-months-old Alberte to the dinner table and we turned to see her staggering toward us holding the child lovingly in her arms, bouncing her gently as she walked in order to conceal a certain embarrassment—but upside down. I began to be afraid of what might happen. I begged her to stop drinking. She hid bottles of rum in the French-fries pan, behind the piles of sheets, in the laundry hamper. She treated her body with the same contempt as she did her aprons, which were torn, stained, crumpled the minute she put them on: neither aprons nor body really belonged to her. She neither asked for nor took any days off, any holidays. Sunday didn't exist; the days had no names. But every now and then, exhausted by hard work and alcohol, she just didn't get up.

The moment came when I had to say to her: "Franca, you must stop drinking or you'll have to go." She turned that tragic face of hers toward me and lifted her hand in an impotent gesture. "Franca, if you like I'll get someone else for a few months, and I'll find you a clinic where they'll help you stop."

"What would be the good?" she murmured.

"Well . . . After all, Franca, you've been happy here, we get along so well, you're fond of the children . . ."

No doubt, her black, despairing gaze seemed to say, but what does that amount to, a mere emotion, against this need for invisibility, for oblivion, for annihilation? Even her emotions didn't belong to her. She was so deprived, so stripped of everything, except a certain feeling of kindliness, of universal and resigned pity, that she inspired a kind of respect. She left. I learned later that the one important albeit fleeting relationship of her life had been brought to an end when her partner presented her with the same ultimatum; and she had let him go exactly the same way, without making the slightest move to stop him. She had never possessed him, so how could she hold on to him? A great statue of black stone, eaten away by erosion, alone in the middle of a desert. Likes and dislikes, desires, pain, everything stripped away to leave only the bone. Nothing left but a naked quivering—her soul?

I remember Franca taking a pile of plates out of the sideboard one day. She dropped one and it broke. Unruffled, she simply took out another to make the right number. "Oh, Franca!" "What's a plate?" she said, with a slightly harassed gentleness. One's first reaction was to laugh. But it wasn't funny. She might equally well have said: "What's a life?" Her own. It counted for nothing in her eyes, just like that plate. Terrifying. But if the spark of faith were to fall on that stripped, dried carcass, what a blaze there would be! In the end I came to envy her disregard for the world, to feel myself weighed down and bloated with possessions in her presence. At midnight once, in a half dream—slightly drunk too, I suppose—she was doing the washing or the dishes. I said to her: "Franca, you don't get enough sleep." "What does that matter?"

she replied, with such gentle surprise that I didn't dare point out that she was keeping me from sleeping too. What did it matter?

Indifference

After Franca's going, I meditated briefly on indifference. The "holy indifference" of St. Francis de Sales. The phrase is shocking at first glance. We are so accustomed to confusing faith with impulses of love and kindness. Of course we feel kindly impulses . . . But what then? Then Jacques said something, unwittingly, that threw light on my problem: "When we say we've been too kind, it means we haven't been kind enough." If we can't have gratitude, then at least we expect productivity. We will lend money, spend time comforting, advising, yes, but we want that money, that time, to bear fruit, to be useful. To be visibly useful. Our kindly impulses are often also capitalistic.

The Cat

"Dolores, I'd like a word with you," Jacques suddenly says at nine o'clock, just as Dolores is preparing to retire to her room for the night.

Worried, uneasy, she follows him into the dining room. Jacques's incursions into the running of our daily life are rare, but they are shattering and unpredictable. I am flustered. But, the children duly silenced, one takes one's seat in the dining room.

"Dolores, you know how much I appreciate you," Jacques

begins gravely. "You are very tidy, you are very goodhearted, we are very fond of you . . ."

This avalanche of compliments merely serves to increase our uneasiness. Whatever can it be all about?

"However, we all have our defects. In your case, there's no point in trying to hide it, a certain roughness of manner . . . an occasional coarseness in speech . . ."

Dolores blushes. We look at one another questioningly. Who is the informer? Pauline? Alberte? Has Dolores been a little too quick with her hands? Has she been carried away by her powers of invective?

"And sometimes, you understand, a sensitive creature may be very much upset by . . . Well, you are in the habit of shouting rather loudly."

"The children . . ." Dolores begins.

"Who has . . ." I break in simultaneously.

Jacques raises a pacifying hand. "I'm not talking about the children," he explains gently. "I'm talking about the cat."

"The cat?"

We are thunderstruck.

"You must admit, Dolores, that the cat is no longer house-trained."

"Now that's true," Dolores cries vehemently. "Only yesterday it did it again. It did weewee all over Pauline's shoes, the little beast!"

"So. And the fact is, Dolores, that the cat has been doing things like that only since you came to us."

Unqualified stupefaction freezes Dolores's face. I choke a little . . . stifling back my sudden need to laugh.

"A cat is just like a person. It needs affection. Now I know that you've got a heart of gold, but, you see, Taxi doesn't. You've got to get it across to her. Because when you shout you frighten her. You won't let her go to sleep on the beds, and the result is inevitable: the cat has become neurotic."

"Well, I never!" Dolores exclaims, her Spanish accent swamped by the acquired foreign phrase.

"She needs affection. She is trying to attract your attention, perhaps get revenge. So she falls into dirty habits."

The idea of revenge attracts Dolores immediately. It is a notion she is familiar with.

"You mean she's doing it just to get on my . . . nerves?"

"Exactly. You must . . ."

The children, packed behind the door into the bedroom, are eavesdropping, spellbound. I have to shove them aside to get through.

"What's happening? What's she done?" they want to know.

"Papa's raking her over the coals," Pauline says in know-it-all tones.

Alberte is very pale. "Poor Dolores!"

"No, no, Papa isn't scolding her, he's explaining something to her," I put in.

"What something?"

"About the cat."

"I'm going to go weeweeing everywhere as well," Vincent cries, having followed the discussion to the letter. "Then she won't call me a little beast any more, she'll call me sir."

"Would you like that?" Pauline asks him.

"Not every day," Vincent admits.

In the dining room the discussion continues. Dolores will always fall head over heels to please you if you appeal to her feelings and her reason.

"But what is a complex, Jacques?"

Jacques begins to explain. It is eleven o'clock: I go to bed.

Dolores to the cat, curled up on her clean sheets: "Get off there, you little beast!"

Then immediately: "Oh, I'm so sorry! Down you come, little pussy."

We exchange glances. The smiles have to be repressed. Respect for the master of the house.

Taxi has a kitten. Just one. We call it Yo-Yo. Taxi has clean habits again.

Dolores: "But it is true. She did have a complex."

She now looks upon Jacques as a sort of magician.

Telling Stories

When she was very small, with two brothers older than herself, Alberte was forever making accusations against everyone and everything. "Daniel pinched me, Vincent took my pencil . . ." And then one day, carried away by the heat of her own invention, she added: "The cat swore at me!"

The house at Gué-de-la-Chaîne, on the edge of the forest, experienced a moment of glory one day when a wild sow ran across the meadow, pursued by the local farmers' dogs. The children followed this event with passionate intensity. Alberte's version of it went: "I seed a sow, I seed a boar! The sow killed Monsieur Brosse's dog!" And then, perceiving our interest and our credulity, she threw in for good measure: "I seed a elephant . . ."

Gilles and Pierrette have come to dinner. Unintentionally, I pull open a drawer that is crammed with unopened buff envelopes: bills, tax forms, notices of fines, even a few summonses. "I thought this sort of thing had gone out with Balzac," Gilles says with a mixture of wonder and horror. We are a little confused, like someone suddenly discovering he has a talent he knew nothing about, yet sensing the danger of its becoming an affectation.

Confirmation

At a quarter to six Vincent calmly announces: "In a quarter of an hour I have to be at the church."

Dolores, lifting her nose from her newspaper, and equally calm: "What for?"

"It's my Confirmation."

"My God!"

The newspaper falls from her hands, and Dolores goes pale. "Why didn't you tell me earlier?"

"I lost the piece of paper."

No time for lamentations. In the wink of an eye Vincent is whisked away, washed, and combed. No suitable trousers. The only thing that's clean is a pair of jeans, which he pulls on anyhow.

"Now run!"

"I need a godfather," Vincent informs her hopefully.

"But Papa isn't here! And you've only got five minutes! And . . ."

At that moment a hirsute Daniel emerges from his den, long hair flowing, dressed in a flowered shirt and a red shot-silk waistcoat.

"Quick, to the church!"

"It's against my principles," the young man announces.

Vincent's eyes fill with tears. "I'm going to be the only one without a godfather!"

Daniel grumbles, and off they go. A large and meditative congregation. Sailor suits, bows in hair, fathers, godfathers, uncles, all fully conscious of their duties. Daniel realizes with horror that he is going to have to walk out, alone, in front of hundreds of double-breasted suits, wearing his flowered shirt. He tries to button up his jacket. There are two buttons missing. He hesitates to borrow a comb, goes on hesitating—and the moment is upon him. Deeply dismayed, he follows the young bejeaned confirmee up the aisle, raked by astonished and indignant gazes. Vincent, perfectly at ease, kneels down, gives his responses, and returns to his place untroubled by the slightest suspicion of the commotion that has shaken the parish. I heard the whole story that evening, as soon as I came in, from an indignant Daniel: "And he hadn't said anything to anyone!"

"Oh really, what a little wretch you are!"

"What did it matter?" Vincent asks, opening his beautiful eyes very wide. "I was in a state of grace."

Then our parish priest, next day, as I stammered out my apologies: "But it was nothing, my child, I found it really very touching." (A pause.) "Of course, it was a shock for Monseigneur . . ."

And Vincent, in answer to his father's telling him off: "But, Papa, there has to be one little poor boy in the parish."

Did he mean to be funny?

Catherine

Catherine (sixteen years old) was Dolores's predecessor in our house. She never did any washing up until we had run out of clean crockery. In consequence, the kitchen became a stage forever set with monstrous edifices perpetually on the verge of collapse, of murderous subsidences comparable in their intensity to seismic phenomena.

"Catherine, you really must do some of the washing up."

"Yes, I'll do it now, Françoise."

I go out. An hour later I return to hear melodious sounds emerging from the kitchen. I open the door. Lapped by the still dirty plates as a rock is lapped by waves, Catherine is perched on a high kitchen stool, cheeks red and puffed out, her hair framing her delicious little angel-musician's face, blowing on her flute.

"Listen, Françoise! I've worked out the tune of *Ma petite est comme l'eau*, all on my own. Isn't it pretty?"

"Enchanting, Cathie dear."

And gently I pull the door closed behind me.

"It proves she's happy with us," Jacques comments. "And what could be prettier than the sound of a flute? We must see to it that she has proper lessons."

Consolación

Consolación is leaving us. What a sad ring that has: "Consolación is leaving us!" She is twenty-three and very pretty. She has come to collect her luggage. One of her girlfriends has come along to help her. She is wearing a pair of green ballerina shoes that I seem to recognize. Consolación follows my glance, blushes slightly beneath her dark skin, and throws herself on my neck without a word. Goodbye, Consolación. She was infinitely graceful, with a way of pushing and pulling the vacuum cleaner that was hers and hers alone.

A gazelle. Green eyes. Terrible taste that suited her to perfection. Four years later I met her again at the hairdresser's.

"How are things, Consolación?"

"Oh, everything is fine!"

She is covered in awful jewelry, dripping with furs; beautiful like a wild animal in a cage. We emerge from the shop together.

"Which way are you going?"

"Oh, I have my . . ."

A huge car draws up in front of her, driven by a chauffeur. She blushes a little, throws herself on my neck without a word, and vanishes. Dear Consolación.

Vincent: I'm thinking about the first person who ever sang.
Me: Well?
Vincent: I can understand talking. Because you would get hungry, or thirsty; so you begin to grunt and groan like animals, and then you get on to speaking. But think of the first person to sing, in that cave, with the wild animals outside making you afraid . . .

One should know how to listen to children. And keep quiet.

My Aunt

My aunt (ninety years old): I'm depressed, I'm bored, what do you expect me to think about at my age except death? I told Mme M. as much, I complained about it to her, and do you know what she said? "I'll send my Abbé Henry round to see you." As a way of distracting someone from death, what a stroke of genius!

Disorganization

Year after year I become more and more disorganized. I am three years behind in my taxes, three months behind in my correspondence. I think less and less about my old age and how to save for it, though I gave things like that proper consideration when I was twenty. I invite friends to eat out with me at the end of the month; I play the guitar while the washing piles up; I hold "poetry evenings" with my children during which we sit surrounded by candles reading everything we can from Hugo to Cendrars and munching biscuits, instead of going over their Latin. I forget "useful" cocktail parties and art openings and end up in a cinema seeing a Graeco-Roman beefcake epic called *The Titans*. It's crazy, the disorganization that has crept into my life since my conversion.

There must be some connection.

And yet in that dawn of conversion, what a beautiful first morning back at school it was, what neatly arranged new exercise books, what white pages, what resolutions! What examinations of conscience, what fervent glances at the Master up there, so grave and stern in front of his blue board: "Will it do?—you could do better." Always that qualifying comment following you in all your efforts, through every backsliding. Write, write, write, polish, cook, read, attend political meetings, go to Mass, clothe the naked, comfort those who are sick at heart . . . "You could do better." To have made confession with true despair; that's almost the same thing, of course. "I've lost my temper, I missed Mass once, I've spent money on idiocies, I've . . ." But still, it isn't quite the same. Something is missing; the new exercise books have blots on them, the writing is no longer the best copperplate, there are errors of grammar, things crossed out . . .

Then the tragicomic misunderstandings. Instead of concentrating on the noble and the beautiful, I have been reading bland and soothing nonsense . . . "Father, I've read bad books, I've wasted my time . . ." "My child, you have soiled your mind, the body is the temple of God, you must respect it; such reading predisposes you to sin . . ." Oh, heavens, now he thinks I spend my time reading pornography! How is one ever to be understood?

I say to myself as I get up: what's for today? Writing—
that, of course. Two manuscripts to read. A smallish pile of
washing. Take Pauline to the dentist. Shopping, just like yesterday; dinner to get, just like tomorrow. The entire day filled,
stuffed to bursting like a shopping bag full of utterly disparate
objects: tomatoes, pocketbook, Omo, ballpoint pen; and at the
end of it all, the frustration, the lack of satisfaction, the uselessness of it all falling back on me, like a heavy lid, as night
closes in . . . That is my moment of angst: I never like the
night until I get to the morning end of it . . . Is that it, then,
a Christian life?

All right, I do what I can. I have nothing, as they say, "to
reproach myself with." But how dismal it is, having nothing to
reproach yourself with. How empty. And what can you do
about it? Martyrdom isn't given to everyone. To start with, you
have to have the opportunity. And would it be a solution anyway? Look at those hermits. They prayed. Then what? They
went locust hunting. They had their herb broth to make, their
sidelines like pulling thorns out of lions' feet—and the opportunity to do that could scarcely present itself *every* day—and
then what? Meditation in front of a skull, a big book read and
reread a hundred times (you rarely see more than one in
any of the pictures) . . . All that can take six, perhaps eight
hours a day if you really drag it out. But they're supposed to
have slept very very little. Did they say to themselves at night,
in their grottoes: "Saint Jerome (or Saint Simeon), *you could
do better*"? Or perhaps: "What's the point of this life? I would
be much better occupied in the city, putting down all those
rhetoricians and getting on with my writing." (St. Jerome did
leave his solitude after many many years, to put down a
rhetorician whose arguments offended him.) Perhaps St.
Jerome was a special case, perhaps there were jolly hermits
too, innocent and cheerful hermits who went out picking wild
flowers and taught their lion clever tricks. ("Jump for Nero!"
No reaction. "Jump for Jesus." And he jumps. Reward: a

locust.) But where would I find the time to go picking wild flowers?

There is the obsession with work. Shall I be well enough to work tomorrow? Or shall I be kept from working by a migraine, by nervous lethargy, by a telephone call, by a visit? I wake up, I feel myself all over. In the mood? No? That urgent debt, that letter that must be written, that request I have to make, ouch, they return suddenly to haunt me as I brush my teeth. Well, that's just bad luck. Grit them (the teeth). Keep going willy-nilly, with the migraine, with the angst, with those little mosquito obsessions buzzing inside. Perhaps there'll be a moment of exaltation all the same. Keep at it, humming a hymn to exorcise those ghosts (overdraft, unmade beds): "Onward, Christian soldiers . . ." or "In the valley of the shadow of death I shall fear no evil . . ." Soon vanished, the exaltation, when faced with so many words, words heavy as flagstones too heavy to lift or falling back as soon as I do lift them: Sisyphus. But Sisyphus is Pagan Antiquity, not Christian at all.

When the rock has rolled down again a hundred times, it's back to everyday life: shopping, housework, inspecting the work of Dolores, of Franca, whose incompetence hits you in the eye at every step. Now the second obsession confronts you: polish. Difficult to overcome. In Flanders you're born with polish in your blood. I look at the dusty sideboard, the dull floor, the plastic car crushed in a corner, the dog's bone, the bird cage in need of a good cleaning: total distress takes over. I shall never get to the end of it. When my papers are organized, the house is not. When the house is organized, then my cooking goes to pot: mincemeat and frozen vegetables. When I sew on a button, that means a letter not written, a lesson not learned, a load of washing not done. Be good-tempered, sing hymns, live in God's freedom—what if there are balls of fluff under the beds!

"I need more time, more time . . ."

"Oh yes!" Pauline agrees. "Then you could learn the guitar and play for us when we sing."

A battle is joined inside me. Polish or good temper? Polish or gaiety? There is the sense of duty. But which duty comes first?

I learned the guitar (more or less) and sacrificed the polish. Jacques adds his stone to the edifice: "What are debts, after all?" he asks. "Credit," he answers. The Catholic Aid Society, which seems to have a very favorable opinion of us (along Salvation Army lines), sends us the strangest recruits. An OAS legionnaire who has escaped from prison; an old lady who can't pay her rent. "One must always give," Jacques says, beaming all the while (though he informs the legionnaire that he is a Maoist, to redress the balance). Next day we receive the twentieth demand from the social-security office or the income-tax people. I have learned to watch, without trembling, the pink or green slip emerging from its envelope. Our path to God quite obviously goes by way of love and improvidence.

From time to time I still suffer fits of orderliness. I sort out papers, I list the books lent and not returned to the bookshelves. And I polish, I polish furiously all day long. But I am perfectly aware that it is a sin, because when Pauline sighs, "To think we could have gone to the zoo and done some sketches . . ." I answer, shamefaced: "You're quite right. We'll go next Sunday."

The terrible comment begins to fade. "You could do better" —yes, of course I could, but after all, the Christian Way of Life is not a race or a competition. I have lots of things to reproach myself with now. That, I feel, constitutes a genuine moral improvement.

As a child, Daniel was possessed of a marvelous candor, though a candor much more akin to innocence than to purity. At his first confession, when the priest asked him if he had any "bad habits," he said yes, and was amazed by the seriousness with which this admission was greeted. He even questioned me about it.

"And *do* you have bad habits?"

"Oh, yes," he said with some embarrassment. "I bite my nails. But I didn't know it was a sin."

To a friend who asked him with that harsh and ignorant malice that children have: "Do you know what it means when a woman strips off in front of a guy?" he answered with dreamy gentleness: "It means she trusts him."

He was a marvelous child. He has become an entirely bearable adolescent. Which perhaps makes life even more difficult.

A Visitor

Nicolas sold newspapers and secondhand books. A door-to-door life. Sometimes it was market research; he went around asking housewives why they preferred powdered potato to condensed milk, packets of soup to soup in cubes . . . He came, he stayed. A welcome: one must at least give that, if that is all one has to give. He would come for a meal, always unexpectedly (because if you invited him he didn't turn up), and then talk, interminably. He saw himself as a case history. He was always going to see psychiatrists, but every interview with one of them was a contest, a battle from which he invariably emerged the victor, having succeeded in warding off every attack on the neurosis he then displayed to you like a trophy. At one point in his life he had been in civil service; but he hadn't been able to keep it up. "I behaved like a madman, a real madman," he informed us with satisfaction. "I threw away the opportunity of a lifetime."

"Regular employment" was his obsession. He searched for

it with a despairing obstinacy. And then, having found it, he would begin searching with equal frenzy for a way to lose it. He was cultured and intelligent. He found work all right. A translation, a book that needed writing . . . And then the drama would begin. He had such a clear vision of the ideal translation—so faithful, so elegant; of the perfect book, crammed with every available scrap of information on the subject, and yet so readable, so amusing, inspired but well documented, learned but witty . . . And the perfection of the vision always reduced him to paralysis. He used to telephone us. He telephoned a great deal: in the morning, when you had just succeeded in getting the children off at last, when you felt all fresh and ready for work, when you had just heaved a great sigh of relief, when you were just waiting, still a little paralyzed by angst, for the sediment of your worries, your inner agitation, to settle once again to the bottom of the slowly clearing water. It was as though he sensed all that, as though he wanted to gulp it down, that fragile peace descending, snatch it from us, despairingly, by force, because we didn't want to give it to him.

And how we clung to it sometimes. "You take it," I would say to Jacques as the unquenchable, monotonous voice continued the endless account of his failures, of the translation that lacked the rhythm he wanted, of the night "abominable" things had occurred, of the friends who had let him know they'd had enough, yes, and more than enough, of his troubles. Jacques would take the receiver, more patient than I, more resigned, but with a little twitch, a sudden crease at the corner of his mouth through which I could sense all the vitality, all the freshness of our day leaking away. And sometimes, furious at his very resignation, with the fury of a housewife confronting some clumsy person who has chipped a plate or a glass and ruined her set, I would take the telephone back, be curt, be cold with our caller, refuse to share with him, because we had nothing for him—let him at least leave us this,

this moment of grace, this moment when we were about to dive into the cool waters of our work . . . But of course, because we didn't want to give him anything, because we didn't want to share, he would cling on, knowing exactly what he was doing, befouling our little oasis, smashing, destroying our china, because who has any right to china, to the beauty of the morning, to order and harmony, when there are others gasping for life, unable even to conceive of such things? And when he was certain, quite certain, that he had succeeded, our devil's messenger would hang up.

Then, in forced voices, we would say to one another: "Right then. Off to work now. See you later." And then again, "Work well," or "Have a good morning," as though nothing had happened. And we avoided looking into each other's eyes.

For something, needless to say, had happened. What happened was that every time, in a way, he was right. He was a mixed-up mess, he was a neurotic, he was a non-stop talker; he was devoid of goodness of heart, and he set traps for people. But all the same, in a way, he was right, and that was his neurosis, the key to his instability, his ingratitude, his constant quarrels with his employers, friends, hosts. Work never does come up to the luminous vision we have inside us, abominable things are happening at every instant, love is made without love, words are uttered without any belief behind them, and friends don't give a damn, or rather they are afraid, horribly afraid that the virus will infect them, that they will have to open their eyes, that their peace of mind, their own fragile peace of mind, will crumble away . . .

And yet, from time to time, an evening does come when everything seems to work, an evening when Pauline cries radiantly as she leads him in: "Here's a nice surprise for you: Nicolas!" and we can smile at him, naturally.

He smiles too, with the hint of a blush beneath his wan, executioner-victim's complexion. He plays with Pauline, he plays with the dog. Work has gone better lately, everything takes on a meaning; the children, the house, even the dog are all irradiated with the spirit of generosity that has suddenly returned, like a warm glow in the blood. And the fear fades; it has never existed. The kingdom of heaven is there, wide open, with a place for everyone, for us, for Nicolas. On such evenings he is quite silent, without a trace of his satanic self. He may even risk a compliment on my cooking, he will watch television, he who is at home nowhere will feel at home for an instant. And we too, we also are at home, at last. Eternity is in the instant, love has alighted among us, so present that it brings us a kind of palpitation, of suffocation, we have waited for it so long!

Never pin down butterflies. Follow them with your eyes, wait till they come back. Believe that they will come back. But when?

Teresa of Avila tells us somewhere that five or six years of her life went by without "any hope experienced." Five or six years. She was a very great saint.

Mme Josette

Mme Josette lives in an ivory tower. She lives on the sixth floor in the boulevard de Strasbourg and never comes down. She is a small, slightly built woman of no particular age, with a plain face. She gives hair treatments. She de-greases your hair, strengthens it, makes it grow again, all with the aid of sweet-smelling herbs. I have been going to her on and off for more than fifteen years now, and in all that time Mme Josette has not changed a jot or moved an inch. As withdrawn from the world as any nun, sententious, sometimes a little grumpy, she has globulous blue eyes full of self-assurance; and a broken nose, a mouth always slightly pinched. Truly charmless. And it is as though she derives a kind of pride from that fact. No need for that sort of thing, she seems to be saying, it's quite superfluous.

The setting of her life is charmless too: monastic, yet utterly without mystery. A house-proud, middle-class asceticism. The three chrome armchairs for her customers, each in front of its basin, somehow manage to convey that you are not in any frivolous hairdresser's salon now but in a properly hygienic, medical establishment. "Hair," Mme Josette informs you, "has acquired great importance in the modern world. No director of a business concern can possibly allow himself to go bald today." I wonder where she read that. The room also contains the cupboard for her herbs, all its little drawers neatly numbered (nothing of the witch about Mme Josette), plastic curtains everywhere, some potted plants, and a picture of Mont Ventoux. In her bedroom, into which I have twice been ushered to make telephone calls, there is nothing but a small, narrow bed, a mahogany table, and a Breton dresser on which a few souvenirs sit in state: a box decorated in pokerwork, some dolls in traditional costume or made of shells, yellowing photos, postcards—I recognized one I had sent her three years before from Normandy—and some books. In the kitchen there is a modern sideboard and a quantity of crockery, partly ordered by mail, partly put together from "special offers." There is a small Formica-topped table, a stool, and the gas stove on which the herbs are simmered. I have never been in the bathroom.

A little girl who lives in the same building does Mme Josette's shopping for her. She herself goes out only once a month . . .

Once a month, in order to consult a fortune-teller in whom she has complete confidence. But what does she ask her? "Oh, mostly I just let her talk. The future, the progress being made in her field . . . I believe we shall succeed in communicating with spirits one day. Does that make you laugh? But it isn't even supernatural. No more than the telephone. They are here, the spirits, all around us; all we need is the instrument—the telephone, as it were . . . Of course I do ask Mme Gulbenkian for a few scraps of advice about my little investments." That's just how she is, Mme Josette, sedate, full of good sense, and just as practical in her relations with the beyond as with her speculations on the stock exchange. She reads the share prices every day, and buys and sells stock over the telephone; and her dealings with the spirits are no less real than her dealings with her stockbroker. "It is so convenient," Mme Josette observes, as she kneads a scalp, "to have no private life."

All the same, there is in fact a love story in Mme Josette's past. It goes like this: at the age of nineteen, when it was her ambition to enter the medical profession, she knew another student of her own age, called Georges. She loved him, but without any hope. She was never beautiful, she says, and moreover she sensed that it was not in her nature ever to possess anything. Georges and Josette went over their notes and studied for their exams together; he passed, she failed. That, too, was "in her nature." He took up with another girl, whose name was Monique. "It was a pleasure to see them together." Josette allowed herself that pleasure, went with them to the cinema, cooked for them when they got home. "I had a family, I was happy." Georges married Monique, Josette was a witness. A child was born: Josette became its godmother. The war came. Georges, being a Jew, was deported. Josette took the lamenting Monique and her baby into her own tiny apartment. "One is so very unhappy when one has something to lose," she observes. "But, you see, I have never had anything." She fed Monique and the child, sent food parcels to Georges, and shampooed away with might and main in a beauty parlor. Monique told a woman they both knew: "Josette is goodhearted, but she is cold." "It's true," Mme Josette says. "I haven't her sensitivity. But I do regret it."

Georges came back, Georges died. "It was terrifying, the way Monique suffered then. Yet I'm quite sure that Georges hasn't abandoned us. Look at the child, how much she looks like him! The whole of nature would appear to us in a most extraordinary light too, if only we knew how to look!" Mme Josette does not use her medium to communicate with Georges. "In the first place," she says, "perhaps he has reached the sphere of light, in which case I wouldn't want to disturb him. In the second place, I feel it wouldn't be very nice, considering Monique."

There is no photograph of Georges on the Breton dresser. It isn't necessary, Mme Josette believes.

Mme Josette does not have television. She reads all the newspapers assiduously from first line to last, consigning their contents to a memory unencumbered by the smallest personal recollection. I have only to tell her that I am going to Bordeaux to give a lecture and she will begin softly, as she rubs lather into my hair: "Bordeaux is a charming city, rather cold, with such and such a number of inhabitants. Many of the houses are more than two stories high and have a garden concealed in their center. The women of Bordeaux are clothes-conscious and are more likely to go to a little dressmaker around the corner than to buy clothes ready-made. Historically . . ."

I interrupt her: "Have you been to Bordeaux, Madame Josette?"

"It isn't necessary to have been to a place to know it," she replies.

Mme Josette knows the addresses of a host of doctors, practitioners of acupuncture, fortune-tellers; she can always tell you where to send your children for their holidays, where to buy a lampshade, where to go for guitar or first-aid lessons. With solitude, a good memory, and assiduous reading, an answer can be found for anything.

"I like my work," she says. "My hands take over, I have time to think."

And: "No, I won't buy a television. It would keep me from thinking."

About what, Mme Josette, about what, I always want to ask; but the feeling that she would find such a question un-called-for stops me.

When you express astonishment at her reclusive life ("But don't you ever feel you'd like to go to the cinema? To see what's going on?" "I read all the newspapers, madame, I see my clients—that is enough for me"), Mme Josette likes to quote a well-known anecdote dating back to the Battle of the Marne. People were constantly asking General Joffre's chauffeur Pierre: "When is this war going to be over, Pierre? What does the general say? Has he mentioned it?" But the general never mentioned it. Then one day they asked and Pierre replied: "Yes, he has mentioned it." "And what did he say?" "He said: Pierre, when is this war going to be over?"

Mme Josette does not believe in the value of direct experience.

"I have always voted no to President de Gaulle's referendums," Mme Josette informs me.

"Why?"

"Those questions he puts to us, expecting us to answer just yes or no, they're never clear. They're not grammatical. How can a man who doesn't know his grammar be a good President?"

What is inside that head? A simple and luminous intelligence? Or a massive and sovereign stupidity? You can never tell, you can never be sure. Her words fall like pebbles into water, compact in themselves, but the circles ripple wider and wider.

Renée, Georges's daughter, Josette's godchild, is to be married to a young German who is a practicing Jew—or, at any rate, his family are. Renée and her mother both aspire to a wedding with all the trimmings: organ, blessings, a long veil . . . The priest is willing, but on condition that young Gunther is baptized. Gunther hesitates. Mme Josette, formally invited to meet him, addresses him as follows: "I myself have no religion, Monsieur Gunther, and I am still waiting for it to come to me. But to change one's religion for no reason is senseless. You're not changing families, after all, are you? Believe me, it is things that do the changing, not we who change things. If it is really necessary for you to become a Catholic, it will happen on its own. If Renée makes you change your religion the way you would change your jacket, it simply means you'll be getting married in fancy dress, that's all." Gunther gives up all idea of being baptized. The marriage will take place in the vestry. Renée and her mother (Monique) no longer speak to Mme Josette.

The Death of My Aunt

She remained so much the same, or at least she declined so gently, that for a long while, since she was just as cantankerous, tyrannical, generous, sharp-tongued, intractable, with now and then an abrupt moment of childish wonderment—"Do you love me, do you really love me?"—as well as dirty by design and with delight, the owner of a black sense of humor verging on the sadistic, and comic, nobly idiotic, possessed of a stubborn independence that she never abdicated, even faced with a body ever more and more dependent upon others, yes, she was always so much the same that we believed her to be immortal. She was ninety-three.

The dominant trait of her personality was without doubt her pride, a pride carried to such extremes that it was bound to lead her into silliness. The more she needed others, the more a punctilious and utterly inflexible sense of honor made it a duty for her to be unbearable to them.

To Jacques: "You know how to look after me, but it doesn't matter what you do—I can still tell that your heart's not in it."

To me: "You have a good heart, my poor child, but how clumsy you are! You try to nurse me and all you do is hurt me!"

To her concierge, a talkative but worthy woman who assumed she was distracting the old lady by chatting to her: "Do you really think other people's misfortunes are interesting?"

If you brought her something to vary her diet a little, a treat, something you'd made for her at home: "That's the one thing I really can't stand!"

Or: "It turns my stomach just to look at it."

In the end you had to laugh.

And suddenly, from that soiled bed covered with crumbs, old tins, old newspapers she would never allow you to touch: "I'm disagreeable, aren't I? That's because it's my nature to be like that, my dears. I have always said what I thought. You'll stop coming in the end . . ."

And in her round, old-bird's eye there swam an ineffable gleam of fearful regret, a comical glimmer masking the relief waiting to well up, for she knew quite well that we would come *in any case*, and it was that "in any case" that she needed for her reassurance, while her vituperation, her crosspatch impatience, her cantankerous greetings were all the product of her independence, of the pride which insisted upon them as a sort of absurd duty she had imposed upon herself so as not to seem to be begging for a favor, so as not to yield an inch to her illness and her failing strength: they were her personal conventions. But when you were really exasperated, really desperate, that pitifully comic gaze reminded you that after all they were *merely* conventions, and that really she was very fond of you.

Sunday

I get up at eight-thirty to make the coffee, determined that this Sunday will be a day of orderliness and organization. I wash and dress. I must stand back from things a little, I mustn't let myself be sucked in by them. I wake the children by main force. Protests. I take the dog out. Breakfast is eaten in a variety of states of undress. Daniel, naked to the waist, sits playing the guitar on one corner of the bed as I set the tray down on it. The dog jumps up to waken Jacques. The two cats appear in majestic procession, then settle down beside the croissants. We have run out of sugar.

The thrush is whistling away at full blast. Daniel's singing is putting its nose out of joint. Pauline has pulled on a pair of pants chosen at random. They are far, far too big for her (are they Dani's? Jacques's?) and hang down to her knees. Despite this, and the fact that they are very evidently Y-fronted, she insists that she is now dressed for church. I ask the children to make their beds (a preliminary demand from which I don't, to be truthful, expect any great result). I receive a reasoned refusal: they would rather rehearse the play we are putting on for Christmas first, "because if we don't do it now it won't get done. But the beds . . ." I am dubious about this argument. They rehearse. Jacques refuses to get up. He has a bad back today (?). He will look after Juanito, who has been left with us while Dolores is out enjoying her weekly "little java," and is now crawling about on the carpet. At ten past ten we suddenly decide to make a dash for church. I cannot find my left boot: Juanito has done a disappearing trick with it. Vincent has an enormous (and very visible) hole in his shoe.

"Put on your basketball shoes."

"I can't. Juanito dropped them in the bathtub and it was full . . ."

They are still there. I retrieve them and set them out to dry. Vincent leaves for church with his sock showing through his shoe, while I have hastily pulled on another pair of boots that are too tight around the leg, so that I look as though I've just leapt off a horse. The girls follow us, their hair like birds' nests; in church Pauline fidgets ceaselessly.

"I don't like church!" she says.

"Why come, then? You don't have to at your age," Alberte tells her.

"I don't like church, but I like God," our precocious heretic replies.

I get home again. Eleven. House upside down. Must go out shopping. Must rush to Batignolles, see Aunt and take her some lunch, massage Jacques with some pimento ointment (a remedy in which I have complete and irrational faith), and get lunch. The children still refuse to make their beds.

"We must go out and get a breath of fresh air first."

But they can't get a breath of fresh air in the Luxembourg without a new ball, because Luc, the dog, always eats them. I disburden myself of ten francs.

Shopping: a heavy box to carry the length of the boulevard Saint-Michel. Daniel needs a few tins of things "a little out of the ordinary" because he is organizing a little pre-Christmas feast with some friends. Short pause at home to massage Jacques. He groans. The bed surrounded by packing cases piled high in readiness for our imminent move. I won't be back from Batignolles before two and Jacques is hungry. He doesn't want to wait for me and the children to come back before he can eat. Quickly, some eggs and red wine. Hunger proves contagious: I sit on the edge of the bed, I have something to eat and drink. Relaxation. Twelve-thirty. Quick, to Batignolles. Long journey. I try to meditate on the morning's sermon and find myself thinking about Christmas presents.

I arrive, bearing a piece of chicken packaged in cardboard.

Aunt greets me cordially. "When I want to see Jacques, it's always you who comes," she says, "and when I want to see you, then it's him."

"Yes, that's very unfortunate, Aunt."

Once the principle has been reestablished and her independence affirmed, she sweetens up slightly and even manages to laugh a little as she tells me about her youth.

Finally: "Goodbye, Aunt."

"Already?"

"Well, even now it will be half past two before we have lunch . . ."

"What a strange way to live."

Must get back home. Oh well, a taxi, I suppose. Back at the house. Jacques is dozing. Daniel has retired into his tiny room with one or two friends who are helping him create a fantastic din with electric guitars, etc. The overstimulated thrush is shrieking its head off. Beds still not made.

I make a fondue, because the girls like it and it's quick. There's almost nothing the girls like. Besides, last evening, when Daniel went to the refrigerator for a drink, he left it open and the cats have nibbled at the joint I had set aside for Sunday dinner. I point this out to him.

"Oh, it doesn't matter," he says sweetly. "I ate out."

So we end up with another tray on our bed: fondue and long forks. The younger children are delighted—well, thank goodness for that.

"And having it like this, Papa won't feel left out."

Jacques, who woke up to find one cat on his head and the other on his stomach, bursts out laughing. Harmony.

At the last moment we realize the fondue burner has run out of fuel. It is half past two—at least. Everything is closed. The children rush around the other flats in the building trying to borrow methylated spirits from our neighbors. They bring back a miniature calculating machine (a Scotch-tape premium), a folding tape measure, an old copy of *Pieds nickelés*, two Christmas tree decorations, three toffees, and a lollipop. The neighbors must have thought they were collecting for the Little Friends of the Poor. Finally, giving up in despair, we pour the dregs from an old whisky bottle into the burner. It doesn't burn as well as meths, but it could be worse. Jacques comes to life again after a little white wine. Daniel's contribution consists of an account of the meal he ate out. Universal good humor.

In the afternoon we rehearse our play. Pauline, who is playing the crocodile—with great talent—has just lost all her
front teeth. Consequently, whenever she says, in fearsome
tones, "Look at my teeth," everyone collapses in hysterical
laughter.

"Crocodiles have milk teeth too," she informs us.

This starts a lively argument. Do crocodiles have two sets
of teeth?

Seven o'clock. Tray number three, on which I pile any food
at hand: sausage, hard-boiled eggs, some leftover spinach,
which we eat out of cups because of a sudden concern over
the amount of washing up we are leaving for Dolores. We
watch a Western on television. I have to admit that it is engrossing. So engrossing that by the time I realize the children
have all been undressing with their eyes firmly fixed on Mar-
lene Dietrich, it is too late; their clothes are now lying in a
heap on the floor with Luc on top of them. Jacques explodes.
The explosion is brief, totally ineffective, but ritually required.
Pauline, aware of this, pretends to cry, out of pure respect
for the conventions.

". . . Children with no manners! . . . Haven't even made their
beds! . . . Taking advantage of their parents' being tired! . . ."
Etc.

But our little darlings remain quite unmoved, pick up their
clothes, carry them into the dining room, and dump them in
the exact same heap on the sideboard, where it is the cats'
turn to make a bed of them. Well, it's cleaner than the floor
and the dog, at least. Then they troop back in for evening
prayers with such joy, such serenity that they irradiate the
whole room with pleasure.

"I feel these last days here are going to be an apotheosis,"
Jacques says, now quite calm again.

We move in three days' time.

Sleep at last. But almost at midnight we are awakened by
a suddenly worried Daniel asking if the alarm is on. We chat

for a moment, someone suggests that some fruit juice might be nice, and I get up again.

On Monday morning I leave the flat very early. I have to make my mind blank again, void again . . . But as I walk through the three rooms to the bathroom, one after the other, like sentinels taking over watches, the little voices rise out of the darkness.

"Is that you, maman?"

"Give me a kiss . . ."

"Where are you going?"

My timetable is always the same, yet every day I am asked: "Where are you going?" One day, in irritation, I snapped back at Alberte: "To a ball, at the Palace."

She answered simply: "Oh, have a nice time," and went back to sleep.

The House Is Made of Cardboard

> *"The house is made of cardboard,*
> *The stairs . . . are made of paper,"*

Vincent sings. That's exactly how I feel. Everything supports the impression: the chaos that reigns in every room; the rag-bag assortment of clothes my children wear (Daniel is going through that adolescent phase when his long hair brushing his shoulders, his many rings and chains combine to make him look like a young barbarian chief or an extra at the Opéra-Comique); the irregularity of our income, aggravated by the irregularity of our consumption (alternately over- and under-estimating our resources, we start the month by eliminating laundry, tobacco, stamps—one summer, in the grip of a furious bout of thrift, Jacques took it into his head to live wholly on milk, and ended up with jaundice—then find ourselves giving dinners for twenty at which the rich fumes of caneton à l'orange rise from our cracked crockery and Volnay is served in those glass jars you buy mustard in); the unfortunate habit we have of choosing maids by appearance: "An interesting head . . . She has character," Jacques murmurs, head tilted back, eyes half closed as he sizes up the bewildered candidate. And on my side it is mere liking, fellow feeling, that plays the largest role in those thoughtless impulses that drive me to hire an aspirant flutist to wash my dishes, an unmarried mother afflicted with twins to dust my flat, a likable drunkard accustomed to army canteens to do my cooking. This method, based upon aesthetics and elective affinities, has rarely produced good results, at least on the level of household management. The former model spent her days off wearing my shoes; the drunkard carried my youngest daughter (Alberte) head down and tried to insert her into her high chair the same way; the flutist managed to burst several hot-water pipes by a secret method that she always refused to divulge.

We are eternally in conflict with such various and very impressive organizations as Social Security, C.A.V.M.U., and U.R.S.S.A.F., to say nothing of the direct and indirect taxes on which we are always behind, and the fines that continue to pile up; and my feeling of insecurity is only increased by the perpetually missing buttons, the socks and pants without elastic, the burnt-out lightbulbs that no one replaces, the door handles unscrewed and missing. (Do door handles get unscrewed in other people's homes? I have *never* found a door handle missing in any normal family. Where do they find the time to replace them? But then, neither have I ever succeeded in identifying our mysterious door-handle-unscrewer, the perpetrator of so many other acts of vandalism.)

The house is made of cardboard . . . I have often asked myself: Is it my fault? Is it normal? The staircase is made of paper . . . The entire house, it seems to me, is made of paper—

the paper that I scribble on so patiently and that then so totally escapes my grasp, the children's drawings scattered all over, the canvases that Jacques stores in piles under the stairs, the open books, unfinished poems, collages, even the shimmering and wholly valueless knickknacks that find their way into our house and manage to survive so very long there, better preserved than any precious little Dresden figure ever would be (no Dresden figure would last a week): all those things that make up the brightly colored, frail, and fluttering fabric of our house.

Everything in it gets broken, gets dusty, disappears, except for what is most ephemeral. There is no order, no time, no menus; and what kind of work is it that consists in patiently covering cloth with paint and paper with black squiggles? Moreover, by a kind of natural justice, our children manifest the greatest ability in the confection of cardboard mobiles, and draw, write poems, run up collages, make up plays, dance, sing, laugh, and weep with the greatest facility, but fail to brush their teeth, forget their satchel when they go to school, bring back bad reports with disarming smiles, and are generally ready for everything in life with the sole exception of what is generally looked upon as a normal existence for school children their ages.

Friends come and go, stay for dinner or lunch. Even animals move in on us, apparently of their own volition. A stray cat, a dog given as a present. A goldfish (won in a lottery) that has now attained the respectable age of four and a half. A pigeon with a broken wing took shelter one day in the staircase of our building and as we came home began painfully to clamber up, step by step, until it finally halted outside our front door. There was no possible room for doubt: *it was coming to stay with us.* Vincent put it up in his room for three months. It very quickly became tame, and used to nestle down on his pillow, beside his head, for the night. A touching sight, provided the observer could not also see the state of the tiny room, the grain scattered everywhere, and those stains that inevitably accompany pigeons and which the newspapers commonly characterize as "dishonoring" our statues. Vincent's room was in a state of total dishonor.

And that still leaves the accessory animals: the terrapins given us by Bobby, who teaches a beginners' class in classical dance ("A good Latin coach would be more use to you," Jeanne points out, but are we to blame if our friend happens to be a dancer, not a Latin tutor?), occasional hamsters, puppies "entrusted" to Dolores by neighbors who—lucky for them—are getting away on holiday, the song thrush (oh, so many!) that the dog will eventually eat, the rabbit which Dolores won in a raffle and which rendered all access to the second bathroom we are so proud of utterly impossible for two solid weeks. Dog, cat, pigeon, rabbit, everything you need to make a nice counting rhyme. Paper house, house with ever-banging, flapping doors—I try in vain to keep those doors closed, to caulk all the cracks through which everything runs away, is lost, or finds its way in. But is it right to close, to caulk, to arrange in rows, to immobilize one's world?

Good Intentions

And when we were married, Jacques and I, it was with such good intentions! We were putting our lives in order at last, and they were going to stay that way. For a while we were quite drunk with the idea of the sensible, practical life that lay ahead. We would cease to be children, we would become the model adult couple our children (already certain of their places in this world) would need. It was an orgy of practical fantasy, an inside-out romantic dream that procured us the most intense pleasure. Enough of Venice and Mozart! Our talk was all of sideboards, laundry baskets, budgets-to-be. When we went out together, it was to the Bazar de L'Hôtel de Ville to buy chromium-plated taps much cheaper than the ones sold by the local ironmonger (we saved 95 old francs a tap). Later we found ourselves in a Chinese restaurant spending ten times the cost of the taps. But we were still under the watchful eye of our models, that ideal and ghostly couple who haunted us, so that even in the restaurant we pretended we were there "to talk things over seriously."

We would come home very late, tipsy on bad red wine but clutching reams of paper covered in scribbled figures that we then immediately misplaced.

Why did that ideal couple never materialize? Why were those rigorously drawn-up budgets never applied, those ingenious do-it-yourself projects never taken further than the rough-sketch stage, those general principles (Jacques: "No animals, ever." Me: "Do one room thoroughly every day") immediately jettisoned? The animals arrived, the rooms became cluttered with things (another general principle was NO KNICKKNACKS!), which made cleaning them nearly impossible . . . It has all grown up around us like the proliferating vegetable life of the jungle. We lived for ten years on the illusion that "we need only move." And then we moved . . .

Digression on knickknacks. Dolores says: "If only they were worth something!" Ah, we use their very worthlessness as our only excuse.

The process was simple, looking back. The taps were never fitted. The handles of the doors vanished one after the other. The windows ceased to meet, despite their docility during the reign of the previous owner. The washbasin, finding itself no longer treated with the respect it merited, stubbornly stopped itself up and stubbornly stayed that way, despite the weekly ministrations of a plumber whom age and drunkenness never discouraged from pestering me with amorous advances. The bathtub was more accommodating: it provided us with hot water in abundance, it welcomed us for hours on end into its bosom, sometimes several at a time; but in order to make it clear nevertheless that it would not allow too much familiarity, it refused—through the intermediary of a recalcitrant plug handle, refusing to connect with the plug firmly stuck in its depths—ever to empty itself.

"We must have this stopper thing changed," Jacques would say to me in a preoccupied voice as he lay in the tub reading *Le Monde*.

"Yes, darling, of course . . ."

But the plumber felt differently: "Now really, my dear, you can't go on calling a fellow like this just for a plug. You can manage with it as it is, can't you? All you need do is pull it and *hold* it while the bath empties."

So we pull it and hold it, Dolores or me, bent double over the edge of the bath, our faces contorted with the effort, one arm immersed to the shoulder in the by-now-icy water that does eventually, albeit very slowly, ebb away. But more often we do not hold it, and the bath remains full for several hours, providing the children with an opportunity to launch a fishing fleet on it (shrieks when we do decide to empty it) or Juanito with the chance to make scientific experiments: the immersion of a cat, of a salad bowl, of a volume of our Pléiade Balzac, which, having undergone three or four duckings and then being dried as many times on the kitchen boiler, has taken on the twisted, tortured aspect of a marine trophy, of some age-old Greek amphora, of a coral-encrusted crab. But we do get on quite well with the bath, all the same; it is like an old lady, capricious, but kindly too, in her way.

I could never say as much of the two chairs that suddenly let you down, of the food cupboard, particularly sly, which still pinches our fingers despite all the kindliness and repairs lavished upon it, or of the refrigerator which even in its earliest youth stubbornly insisted on producing quantities of murky and inexplicable water during the night, dousing the food committed to its charge, and which has grown no more continent with age. The sideboard has lost its keys on numerous occasions, and what is one to do at a quarter past one when the children are stamping and champing—I'll be late for school!—and one is deprived of access to one's crockery? "Sandwiches," said Cathie, our guardian angel whom nothing could ever faze. Of course. For the children it was a perfect solution, as is anything that is out of the normal run, and while we were stuffing them with bread and cheese, Taxi, the cat, was able to feast on horse steak. Later, disappointed no doubt at the failure of its vendetta (it has been kicked so often!), the sideboard disdainfully disgorged its key, which it had been concealing in a rolled-up table napkin.

That time it had lost, but it would get us next time. Next time came, and within its hermetically sealed flanks our crockery could be heard shifting in inexplicable but only too destructive avalanches. Several soup plates, boldly set atop a pile of cups with an aerial sense of architecture that betrayed Cathie's touch met an early end in that incident. "It's just like Milhaud's *La Création du Monde*," Alberte observed, rather pedantically. But Pauline was uttering cries of joy: amid the wreckage she had found her silver christening mug, which had been missing for several weeks. Pensively, Cathie considered the disaster area. "You know, one day you're going to have to buy a new sideboard," she commented. She understood us.

I hardly dare think about the lightbulbs. From the rate at which we consume them, you would be led to imagine vast rivers of light, state balls à la Louis-Philippe, the Galeries Lafayette at Christmas, Orly, the Ritz, the Elysée Palace. In our house they take delight in abrupt explosions, in mysterious disappearing tricks, in amazing metamorphoses, in perverse experiments. Painted blue, daubed with yellow, like Achilles they prefer a short and glorious existence to a long but obscure life under a lamp shade (though as it happens we don't have any lamp shades, only plastic globes whose advantage is that, once heated to the right temperature, they acquire a softness and plasticity that make it possible to mold them like Plasticine). The secret life of the lightbulbs in our house would need a whole book. And we have become resigned to treating them like young ladies from the corps de ballet in a Balzac novel, like mistresses that cost you far too much, always deceive you, always leave you, but are nevertheless quite indispensable. But what really upsets us is the curtains. Why is it that in the houses we live in there are never any curtains?

Curtains

One day of acute distress in Normandy, in that country house whose mere mention seems to confer a patent of respectability ("my country house," or "our little place in Normandy," phrases that really warm the cockles of the heart), I was nevertheless obliged to face the fact that, despite all our waiting, despite an intensity of expectation worthy of the Three Wise Men, the curtains had still not arrived, were still not hanging at our rustic casements. And yet I could envisage them so clearly, the red and white of the neat check, so rustic and milkmaidy— though, admittedly, Jacques saw them more as striped, white and green, a disparity that gave rise to many a sunny discussion, just like the ones newlyweds have, discussions immediately complicated by the views of the children, all of whom were hoping for sprigs of flowers; it was all so terribly nice, rather in the spirit of those American films in which you meet the perfect average family surrounded by kitchen gadgets . . . But the curtains didn't come, despite our optimism.

In Paris we had lost heart a little over the years. It had become more and more evident that the curtains were not going

to come. The neighbors had become accustomed to seeing our
children pulling on their Aertex pants, and when we ourselves
were suddenly overtaken by a fit of modesty, there was always
the hallway, which had no window. But out in the country,
encouraged by the green meadows, by the apple trees in blossom or laden with fruit, hope would rise again. The house
cried out for curtains—that was an undeniable fact. We almost
expected to see them arriving like a flight of swallows, skim-
ming in through our windows one sunny day. From time to
time, with just a hint of impatience tempering his fundamental
optimism, Jacques would say: "You know, it really is odd that
there are no curtains in this place." And I would agree. We
would leave the house to go to Mass, to go to the market. We
would leave, then return, the car full to overflowing with
cabbages, with caramels, with magazines (don't forget Dolores's picture romance!) and cigarettes, the docking of a back-
from-the-weekly-shopping conquistador—but no curtains.
With every passing week their absence struck home with
greater force. Within my breast the house-proud spirit of
Flanders groaned in anguish. And at last the day came when
the cruel truth pierced my heart, like the ray of light that
struck home to Paul of Tarsus, leaving me shattered, yet resigned at last before the decree of fate. We just never would
have any curtains.

The simple fact is, curtains will have nothing to do with
certain people. People whose crockery never matches. People
whose fireplaces smoke and whom sideboards cannot abide.
People into whose hair no comb will bite, hair upon which
even the most carefully done permanent has no effect. ("What
do you expect," they ask me in despair, charming Mme Eliane
or nice M. Jean-Pierre who occasionally try to civilize my hair.
"You brush it once and there we are back to square one again!")
Those same people unfailingly have children whose teeth are
crooked, whose shoelaces are always undone, who always have
an inkstain on their best pullovers, buttons missing every-

where, and *The Three Musketeers* hidden in their satchels between a lump of chewed chewing gum and a key ring. What is one to do? Oh, my dream of polished Flemish interiors! Of shining porcelain! Oh, homely spirit of bright-glazed jugs, gleaming floors, Sunday clothes! Solitary tulip in its vase, book left lying on a table and found still in the same place! Sweet linen cupboards!

I wept. I prayed. I wrote a poem. We still have no curtains.

A friend made me a present of an account book. Then of a monstrous clip to keep my mail in, blazoned with the threatening inscription: "Don't forget." Then of a very pretty blue bird intended as a receptacle for the many pins that inhabit our house like eels in the ocean, forever spawning and migrating, to the peril of all concerned. But the friend started to slide into compromise. His latest present was a paper flower, totally devoid of utility. Another opportunity down the drain. Another possible source of help infected.

Things

But there are some things that do like us. Kites, for instance. Mexican money boxes, a series of tiny mocking faces strung up over the piano. And musical instruments. For my eldest son, that means banjo, guitar, saxophone, clarinet, bongos, and various other percussion instruments from time to time. For my daughter Alberte, it means the piano; for me, an accompanist's guitar; for my husband, a violin that he scarcely ever plays but from whose plump presence he draws some sort of secret satisfaction. And in the person of Catherine, the angel from Normandy who passed her adolescence with us, from the age of fourteen till the age of eighteen, we possessed a most persevering flutist. Dolores is our queen of the flamenco. Daniel continues to preside over ephemeral but very noisy jazz combos. (One of his most successful was forced to break up after having disappointed a frenzied crowd at Arcueil-Cachan one July 14, partly by playing too often in discord and partly by eventually collapsing in a drunken stupor all over the tri-color-decorated dais.) Lastly, we once acquired an Indian thrush that was supposed to imitate the human voice. But, having first expressed its carefully calculated scorn of us by barking like the dog, it turned its attention to the musical field, decided that the radio and television were its rivals in our home, and trained itself to produce piercing and supra-ornithological sounds up and down a scale so vast and so varied in tone that it compared favorably with the voice of Yma Sumac, descendant of the Incas, American nightingale.

Other things that are happy living with us are: dolls, kaleido-scopes, empty jars (without lids), oddly shaped bottles (the objects of a collective hope that they will one day transform themselves into lamps), shoes. (No pair of shoes, however worn out, can ever bring itself to leave us. In the end, worn out with hoping, Daniel, who is an enterprising boy, nailed them up, temporarily but in quantity, on the walls of his room. That way at least we knew where they were.) Also string, rolls of Scotch tape, bashed-in wicker baskets, squares of mul-ticolored cloth (too small to be used as bedspreads), shawls. (How can you go out in a shawl three yards long? Still, the cats are very fond of it.) And books, brooches, stretchers with-out any canvas, canvases without frames, rusty cocktail shakers and pastry knives that have appeared from nowhere, and medi-cines that no one takes. Bent nails. Files in which nothing has ever been filed. No fountain pen or toothbrush has ever been disloyal enough to abandon us. Keys, apart from being given to practical jokes at our expense, also never cease increasing in numbers; a great many of the ones in our house, big and small, have certainly never belonged to any lock. Some of them are no bigger than your fingernail.

Were we a Lilliputian family in some former life? I gaze down at one in a dream. I have never owned a jewel box, or any box that had such a key to lock it with, any coffer or casket of microscopic size . . . A money box? A case for a tiny golden comb? The sewing box we have always dreamed of but, like the curtains, have never seen arrive? "Don't worry," Pauline says, surprising me at my reverie. "It will grow up too, like the others. It's just a bit backward, that's all."

Politics

Mme Josette: If I went out at all, I should certainly go to the demonstration at the Trocadéro, because I'm a Gaullist.

Me: You're a Gaullist? But you say you've always voted no on the referendums.

Mme Josette: And why not? That was a matter of grammar, as I've already told you. Your students, your Cohn-Bendits, what horrors!

Me: So you're against the students then, Madame Josette?

Mme Josette: Of course I am. All they do is talk and make a lot of noise instead of doing something, instead of pushing all those monsters out and taking their places, instead of having a go at changing all the things that are wrong. Look at all the promises we have made to us, revaluation, revaluation . . . And then what? Inflation. And if you still can't buy anything, then what was the good of revaluing? I stop to think about these things, you see. It's our buying power we need to have increased, not the face value of our money. And the way it's all organized at the moment—well, there just isn't any way of increasing our buying power. It's the middle men we've got to eliminate, it's the whole system that needs reorganizing.

Me: By force?

Mme Josette: Why not? They'd do better to seize power, those students of yours, than to stand around speechifying at the Odéon.

Me: You're more of a revolutionary than you think, Madame Josette.

Mme Josette: Me? I'm a right-winger, like all my family. But I think things out.

What she says is true. Solitude and reflection have made Mme Josette into a being apart, totally original, perhaps poorly endowed to begin with, but able at last to develop without any constraints, and utterly ignorant of the meaning of her transformation. The idea that she is "a right-winger," like her Breton dresser, is an inheritance from her family; she preserves both out of piety, and without seeing them for what they are. She is an astonishing example of Simone Weil's noble pages on application. That one faculty is all she possesses, and from it she derives an inner life sufficient to satisfy her completely. There is nothing else she craves. "The workers are demanding longer holidays again!" she says. "Holidays! Why should you need holidays if you have a job you like and time to think? The trouble is they haven't got either, so they can't think what else to ask for. You can see how everything needs changing."

Sometimes Mme Josette frightens me a little.

Flowers in the Morning

Jacques and Daniel are in the habit of expressing themselves with great firmness on the subject of their political views.

Jacques employs a typically Catalonian violence of expression in the service of what are really, underneath it all, rather staid opinions, while Daniel expresses the most extreme of arguments with a Nordic coldness. Third parties caught in their crossfire are swiftly reduced to bewilderment, panic, even a kind of mental vertigo, and if they venture to betray any kind of third opinion they are forthwith vehemently hauled over the coals or icily condemned, with the result that they give up trying to say anything in the face of this double onslaught or else they end up spending a rather miserable evening. I always try to calm down the attackers, but in vain.

"If we're not going to talk about things worth talking about, then why meet at all?"

What do you say to that?

Recently I invited a friend of mine I hadn't seen for some time to one of our Sunday dinners. She is a pleasant, pretty young woman, but unfortunately announces loudly at the very outset, poor simpleton, that politically she is "completely demobilized." Jacques's eyes flicker to life, Daniel's features freeze. The attack is about to begin. In vain I try to deflect the conversation into some other channel. Too late. Especially since my guest, expecting no more than a few anodyne exchanges of views, refuses to take evasive action, ignores the lifeline I have tossed her, and goes on professing an elegant scorn for the excesses of fervent political commitment.

Jacques moves in to the attack, using a still quite moderate vibrato. Daniel's voice sinks to a deep and gently thunderous bass. They are taking their time to warm up; then, after ten minutes or so, they confront one another in earnest, bouncing the unfortunate and quite bewildered victim between them like a ball. A note of violence enters the conflict. Jacques raises a forefinger, points it accusingly, and Daniel's hand is immediately laid gently, protectively on the visitor's arm. It is a trial, a trial in which the role of prosecution is assumed in turn by each side, whereupon the other immediately switches to defending counsel. Defended, besmirched, accused of the worst hidden intentions, forgiven in recognition of extenuating circumstances she had never till this moment dreamed of, the victim herself is quite unable to get in a single word, or even to eat the plate of couscous I have placed in front of her and am now watching grow so sadly cold. In despair, turning for help to my lifelong friend Andrée, who is stoically accustomed to our outbursts, I try to create a diversion.

At the top of my voice I cry: "Andrée, have you seen *Easy Rider?*"

"Yes," she screams back. "I rather liked that sequence where . . ."

For a moment our guest tears herself away from the fearful fascination of the two jousting champions. "Yes, I enjoyed it tremendously too," she says.

Bobby, at the far end of the table, an ardent lover of harmony as befits a classical dancer, perceives the purpose of my interruption and attempts to come to my aid. "That's an American film, isn't it?"

"Yes, I saw it in New York," our guest tells him.

Daniel doesn't let the admission escape him. "You went over there for that specific purpose, I take it?" Then to Jacques: "She thinks that America . . ."

"She thinks nothing of the kind!" Jacques retorts violently.

In proud confrontation, the one splendid in his restraint, the other overwhelming in his ardor, I cannot help but admire my son and my husband, the vitality that infuses their conflict, and the profound agreement that surfaces between them from time to time like the truce of God, only to be immediately broken by an even more violent series of attacks and ripostes. Our visitor, to be honest, is no more to them than a pretext, a plaything to be tossed to and fro, and it is simply their magnificent moral and physical health that imbues what is really a purely formal controversy with such a fine intensity of fury.

But "you can't expect all conversation to stop just because we happen to agree, can you?"

"Will you have a little more lamb, a few more vegetables?"

I might as well save my breath. Her appetite has gone. Whose wouldn't have?

"This type of person is a source of defeatism pure and simple . . ."

"I beg your pardon: you mean of concealed fascism, and all the stronger for being unconscious . . ."

"All the same, one must admit . . ." Jacques's voice rings out.

"Once you've admitted one thing, you might as well admit everything," Daniel remarks gravely, a budding Fouquier-Tinville.

I cry out with the energy of despair: "And *Pigstye*? Have you seen *Pigstye*, Andrée?"

Alas, Andrée too is inspired by a warlike ardor that passes unnoticed only because of the sheer volubility of the two contestants. Instead of answering my question, she turns to Vincent and his little friend Sylvie, aged thirteen, who want to know: "What are they saying?"

"What are they saying, my dear? But the whole of man's responsibility is at stake, my little ones. Don't you see that . . ."

All is lost. I go out to fetch the cheese, escorted by a groaning Bobby clutching his curly head in his hands: "Dinner, dinner, it's more like the end of the world!"

My friend left at about ten, still very polite, but pale, with dark smudges under eyes, and saying she had a migraine.

"How lively it is in your house!" she remarked politely as she went out.

Next day, in the bathroom, with the ebbing tide, Jacques and Daniel were seized with remorse.

"We ruined her evening . . ."

"And she was really so nice . . ."

"A pretty kid too, and not stupid . . ."

"She'll never dare come again . . . What can we do?"

"If we telephone her to apologize, she'll just think it's some kind of a joke . . ."

Jacques suddenly lit up with a thought: "We'll send her some flowers."

"Not such a bad idea," Daniel agreed. "But I thought we were so broke just now."

"Never mind that. We'll write something nice on the card. Yes, a big bunch of flowers!"

The expiatory act was duly performed during the day. And that very evening we all went together, Jacques, Daniel, and myself, to a formal cocktail party given in honor of my mother. Daniel met a girlfriend of his who had recently become engaged. They stood talking alone in a corner. After doing my duty rounds, I saw that Jacques had joined them.

I began to walk over myself, and as I came closer I heard: "I admire you for having such convictions. I have none at all, you see. No, really, none whatever . . ."

I almost ran the last two steps. "Now be careful! Remember!"

They both nodded at me reassuringly. Then my mother harpooned me and dragged me off to meet some newcomers. I left them with dread in my heart. Twenty minutes later I returned to find Jacques extremely animated, Daniel far too calm, the girl much too pink.

"I must leave you now," she said with evident relief. "I must go and talk to some of the other guests."

I threw my husband and son a suspicious glance. Their eyes refused to meet mine.

"What have you been saying to that poor girl?"

"Oh, nothing . . . not a thing . . . a little discussion . . ."

"Come on, be honest! Is it flowers in the morning?"

"Yes, I'm afraid it's flowers in the morning," Daniel confessed. It's going to cost us a fortune, by the look of it.

Religion

My aunt was married in 1914. Six months later her husband, whom she loved deeply, was reported missing. "It was God's will," she remarked once. "But I can't say I'm grateful to him for it."

Left a widow, without ever a thought of remarrying, she took into her dark and far from clean ground-floor apartment, fed, kept, and tyrannized over successive members of the family in their times of need, taking care that they should always feel able to leave her without bearing too heavy a burden of gratitude; her sharp-tongued observations, her insulting conjectures on the subject of their morals and their self-interest took care of that. She was determined to deny even the sweet delight of helping others that was the chink in that closed, cantankerous, but fundamentally generous soul. The relationships she set up were harsh, ironical, pitiless; she repressed like a tyrant the need for affection that had survived in her from her orphaned childhood. No year passed, as long as she could still walk, without her going to lay flowers on the grave of the cousins who had brought her up "out of charity." "I owe it to them, though I can't say I miss them."

Moreover, she kept an extremely meticulous account of all birthdays, all the gifts, all the little attentions that were "owed," and the slow torture of the paralysis that extended a little more each day over her limbs was certainly less agonizing for her than the fact of no longer having "to pay back," of no longer being able "to pay back."

Though savagely thrifty, indeed parsimonious where she herself was concerned, she distributed the proceeds of her meager war-widow's pension and her post-office superannuation with aggressive generosity. It was vital for her to believe in the mercenary motives of those who came to visit her. (Take this note, take that vase, that picture, that knickknack you said you liked, yes, yes, I insist!): love, kindness, pity—they would all have been too heavy for her to bear. And yet, when she had finally worn you down, when you noticed the tears of exasperation in her eyes and agreed to accept the obligatory gift, she had a way of thanking you, pitiable and joking at the same time, that made it very clear how far she was from being a dupe of the comedy she was forcing you both to act out.

And so, when she had nothing left to bait her hook with, she began to promise us heaven as our reward. "The Lord above will forgive you a great deal because you've done your duty toward me." She herself, whatever the circumstances, had always done "her duty," always taken the greatest possible care on every occasion that no one should ever think she was acting out of any feeling of kindness or sympathy; that would have diminished her in her own eyes.

God kept an account book up there; he would know exactly how much to "pay back." She would neither want nor dare to ask him for more. She was insistent upon having the formalities of her faith respected. On one occasion, the abbé who came to give her Communion found that he had no white napkin and decided to do without one. "But without a white napkin, does it *count?*" Her faith was total, scrupulous to the *n*th degree where observances were concerned, blind as far as the spirit went, yet faithful and stubborn all the same. She was the most insensitive person in the world. She wounded all those close to her ten times a day, all the big-hearted concierges, the grand ladies doing their Good Works, the savagely treated cleaning women—who took their revenge with venomous and vulgar retorts, then still came back for more, faithful as all the rest. It was horrible, yet fascinating.

Tongues, in her apartment, could be swords.

A cleaning woman: "What with the way you suffer and the way you make others suffer, you'd be better off dead!"

Aunt: "Of course! So that you can find where my savings are hidden and make off with my week's funds, eh?"

They were only half joking. And we who weren't as tough as the cleaning women, we left the apartment with our hearts in shreds. Were we perhaps wrong? The coarse old concierge, the sharp-tongued cleaning woman, the "visitors" who stopped their noses against the stench of that dark hovel, the old drunken woman she took in for a while, who stole her thousand-franc notes (a fact she feigned ignorance of), none of them abandoned her.

The old drunk, Mme Hélène, was a former music-hall singer who had once, so she claimed, been kept in a grand style. When my aunt took her in, she was living on a staircase with her cat, and was the mistress, we were told, of a coal merchant who allowed her the use of the staircase in return for certain services. Two monsters. All bloated and flabby, she would get so drunk she sometimes had to crawl around my aunt's apartment on all fours, then would collapse in the hallway to the kitchen and go to sleep there with the gas or the lights all on. We were afraid she'd burn the place down or asphyxiate them both, so we tried to persuade my aunt to get rid of this nerve-racking companion. She refused with a kind of terror. "It's bad luck to drive a needy person away! No, Jacques, you mustn't do it!" He wavered for a long while, then made Mme Hélène a present of a week in a hotel, after which she went back to her staircase. The day of my aunt's funeral, Mme Hélène, totally drunk but weeping copiously, her hat all askew, was there in the church; the concierge and the cleaning woman hadn't dared go past the vestibule. I would have been truly glad to have had them all with us as we drove out to Père-Lachaise; but it seems that was not compatible with the "etiquette" required by the pitiless undertaker's man in his black tie, a black band around his sleeve, who was to "lead the mourning."

Poverty

Marie-Louise was the last cleaning woman my aunt had living in. On the day my aunt died, while the body was still lying on the bed, Marie-Louise had packed her own things, stripped her own bed, and was all prepared, with military discipline, when we arrived, at about ten in the morning, to make the necessary arrangements. She had helped her employer through her death throes and helped lay her out and then had readied for her own departure.

"Shall I go right away?" she asked, her small cardboard suitcase at her feet.

"But do you know where you'll go, Marie-Louise?"

"No, oh no."

"Have you any money?"

"No, oh no."

Yet she was all ready to leave, then and there, to find herself out in the street at a moment's notice, this woman of sixty who had been so kind to our aunt. No money, nowhere to lay her head, and to her it seemed perfectly natural. She had lost her husband, she had never had a child.

"I may find some offices to clean, though with this strike . . ."

We protest. There's no hurry: the rest of the month's rent is paid, there are papers that will have to be sorted out, a few pieces of furniture to be moved; there's really no reason why she can't stay another week or two. She is quite overcome with surprise, disconcerted almost. Oh, it's not that she has any doubts about us, about our *kindness*, she explains (kindness— not throwing out into the street at a moment's notice an old woman who has done you a service); it's just that that's how it's usually done . . .

Where did she acquire this firm conviction, which all our expressions of astonishment are unable to shake?

"But people aren't as unfeeling as all that, Marie-Louise! You don't seriously think . . ."

"Oh, of course I always knew how kind you was, Monsieur and Madame Jacques! But I said to myself, Well, it's the practice, isn't it, and as I'm no use here any more . . ."

It was impossible to make any impression upon her conviction, ingrained in her very flesh, that it is natural and normal to be tossed aside like a broken tool as soon as one is "no use any more." It was impossible to make her understand that by allowing her to stay in that apartment for a few more days we were doing no more than simply recognizing her right to be a human being. Had we insisted further, she would have found it almost distasteful.

It is at this point that words become impossible, that true poverty begins, the poverty that has impressed itself so totally on its victim that he or she has become one with it, would be deeply hurt if you tried to find a way of wrenching it away. That was the extent to which Marie-Louise had given up any idea that she could possibly have any rights. To prove to her that she did have rights, that it was a duty to have them, would have been an act of cruelty. Admirable? Horrible? "Life is a terrible thing," Cézanne sighed. Those thanks, and the approval of the concierge—"It really is so kind of you"—seem to me now more terrible than any number of more sensational injustices. Mme Hélène, the drunken old singer, had also allowed herself to be shown the door without making the slightest fuss, but that was because, like Franca, "she preferred her drink."

In a way, with her hat askew, her noisy drunkenness, and her staircase home, Mme Hélène made me feel less bad than gray, hard-working Marie-Louise; after all, she was a kind of celebrity in the neighborhood. She clung to her wine in the same way that our aunt clung to her evil temper; these were their ways of fighting back at old age, at poverty, at injustice.

Mme Hélène sang sometimes, and our aunt occasionally laughed. Marie-Louise never did either.

The Church has made poverty a virtue, I tell myself. But not poverty like Marie-Louise's.

I refuse to believe it. Would claiming her lawful right to live mean giving the lie to the spirit of poverty? To believe that, to make others believe it, would be to betray the spirit in obeying the letter.

And yet poverty is a virtue—one that the Church preaches above all to the poor. Which is odious, but very just. It is nobler by far to renounce voluntarily what has been taken from you. The poor man who renounces the riches that he lacks—that he lacks through injustice and because he has been deprived of his rights—is a saint. The Church speaks for the saint lying dormant in all of us. The Church is right *and* odious. And we who make use of words—our wealth—to say that words are nothing, we too are odious, and quite right.

It was when we wanted to shake Marie-Louise and say: "You have rights! You are being treated unjustly, and so many others along with you," that we were Christians. But because we would then have had to go on, to be cruel, to make ourselves odious by adding: "And now, in the name of a God you do not know, we want you to accept the injustice that we have just revealed to you"—because that would have been saying, really: "Become a saint or starve to death"—and because we were neither unfeeling enough nor saintly enough, we didn't say anything at all.

The Church says it for us, and God knows how it is exploited, this odious, this unjust way of being right. And that exploitation is the spit on His face that we have neither the strength nor the right to share, because we are not saints.

Posters

And because we aren't saints we believe that situations that can only be resolved by saintliness ought not to be tolerated. With the result that we put up posters, hand out pamphlets, and (sometimes) attend political meetings.

"But is all this protest in keeping with the spirit of poverty, of renunciation?" I am asked by Jeanne, a young and pretty friend who is still, most charmingly, what used to be called "devout." That same concept of poverty. But since there is "poverty of spirit" even when the desire to acquire things, to possess, no longer exists, perhaps such poverty can also in fact be attained by the satisfaction of certain economic needs. Could one not argue that the abolition of the desire for acquisition can be achieved by satisfying people's basic needs: housing, reasonable working conditions, and even the possession of a car, a television set, a refrigerator? The important thing really is that there should be a ceiling, a limit to this need to possess that masks our need to be. How many of us haven't at some time known a person who has everything he or she could possibly need, and yet is always searching desperately through all the many gadgets our society has to offer in the hope of finding something to want? It is quite clear that the desperate search is a means of masking the terror of having nothing left to want—and that, whatever one's material circumstances, constitutes *poverty.*

A terrible situation. To reach the end of one's material desires, or even to discover that these desires can indeed have a limit, is for many the edge of the abyss, the moment when they must face themselves, face God. This would explain the total confusion that has occurred in countries where an attempt has been made to set a *ceiling* of this kind, countries in which, moreover, a relatively high standard of living is the norm. I am thinking of Sweden, for example: the suicide rate in such countries is shattering proof of the difficulty inherent in the confrontation with one's self that results from the satisfaction of all one's reasonable natural desires. We find few or no suicides in situations where the difficulties presented by material circumstances provide immediate and legitimate goals to strive toward. Want must be vanquished. But we must also rout false poverty, the psychosis of poverty created by the consumer society: one is poor when one lacks proper housing or a living wage; one can also legitimately feel poor, in certain contexts, without a car or without a refrigerator; but the great consumer society can actually make you feel poverty-stricken if you happen to lack a certain size screen, color television, an electric barbecue, a rock garden, a swimming pool, a Louis XVI bath, because *there is no ceiling*. To eliminate the material difficulties of life, to keep anything from coming between mankind and the pure difficulty of being, to abolish all excuses is both an act of kindness and of cruelty. There is no way around the dilemma. For once those satisfactions have been provided, once that *ceiling* has been set, the society concerned must almost inevitably be overtaken by an agonizing crisis, since it is now deprived of the excuses formerly provided by real needs (now satisfied) and false needs (now eliminated). Must not a period of purgation, as the mystics call it, ineluctably follow?

"In other words, you're just taking another route to get to the same point. Whether to be a saint or not," Jeanne comments, not without irony in her voice.

"Perhaps. But it's the route I prefer."

Efficiency

Alberte: Altogether, then, Jesus Christ was at work only two or three years, wasn't he?

Pauline: But before that he worked as a carpenter.

Alberte: They killed him almost right away, so he didn't have time to do very much.

Pauline: He wandered around and told people beautiful things.

Alberte: He could have organized houses where they give poor people soup, like St. Vincent de Paul.

Vincent (sententiously): Man does not live by bread alone.

Me: Even if you start lots of canteens and hospitals you can never feed and nurse everybody.

Alberte: So you mean it's not worth trying?

Me: I don't mean it's not worth trying. I mean that these things are relative. I mean that you can never make everything perfect once and for all. That what you do is always proportionate to what it's possible for men to do.

Alberte: All they have to do is all get together.

Pauline: All who?

Alberte: All the people who want to start canteens. Aren't there just as many people who want to run canteens as there are people who are hungry?

Me: Perhaps not. And perhaps they're not all in the same place, or don't know how to go about it, or can't agree about the way to go about it.

Vincent: There you are. People can never agree about anything.

Alberte: They ought to be forced to.

Me: But if you assumed the right to force them to do good, you would also be assuming the right to make them do evil.

Alberte: Yes, but if you don't force them to do something, nothing would ever get done.

Vincent: You, you're just a dictator!

Pauline: It's true, she is. She always wants me to play the game she wants to play.

Alberte: You wouldn't like it if you had to play alone.

Pauline: Neither would you!

Alberte: I'm older than you!

Pauline: I shall be ten too, one day!

Alberte: But I shall always be two years older than you.

Pauline bursts into tears. "It's not fair," she cries. And then suddenly the sobs modulate into hysterical laughter: "That means you'll die before me, and then I shall catch up!"

Alberte is left speechless.

Vincent: In the end, what's relative is that you wear yourself out at . . . well, for example, nursing people who are going to die in any case.

Me: Yes, exactly.

Pauline: But all the same you must nurse them, it wouldn't be nice not to.

Me: Of course! People must be looked after, and fed, and have somewhere to live, so that they can have a chance to think about something else apart from food, or where to live, etc.

Alberte: Oh, you, you just think life's made for thinking about things all the time.

Me: Perhaps I do. What about you?

Pauline: I think it's for laughing!

Me: But laughing, that's joy, that means you're praising what God created, telling Him that life's really not bad . . . Only we mustn't forget that everyone else isn't laughing at the same time.

Vincent: Laughing's relative too.

Me: Exactly.

Alberte: And being a Christian? Isn't that relative?

Me: It's relative as far as what we try to do is concerned. It isn't relative as far as the whole concept . . . well, in relation to God. *[I am beginning to get in a muddle.]*

Alberte: I don't believe that the people who see us ever feel they'd like to become Christians like us.

Pauline: Why not?

Alberte: We're always in such a mess.

Me: But being Christian doesn't necessarily mean being well organized.

Pauline (with overwhelming conviction): Oh, goodness no!

Me (panic-stricken at what I've said): But of course that doesn't mean you shouldn't be either. St. Augustine says: "Love, and do what you will."

Alberte: That makes things pretty easy.

Me: It isn't all that easy to love everyone.

Alberte (subsiding): Then I'm a good Christian, because I do love everyone. Even Paulette, you know, the girl who plays the piano better than me and is Mme R.'s *[her teacher's]* favorite.

Vincent: Mother is a good Christian too. She loves us and we do what *we* like.

Poetry Evenings. Upbringing

What we rather grandly call our poetry evenings also have an important material aspect. We must have orange cakes and gingerbread, ginger cookies and sour balls, or else some of those imported chocolate finger biscuits that are in fact just like fingers wrapped in chocolate (the main attraction, according to Pauline), and also Coca-Cola or Evian Cassis, a huge candle on a tray—an unruffled evening when everyone is relaxed. In short, we need a great many things to appreciate poetry. Still, we manage to meet all these conditions about once a fortnight, and then we all get together on my bed, an immense raft that has survived many a storm and upon which we all invariably end up.

Sometimes, as in the conversation I have just recorded, we tackle some important problems. Sometimes, when a feast day is approaching, we read from the Bible. Most often, we just read our favorite poets, with great eclecticism. Daniel, who has a beautiful, resonant voice, specializes in Victor Hugo. We hang on every word. Jacques prefers a leavening of sarcasm and reads Cendrars. Alberte is crazy about Aragon, and Vincent reads poems from the Chinese, translated by Claudel, with a subtlety that ravishes me. Pauline says: "The two most beautiful poems are 'Booz endormi' and 'Le Hareng Saur'"—an absurd selection that is just like her.

"The odd thing is, with the way you bring them up, still none of your children can spell," Jeanne observes.

And it is true that Alberte, who at the age of eleven is capable of giving a very cogent explanation of "*Aboli bibelot d'inanité sonore*," has been known to write "telephone" with an *f*. And Vincent, who possesses a nonstop fund of subtle puns and word play, has handwriting like a spastic spider's and never remembers to make his participles agree. The fact is that when I explain Mallarmé to Alberte she finds it so engrossing, in the way she might a crossword puzzle, that I become engrossed too and consequently rarely think to give her the dictations she ought to be having. And while I am singing folk songs, arguing about films, admiring their drawings and handicrafts, it usually goes quite out of my head that I ought perhaps to look in their school bags, go through their notebooks . . .

Hence the vague remorse that gnaws me. "The way you bring your children up." Jeanne seems to take it for granted that Mallarmé and the guitar, our chaos and our catechism classes, our pets and our poetry, are all part of some predetermined plan she disapproves of but nevertheless respects as the end result of a conscious determination. Alas! Am I in fact bringing my children up at all? It is perhaps time I began to think of doing so.

One day a woman said in my presence: "You can always tell whether a child is well brought up or not by its shoes." I blushed.

The Saga of Daniel

I was eighteen when Daniel was born. I bought quantities of the most up-to-date equipment: folding bath, thermostatically controlled bottle warmer, sterilizer . . . I was never quite clear how to use them. The bath, yes, but the sterilizer! Daniel never seemed any the worse for my incompetence. I used to take him into cafés sometimes, where he was glanced at with some surprise: it wasn't the fashion in those days. He was a precursor-baby, a hippie baby before hippies were heard of. When I went out dancing, he slept in the coat room, curled up in the middle of the coats. We were very fond of each other, with just a hint of amazement on both sides at the capricious fate that had seen fit to yoke us together.

At five he demonstrated a precocious protective instinct by yelling in piercing tones in the métro: "Let my mother get past." At eight, when he decided that I was late coming home in the evening, he did "his" shopping and made "his" dinner without assistance. He had left me completely behind. At nine we had a few battles. He refused to go to school, to wash, and to eat fish. One day I dropped him fully clothed into a bath; another day Jacques carried him all the way to school on his back, with Daniel yelling blue murder the whole way. These attempts to instill better behavior into him met with no success. What's more, his behavior suddenly improved all on its own. We decided not to interfere again.

At ten, at secondary school, when he was asked to write a composition on "A beautiful memory," he began it ingenuously: "The most beautiful memory of my life is my parents' wedding."

At fifteen there was a rock-'n'-roll phase. His room filled up with 45 rpm records. At sixteen he began to display a lively interest in the opposite sex. Young ladies whose Christian names I didn't even know were always disappearing into his room, swathed in vast and grimy raincoats, like lady spies in B-feature movies.

He began playing the clarinet. And drinking a little.

At seventeen he became a Buddhist.

He began playing the tuba. His hair got longer.

At eighteen he passed his baccalaureate. Shortly before that, there was a period when he was always covered in jewels, like a Hindu prince or a movie extra, a ring on every finger. I waited in silence, open-mouthed, utterly fascinated, as though watching a plant growing, a caterpillar pupating.

The jewels disappeared. He began playing the saxophone and the guitar. He hitchhiked 2,500 miles, spent some time with the tribes that live in the Mauretanian desert, saw an elephant in the wild, traveled lying on his stomach in a goods truck, half asphyxiated by the dust, and discovered with his own eyes that Dakar bears an astonishing resemblance to Knokke-le-Zoute, Belgium.

He returned home more or less without shoes, his own having crumbled away in the desert heat, but the possessor of enormous prestige in the eyes of his brother and sisters. He cut off his hair and began studying for a degree in economics. That is the saga of Daniel.

Where is the upbringing in all that? If Daniel, who will be twenty-one this year, is a good son, a good-looking boy, serious yet with a sense of humor, endowed with both imagination and common sense, did I have anything to do with making him so? No, nothing, nothing. And yet yes, something, one tiny little thing, the only thing perhaps that I have given him, yet the only thing too, I sometimes tell myself with pride, that it was important to give him: confidence.

Which doesn't mean that all our problems are over. Daniel has just bought a monkey.

In the Train

I was bringing Vincent back from the health farm in Besançon where he had been forced to spend six months.

A widow, a post-office clerk, started telling me all the trouble she'd had bringing up her children. Especially her son, a school teacher who'd had to marry a very young girl from Marseilles, "in something of a hurry."

"Their little girl, madame, their little Sylvie, I'm mad about her—well, it's no exaggeration to say she was their first piece of furniture. I was a tobacconist's daughter and a tobacconist's wife, but that never stopped me liking to read; I was determined that my children would have a good education, and I was always at them to see that they did. Well, believe it or not, now they're both in trouble. In spite of everything. The terrible thing is not to sacrifice yourself for others; it's to realize it simply wasn't *worth* the sacrifice. Ah, children!

". . . Yes, a tobacconist's daughter, a tobacconist's wife, and believe it or not, just as you like, I had never smoked. My husband died in 1940, I was twenty-nine. All alone. Of course I had my two children, I worked with them, coached them for their exams, and while I was doing it I said to myself: poor girl, you're working at your own loneliness. And judge for yourself whether I was right or not; here we are, my daughter in Paris, my son in Lyons, and me in Besançon. Well [with a plucky grin], I started smoking.

". . . Still alone, always alone. I'm not about to marry again at my age. With men you have to fit in with their little habits, and it wouldn't work any more; at fifty-seven I've got my own habits. So I got myself a job in the post office. Letters, they're like ideas, there's something alive about them."

She made a pretty gesture with her hands, as though those letters of hers were a flock of birds fluttering about her head.

She speaks very well, this lady, I thought. What does she read? I glance down: the *Memoirs of the Cardinal de Retz.*

"Is he coming home from the health farm, your little boy? I hope he's all better now. But of course, if he were ill they'd have kept him there, wouldn't they . . ."

Babies

Dolores has Juanito, whom she adores but in her nervous states just cannot bear. So she sends him away to her parents, brings him back, sends him away again. Conchita has Manolo, whom she feeds on petits-beurre biscuits and water; he falls ill, goes into the hospital, comes out, falls ill again, goes back in again. Anita has a little baby called Sara, three months old, whom she is sending off to Spain in the care of a Spanish woman she scarcely knows and who is going to look after the baby there in return for a hypothetical allowance. Juanito is robust, Manolo intelligent and affectionate, Sara a sheer delight. And all three of them are good-looking.

Three doomed childhoods. One feels one should judge the three mothers rather harshly. But Dolores, having arrived in Paris as trusting as she was ignorant, was abandoned by a man after they had been together five years, her child just barely born. Since then, she says resentfully, "my womb's blocked up." Conchita, who can neither read nor count, says proudly: "No one in my family can read," and refuses to part from the child she feeds so inadequately. Anita entrusted all her savings to a butler in Neuilly (a station in life that to a maid of all work in the fifth arrondissement, even a pretty one, represents something like prince charming), who, it turned out, was a gambler and lost it all. Their stories are sort of melancholy picture romances. And in fact each girl cherishes the hope that her own story will eventually be a true romance: Dolores's lover will come back repentant to marry her and fulfill her every desire. Conchita will come into a fortune and clothe her little Manolo in nothing but the finest silk (though, I suspect, whatever happens, he'd still continue to be fed exclusively on petit-beurres). Anita will welcome her little daughter back from Spain with tears of joy, having at last, in a dance hall somewhere and with the aid of her miniskirt, found her a rich and powerful father.

Their dreams follow the patterns decreed by picture romances. They dream of themselves as good mothers, all three of them, and at the same time rich, adored, showered with cars, villas on the Riviera, jewels. And the dream of motherhood seems just as unrealizable to them as the dream of luxury. They are always out dancing—Lo forgetting to send Juanito's allowance, Conchita leaving her three-year-old and already-half-tubercular Manolo alone, Anita forgetting even that her Sara exists.

Anita and Lo look upon themselves as victims: Lo of society, which did not allow her to get enough education to become a shop assistant or a secretary; Anita of love, abandoned by her butler and swindled of her savings. But Conchita, slovenly, ignorant, sponged on, dishonest, illiterate, well on the way to making an equally chaotic future inevitable for her beautiful and intelligent little boy, does not think of herself as a victim in the slightest. It is perhaps for her that I feel the most pity. You could say, of course, that Lo works only three hours a day, gets up late, spends all her time in bars and on café terraces, where I see her basking on my way home from the library or the social-security office. And that the little work she does do she does badly. She forgets everything I ask her to do, feeds us from tins, and this spring I had to tell her at least eleven times to arrange for the repair man to replace a broken pane of glass. She asks me to find her part-time cleaning jobs, and when I do she doesn't go, or else she quarrels with her part-time employer because the woman has spoken to her in a certain "tone of voice" or "made her feel" that she's just a cleaning woman. You could say that she is careless, unpersevering, impatient. You could say all that. And that Conchita is simply dishonest, slovenly, and lives in a fantasy world. And that Anita, who never sees anyone but pimps, her partners at dances, or out-of-work barmen, and despises hard-working Spanish laborers, who smell of onion, can hardly expect to meet a man of virtue who will grant her every wish for herself and her little girl, unless she changes her ways.

You could say all that. And then a single word, a single gesture will demolish all you were about to say. Anita hid her pregnancy from her employer because she was already pregnant when she took the job and the employer therefore had the right to dismiss her. "She would throw me out, it's her right," she said, in exactly the same tone as my aunt's poor Marie-Louise. It was natural, it was the law of society, just like the theft of her savings and her being deserted. At bedrock they all know that there is no truth in the picture romances, not for them or for their children, who are doomed from the start— so why make any effort, why make any attempt to remedy a situation that they know in advance is irremediable?

On her way to do two-hours cleaning that will bring her in a thousand old francs, Lo takes a taxi that costs her five hundred:

"But, Lo, that's going to cost you an hour's work!"

"Well, for what my work is worth . . ."

Yet this woman who so loathes getting up that if I didn't keep an eye on her she would send my daughters to school late every day will suddenly start getting up at six in the morning, week after week, just to go help an old man in the rue de Buci, a Moroccan concierge, to take up the mail to the apartments there.

"But why doesn't he take the mail up himself, Lo?"

"Because he can't read."

"The concierge can't read?"

"No. When they took him on, they didn't ask him if he could read or not, so he didn't tell them, and now he's in a state."

"I'm sure he is."

"And the tenants are in a state too, their mail is always late getting to them; so I've been going around with it for a while, till things quiet down again."

"And isn't there any other job he could do, this little Moroccan of yours?"

"Oh, no!"

"Why not?"

"Because he's always drunk."

"Why is he always drunk, Dolores?"

Sensing something less than approval in my tone, Lo is immediately on the defensive: "Well, he's got a right to be drunk, believe me! He's lost two sons in the Resistance [by which she means the F.L.N.] and a daughter in an abortion, so there!"

I am well aware that Dolores looks upon abortions as woman's equivalent of a military campaign, part of her (meritorious) struggle against nature and an unjust fate. But that day I was feeling argumentative.

"But you know, there are lots of people who lose children and don't become drunkards because of it."

"Oh yes, I'm quite aware that there are people in the world with no feelings," Lo answers.

"Why should I be honest?" Conchita demanded in bewilderment when confronted by her employer with the matter of certain stolen undergarments. "Would you pay me more for that?"

After her dismissal she complained to Dolores: "She just didn't like me, that woman."

Whereupon, chancing to be present, I put in: "But if you took her clothes . . ."

"If I hadn't taken them, I suppose she'd have liked me, would she?" Conchita screamed suddenly, her flabby, wan face abruptly transformed by wild despair. No, Conchita, I thought, I'm afraid she wouldn't. Do I like Conchita myself? I'd like to like her, yes, I'd like to; if it were possible to love every human being as if he were unique, then every one of us would be saved perhaps. Undoubtedly. But all I can feel is pity, a terrible, futile pity.

We took her son Manolo to stay with us in the country during the holidays. We filled him up with orange juice and chopped beef, and we felt a certain joy, Lo and I, seeing him grow slowly less pale, more lively, almost gay. As the moment approached to hand him back to his mother, who for all her maternal incompetence was passionately clamoring for his return, Lo looked down at him with despair: "You know what we've done? We've just given him the strength to suffer more, that's all."

I didn't dare reply.

Though I love Lo, and love her very much, I have never been able to wrench her out of her despair. It is fundamental, innate. If I tax her with her carelessness, her drinking bouts, her multifarious abuses (she had an abortion on Saturday, went out on Sunday and danced all night, then came back to begin work without having been to bed), she says: "My mother had six children and was never so much as a minute late for her work scrubbing office floors. And what's she got now that I haven't got, tell me that? What? What?"

Would a better Christian than me answer: "She is happier," or "Her conscience is at peace"? I say nothing. My friends find Lo picturesque. It's all so bohemian, isn't it . . . But Lo and I know. And this silence that exists between us is also a bond.

Silences

It makes me aware that I have not resolved my problem, the problem. I am weaponless when faced with Lo, when faced with a certain kind of despair. Love, and do what you will. But is love enough? Is love sufficient compensation? Is the love of God not perhaps just another picture romance that enables me to avoid gazing into the abyss?

A friend once said to me: "I'd rather adopt a child than have one myself. At least the harm's already done."

That sums up the problem. Repairing, sorting out, combating the world's injustice is one thing. Taking upon oneself the act of creating life, and therefore life's injustice too, is another, and on a quite different level. It is still a gamble, but to make it on someone else's behalf, on behalf of the child you have nourished out of your own substance, that is really burning your bridges, and motherhood always, inevitably, borders on the supernatural. Perhaps because I feel the simple, physical joy of motherhood so profoundly, I experience the risk inherent in it all the more. And am I not perhaps indulging myself in that joy at *their* expense?

In the meadow at Gué-de-la-Chaîne, Vincent, seven years old, is stung by a wasp. He sobs: "But why did it do that to me? I hadn't done anything to *it!*"

For the rest of that day, though ordinarily no one could accuse him of being a crybaby, he keeps on suddenly bursting into tears and asking me why. Patiently, I go through my answer again: "It was only an insect, it was afraid, that's all. It didn't know you meant it no harm." And yet all the time— that stricken little face, those eyes full of hurt surprise—I know perfectly well it's more than just a wasp sting that's behind them. "Why isn't the world all love and harmony?" my gentle Vincent is asking. And he is asking me, because I am the one responsible for bringing him into this world. It's the first time, but it won't be the last. Whenever he is faced with an aggressive playmate, with an unfair teacher, with an ugly scene on television, it is always to me that he will turn. Why? Behind all the words I offer, can he sense my silence? I don't know, little one, not yet.

In the same situation Alberte would have stamped on the wasp in fury, Pauline would have forgotten the sting almost immediately, and Daniel wouldn't have asked me why. He never did. He knew by instinct, child of my defenseless adolescence, that we must all find our own answers. Less a son than a companion, he and my mind grew up together. And silence is what we have shared together best.

"What is an abortion, exactly?" Alberte asks.

"It's when you're expecting a baby and you lose it before it's strong enough to live outside you."

"But sometimes it's on purpose?"

"Yes, sometimes it's on purpose. Who told you about it?"

"It was Lo talking to Anita. She said: 'Concha's found someone to do another abortion for her.' Why did she?"

"I think it's because she's unhappy and didn't want her baby to be unhappy too, like her . . ."

"Then she's killed it, so she's a criminal," Alberte concluded with satisfaction.

Unscarred herself, she is naturally pitiless in her judgments, and ready to believe that the rest of the world is too.

"You could say that if she'd done it with the intention of being wicked perhaps. But I don't think she realizes that the baby might have had some chance of being happy, or useful in the world . . ."

"But you, you were sure we'd be happy, weren't you?"

"Sure . . . One can never be sure, you know."

"But we *are* happy!"

"Perhaps you won't always be, though. I hope you will, but I can't be sure."

"And you'll be sad if one of us is unhappy?"

"Very."

"Perhaps you'll say to yourself: It would have been better if I'd had an abortion."

"I don't think so. It could happen, I suppose, if I had a moment of despair; but it would be a sin. Suffering can make us richer, teach us. We can offer it to God, transform it into joy."

"Yes . . . but all the same it's better to be happy."

"I think that if you're truly religious then it's more or less the same thing. Either you're with God, happy or unhappy, and everything is all right. Or you are cut off from him . . ."

"Yes. But it doesn't give God any pleasure if we're unhappy, does it? It couldn't give him any pleasure?"

"Certainly not. And yet there are a great many unhappy people."

"Perhaps when God sees them all, he says to himself: 'It's a pity I didn't have an abortion.'"

Which Brings Us Back to Upbringing

People will tell me that my children have been very badly brought up. At thirteen, I believed that babies were born through the navel, and I wore white socks on Sundays. I don't believe that just because Alberte has learned by the age of ten what an abortion is, or that it is perfectly possible to "have a baby without being married," that she is really going to come to any harm. What is difficult, I find, is to imbue her with a certain idealism without keeping her cloistered, to teach her not to judge people, yet not have her lose her sense of values.

"You've been divorced, haven't you, Mother?" Pauline asks.
"Yes."
"And that's bad?"
"It's not ideal."
"And it was your fault?"
"It's always our fault to some extent when we can't get on with other people."
"But you weren't married in the Church, so it doesn't count," Alberte breaks in, as always unable to accept that I could possibly be in the wrong.
"It doesn't count as a marriage from the Church's point of view, but it still counts as a sin all the same."
"Oh," Alberte murmurs in desolation.
"You don't think Mother's never committed a sin, do you? She's just the same as us, you know," Pauline informs her sister, apparently as pleased as punch at the notion.
"I'm not a saint, you know," I say to Alberte.
"It's a pity, though," she says tenderly.
Tough on the outside, she is the most truly tender of them all underneath. I am not sorry that these questions are being discussed at a time when she can still bring the luminous simplicity of childhood to such problems.
But what am I to do when I discover that Pauline is going everywhere, including her catechism classes, saying: "Your mother's only been married once, and mine's been married three times! And she could have been married ten times if she'd wanted to!"

Pauline

Pauline is our problem child. As a baby she was an angel of sweetness and gaiety. She slept in our bedroom and never once cried in the night, never once asked for her bottle before seven in the morning. And even while she was asleep she laughed.

But as she reached her fourth birthday we began to perceive that this sociable humor had its other side. Pauline intended to lead a life of her own. At the age of five she was already eating out.

"Are you inviting me to dinner? Are you? When?" she would ask the neighbors with her radiant smile, her eyes like stars. And off she went. She became engaged twice between her fifth and sixth birthdays. Her favorite fiancé lived just off the courtyard of our building. He was out there at dawn, under her window, blowing her kisses that she received with joyful, birdlike squeaks.

She evolved a complicated migratory system, spending the night in different apartments in rotation, perfectly happy wherever she was. One summer we sent her to stay with Lo's family, good, plain people who lived on the outskirts of Madrid and had not a word of French among them. When Jacques went to collect her six weeks later, Pauline was the leader of a whole gang of shrieking, laughing Spanish urchins, ran everywhere barefoot, and had totally given up speaking French. She could swear at you roundly in Spanish, though.

"It's always Pauline this, Pauline that," Alberte said one day with some bitterness. "I'm much better-behaved, and I work much harder. What's Pauline got that I haven't?"

And it's true. Alberte is somber and passionate, intelligent and sensitive, industrious and secretive, utterly dependable, in fact. But Pauline . . . Pauline is joy . . . That's all, and it's enough. Dolores is very fond of her company. She takes her out with her to bars, stuffs her full of olives, crisps, and grenadine.

"Don't you think it's bad for children to drag them around to cafés like that? It spoils her appetite, and think of the things she might hear . . ."

"Oh, what makes you think that? Don't worry, my friends

are very respectable," Lo says. "Besides, if anyone did try talking dirty when she was there, I'd smash his face in for him double-quick."

"Oh, yes! I'd like that," Pauline remarked.

In this way she became acquainted with various North Africans, fruit sellers, fritter sellers, construction workers.

Ali says to her: "What's your name?"

"Pauline."

"That's a pretty name: Pouline. Does it mean Little Horse?"

(He assumes, presumably, that it is the feminine of *poulain*. At any rate, Pauline is intrigued by the suggestion.)

"Yes."

"Then you must help me choose the horses for my treble. Five or seven?"

"Seven."

"Twenty-two or sixteen?"

"Twenty-two."

"Diamond or Raglan III?"

"Diamond."

Ali religiously takes note of her answers and he wins. The next Sunday there are four of them consulting the oracle.

"All right," Pauline says, "but if you win you've got to give me a share."

It's a deal. Next week Pauline is out doing all the cafés along the rue Mouffetard: "Did you win, Ali? Did you win, Béchir?"

And she collects her dues.

Later, when we are going to move, she sighs. "It's not going to be easy for me to find a new clientele!"

Vincent suggests advertising in the newspaper: "Lucky mascot seeks light employment."

Lo has quarreled with one of her floating men friends, Mohammed. She is wearing her obdurate madonna face. But Pauline is inclined toward clemency.

"You must forgive him, Dolores. 'Judge not, that ye be not judged!' What's he done?"

"He took me dancing and then danced five times with that pig Cristina!"

That evening, deep in melancholy, she takes Pauline out for a grenadine on the terrace of a café on the rue de Buci. Horrors! Mohammed is there with a Pernod in front of him. Dolores affects an air of vast disdain. Mohammed looks the other way.

Pauline decides to take matters into her own hands. She goes over to Mohammed. "Mohammed, buy me an olive! Dolores is very sad, you know."

Wordlessly, Mohammed hands her an olive, throws a glance in Lo's direction, then lets his gaze sink back into his Pernod. Pauline continues her ferry tactics.

"Look, Lo, Mohammed has given me an olive. He's very sad, you know."

"I don't know him any more," Lo says melodramatically.

Pauline makes another crossing: "Mohammed, buy me some crisps. She'd like you to talk to her, you know, Lo would."

"All she has to do is speak to me first," Mohammed replies. But a certain irresoluteness is apparent on his features.

Pauline returns: "Mohammed's buying me some crisps. But I have to wait a while for them to come. Would you like some, Lo?"

"I wouldn't take anything from anyone as common as him," Lo says.

Mohammed comes over. "Here are your crisps, Pauline."

"Aren't you going to offer the lady any?" Pauline asks.

Lo deigns to smile. Mohammed too. Whereupon, from the bottom of her heart, Pauline cries: "Oh, forgive each other! Please, please do!" And then, seeing them still hesitate: "Cristina—she's nothing but a trollop!"

❁

Pauline stayed tiny for a long time, with bright pink cheeks, whereas Alberte shot up like a piece of asparagus and was soon as tall as her older brother, Vincent. But now, over the past few months, Pauline too has lost a little of her color, begun to grow taller and thinner, and yesterday, I can't remember in connection with what, she suddenly said: "You mustn't say that, it's a swearword!"

Alberte looked at me, a hint of comical regret in her eyes, and said: "Even Pauline is going to grow up, Maman!"

She felt that there was something a little sad about it. I love her for that.

I can't hide it from them that I "found three different men to marry me," as Pauline puts it. I can't hide it from them that Dolores has "had a baby without being married." I can't hide it from them that Jean and Clotilde are living together without being married. That the tramps who wander around our neighborhood are always drunk and sleep on the benches on the Place Furstenberg. That Sara, a friend of mine, is often "a bit odd" toward evening. That Michel has been to visit us, over a five-year-period, with three different wives. That some of their own friends have changed fathers one or more times.

People will say: "What an environment!" Should I send them to boarding school? Jacques is a painter, so he sees a lot of painters. Should I forbid them to speak? And even if I could, wouldn't I simply create an atmosphere of constraint that would disturb the children even more than the freedom of the conversation they now hear? Every environment has its disadvantages. There is Lo, of course. But at least she is utterly goodhearted and totally honest. Cathie was less foul-mouthed, and so charming too, with her flute! Is it my fault if a friend of the family fell in love with Louisette, seduced her, and then stole her away to live happily ever after in the tenth arrondissement, "without benefit of mayor, of marriage feast, or witness," as Aristide Briant, has it? Is it even so very serious? What *is* serious is the difficulty of making them see that the Christian ideal is something else, making sure that they are not imprisoned by the morality of any particular society, and teaching them how to rise above it.

To rise above the merely picturesque—that is such a convenient, easy way out. Lo and her flamenco songs howled out in the kitchen, the pilferings of Conchita, our thieving magpie, Anita's love affairs, Nicolas and his naïve attacks, Mme Josette in her ivory tower, Luc's Zionism, Jean's waistcoats, Daniel's saxophone, Pauline's swearwords, the domestic chaos, the dog —all that is picturesque. Our paper house is a little bit like Noah's ark, with all its animals, pleasant and unpleasant. Our only virtue is perhaps that we accept them all. But Juanito, Manolo, and Lia; Lo in the early morning, a cigarette dangling from her mouth, moaning "Oh, dear, another day"; my aunt dying in the bedroom she would not leave, her body full of deep wounds, toes twisted like roots (on feet that had become mere things), her bed scattered with old letters (the 1914 ones all mixed up with the 1960 ones), with pieces of bread, stale biscuits, orange peels ("No, don't you dare touch anything. I forbid it, this is my house!")—and, as she groaned: "Waiting for death, that's all, and being completely useless," our telling her that suffering does have its use, and telling Lo that life has some use, and thinking for Juanito, for Manolo, for Lia, that the sentence weighing down on their four-year-old, three-year-old, six-month-old heads is justified: that is no longer picturesque. Is it even possible?

Trying once, twice, ten times to find Nicolas a job, without being able, not to help him—our hopes aren't that extravagant —but simply to ease that spleen, that bitterness just a little; telling oneself that one's uselessness, one's total uselessness, is not important. This steady grinding down of so many many beings in closed, irremediably closed situations, accepting it,

and not for oneself, which might still be possible, but for others
—that brutal question, that inconceivable harshness inherent
in faith—I receive it like a savage blow in my face every day,
and I can't always say yes to it. The picturesque is not always
an answer to the children's whys. If I want to answer I've got
to go further than that, and it takes a kind of courage I don't
always have.

Faced with television and its pictures of war, with the tramp
snoring drunkenly in the warmth of the métro grille, with
Aunt's death rattle, with Nicolas's mental prison, with Lo's
unhappiness, with Marie-Louise's poverty, all of them clinging
like oysters to the harsh surface of the world's injustice, can I
say to them: "Yes, that's all justified, that's all outweighed,
that's all good"? And yet if I did always have enough faith,
enough toughness, enough strength and joy to say it, that's
what a true Christian upbringing *would be.*

Vincent and I are walking past the Magasins du Louvre. The
length of the store front, a vast banner announces: "Vietnam
Week Exhibition."

Vincent: "Have they got bombs in there?"

Does the thought appall him? I glance at him out of the
corner of my eye. Apparently not.

And once I have said yes with all my strength, yes, all that
is just, all that is terrible but it is also good, the world, creation
will one day be justified and redeemed, then I shall have to
face that other question, the question that, in spite of faith and
joy, if we are authentically Christian nails us to the cross: by
telling them that, am I not teaching them simply to fold their
arms in the face of the world's afflictions?

May 1968

"Dolores, you haven't swept under the beds."
"There's a strike on, Françoise! I'm not a black-leg!"

One little boy to another: "My father knows a lot more than yours. My father knows Greek."
"Mine has a bigger car."
"Yes, but cars can get burnt."
In May 1968 even little boys discovered that cars can get burnt. False progress. Conspicuous consumption is a big balloon, quickly burst. Education (a certain kind of education) is less vulnerable. The pride of the nouveau-riche makes us laugh. The pride of the expert, of the technician, of the man who speaks well, who knows what words to use, who is a master of etiquette and polite formulas, is more insidious. All that can't get burnt.

St. Theresa of Lisieux said: "My God, I choose all that you will for me."

But one still has to be capable of *choosing*. And that already presupposes an available *capital* of application, of reflection.

Alberte notes down her impressions of the barricades: "At school I have been told that the students are wicked people who are doing all this to frighten honest people. My parents don't agree with that. I am certain of their good faith, but are they right?"

That last sentence, which a friend finds very funny, pleases me with its mixture of trust and circumspection. It is in its way a reward for all my efforts to mold my children's characters without influencing their judgment.

Matthieu says: "It's a little hypocritical, in my opinion. You say: This is what I think, and now do as you wish. But the more they love you and admire you, the more you are influencing them that way."

In the first place, I don't say to them: Do as you wish. I say: This is what I think, and how you must behave while you're children. When you're grown up, then you will form your own idea of what life is all about and you will have to try to live according to what you have decided, in good faith, to be right.

"But you can't be *sure* that your way of thinking is right. You risk warping them . . ."

"One's bound to warp them, anyway. In fact, it's terrifying, the extent to which even the slightest gesture on our part affects our children, penetrates their very fiber, marks them. You can never be sure of doing the right thing all the time. What always amazes me is that the people who rush with such temerity and so little certainty about the outcome into love, into marriage, into procreation, into politics, into work, expect so much from God along those lines."

"But, in any case, a religious upbringing does leave its mark."

Yes, on that point certainly I will commit myself. I am bound to believe, beyond any doubt, that what I give them is more important than any possible warping it may include. My mother wrote me a very moving letter one day explaining why my father and she had decided it was better not to have my sister and me baptized. Strange as it may seem, that "liberal" upbringing helped me in my religious development. They raised us in their truth and left us free to choose our own. What more can one do? I consider such an upbringing preferable to many dry and joyless "Christian" upbringings in which actions are perpetually given the lie by words and in which constant restraints on the children's liberty lead to passionate rejection in adolescence. Needless to say, a both Christion *and* liberal upbringing would be my ideal. But what a delicate balance to maintain! That short sentence of Alberte's gives me some hope that I may on occasion have succeeded in attaining it. Even though I don't know exactly how.

We know so little about what really counts in a child's education! I believe that a certain whimsicality, a certain resolute independence with regard to certain conventional values that I often consciously observed in my parents, taught me far more than any number of weighty homilies on the superficiality of those values could ever have done. As, for example:

Papa on the Riviera

My father, on holiday, decided to treat me to the luxury of an afternoon's swimming in an establishment clearly reserved for the "very best people." Tiled cabanas, a massage machine, parasols, cocktails served on the beach. Papa withdrew to undress. He reappeared in nylon bathing trunks of impeccable cut, his whole appearance of the utmost correctness, except that the fancy had taken him to keep his shoes and his sock suspenders on. Indignation welled up behind serried sunglasses, then turned slowly to stupor as Papa, with Olympian mien, gazed up and down the beach searching for a beach cushion that exactly suited him, until his regal indifference eventually conquered every eye and he became a cynosure of admiration. They had thought at first they were seeing a tramp, a bumpkin, but in the face of such lordly self-assurance, doubt ceases to be possible: it *must* be Onassis. The waiter approached wreathed in smiles. And I simply admired, as I had when I was only five, while my father in stentorian tones ordered himself a lemonade.

Or:

Mother Taking a Taxi

Mother, frail and blond and all graciousness, bending beneath the weight of her numerous pieces of luggage and followed by my sister, has just arrived at the Gare du Nord after traveling down from Anvers. Taxis are few and far between; the travelers wanting them are legion. A lady in front of Mother takes the last remaining taxi. The horizon is empty.

Mother in firm, albeit gentle tones: "Madame, where are you going?"

The lady, momentarily abashed: "To the avenue Mozart. But . . ."

Mother: "That will suit us very well. Get in the front, Miquette [my sister]. We are going to take this taxi with you as far as the avenue Mozart, and then we will go on in it."

The lady, already in the back seat: "You most certainly will not. I won't have it!"

She is wasting her breath. My sister is already sitting beside the driver (blushing, but sustained by family feeling), and the baggage is already piling up around the lady's feet. Mother gets in. The driver, eyes twinkling, refuses to take sides. The lady: "But I won't stand for it! I order you to get out! I've never heard of such a thing! Really . . ."

Mother, still gracious: "Driver, the avenue Mozart, please."

The driver drives off. The lady begins shouting.

Mother telling the story: "Well, Françoise, can you believe it, she shouted *all the way*, from the Gare du Nord to the avenue Mozart. You'd have thought she'd been kidnapped. Some people are just so *violent!*"

Papa is a storyteller. Mother is a writer. Their comedy manifests itself in very different ways. My father's springs from events themselves, from external circumstances. My mother's is the result of a process of internalization, so that it suddenly explodes into a normal course of events of which she never takes the slightest account. She is not without practical sense; indeed, she will sometimes display the utmost ingenuity to ward off events that turn out to be wholly imaginary. For instance, having been deeply shocked by an account of a number of fires in certain big stores, she decided never to go into one again without a flashlight ("You see, the first thing they do in such an event is to turn off the electricity") and a twenty-five-yard length of knotted nylon rope ("So, you see, I just fasten my knotted rope and I climb down, it couldn't be simpler"). I can only admire such vitality in a woman who, despite her suppleness of limb, is well on her merry way to her seventies.

"But you can't take the rope everywhere. To a cocktail party, for example. And that's precisely when the fire will break out, if there's going to be one!"

"How fatalistic you are, Françoise! I'm just bettering my chances, that's all. It's a question of statistics."

Mother runs into a friend in the boulevard Saint-Germain. "You're looking very well."

"Yes," Mother replies. "I've just spent the most extraordinary night with Confucius."

"With whom?"

But Mother has already gone, as always stepping jauntily, like a young girl.

In Switzerland, with Papa, in an ultra-modern hotel in which the glass doors open and shut automatically (regularly trapping unfortunate Indian visitors), and the luggage is brought to the departing traveler on an ingenious system of moving belts, with the result that it is constantly being crushed, lost, delayed. Papa observes the system with ironic eyes.

After we wait for our luggage for thirty-five minutes, he observes to a much braided attendant who has scorned our requests for action: "Well, you may have the best watches in the world in Switzerland, but the very least one can say of them is that they run slow!"

The braided attendant attempts to wither us with a look, but the little Italian pages, less personally involved with the cause of progress, burst out laughing. We leave the hotel avenged.

In a discussion with a pompous gentleman who is boasting rather loudly and too often that he was in the Resistance, Papa remarks: "Yes, I was in it, too. But as an amateur, of course, not a professional."

If one has parents one can laugh at and be proud of too, isn't that an education right there?

My grandmother did paintings of flowers. Without any great talent, but enthusiastically. One day, when she was well over sixty, she arrived at my parent's house in a state of great excitement.

"My dears, I've discovered an extraordinary painter! I'm quite overwhelmed! I've seen Van Gogh's *Sunflowers*! I'm changing my style!"

And here is a story about her that seems to me edifying in the fullest sense of the word.

Toward the end of her life, sentenced by her doctors to stay in bed, she would trick her nurse and get up before dawn, very cautiously take out her paintbox and sneak out as quickly as she could, like someone intent on an illicit pleasure, to sketch just one more landscape. Does the fact that this story is not about a painter of genius but about a modest woman wholly without ambition, who loved beauty in her own simple and unpretentious way, make it less edifying? For me it makes it even more so, perhaps.

❀

Girls

Daniel sometimes brings his girlfriends home. They play their instruments, eat, or watch television with us; then their visits become less frequent and eventually are no more. We miss them. At every first appearance we start work on the foundations of yet another great love story. Where did he meet her? Does she play an instrument? Does she sing? Does she like children? At the sight of a blond head glimpsed for a second through a half-open door, Pauline once cried: "Oh, are you engaged at last, Daniel?"

Daniel finds that there are things to be said both for and against the warmth of our welcomes. The fact is that, although we follow him enthusiastically into his infatuations, we are unfortunately slower than he to shake them off. We wept for two Micheles, a Marianne, a Fanny. Simone consoled us for a while, though we didn't take to Pascale. Sara we liked a lot, and could have wished that Daniel had at least allowed us time to get to know her.

"But why aren't you seeing Jeannine any more?" Pauline sighs. "We were very fond of her, all of us . . ."

Daniel bears our interest patiently. Recently, however, he has taken to issuing warnings when he brings a girl home: "Don't get too fond of her, eh? It's not serious. No slop!"

Daniel: "It's got so I don't dare bring my friends home. You give them such a warm welcome that later if I want to quarrel with them I can't!"

Mother

Mother has a passion for medicines. Something of a witch, she weighs their virtues, decides on dosages, administers them, and then throws in for good measure a recommended list of dietary and other precautions that apparently are intended less as a means of inducing good health than as a kind of learned and hygienic entertainment for the patient. When she says: "I wonder if a quarter of a Corydrane taken with half an Equanil might not give a rather interesting result . . ." she has the look of an alchemist prepared to risk an explosion to make a valuable discovery.

Mother: "I'm a little tired this morning. Yesterday evening, you see, I was just passing through your father's study, and there on his desk I saw this medicine that was completely new to me. Well, naturally I was tempted. I took just one capsule . . . Well, I slept very badly, I can tell you!"

The pensive look on her face nevertheless expresses genuine satisfaction at having undertaken a painful but rewarding experiment.

Papa

Papa admits to having a few doubts about the length of Daniel's hair. But when all's said and done, no, it's not really serious. Daniel has a thousand good qualities that his hair may perhaps conceal from some people's eyes, but never from ours. We may have been just a little worried by some of the stages he went through (jewels, saxophone, late nights, bizarre robes), but through all those eccentricities he has always retained a certain solid, reassuring quality. What is it? I rack my brains.

Then Papa supplies it: "He's not sensible, but he's always serious."

There is a whole philosophy of life in that definition.

Mother

An ardent student of philosophy, Mother finds it difficult to understand that other people don't share her infatuations and her outrage on the subject.

"What did you do yesterday, darling?"

"We had dinner at the P——s."

My mother's face darkens with consternation. "Oh, darling! Hadn't I told you? Oh, I should have, I should have . . ."

"Told me what?"

"Just imagine, a fortnight ago I met P., we talked. We began going into things really thoroughly, you know, and I discovered . . ."

"What?"

"That he isn't a true Platonist!"

Isabelle, Cuba, and the Revolution

"Marie," Mme Josette says, "was the most intelligent, Isabelle the prettiest."

"And you, Madame Josette?"

"Oh, me . . . I was the quietest."

Mme Josette's saga unfolds slowly, week by week, sometimes shot through with a gleam of poetry. Sometimes I sense the presence of an expectation, of a hope; sometimes there is nothing there at all, nothing but that long, resigned silence, that gloomy night of the soul that she continues to endure with blind patience. Throughout the fifteen years that I have been going to her, on and off, to have my hair treated, she has been spinning that slender gray thread, her life. But there are so many shades of gray.

"We always went to stay with an uncle for our summer holidays, down in the Landes. The wells there have no walls around them, you know, just grilles over the top so that children and animals won't fall in. But sometimes they forgot to put them back, or else she used to pull them off herself, I don't know. But what I do know, what I remember, is that Belle used to swing to and fro over those wells, using just her arms for support, her legs hanging down into the hole over the water. To and fro, to and fro she used to swing. I practically died of fright, you can imagine. I didn't dare go over to her for fear she'd fall in; and she just laughed, she just tilted her head back and laughed: 'You're scared! you're scared!' I certainly was scared! And at school, in the convent, she climbed up on the chapel wall. 'You've made me unhappy! I'm going to jump off!' The sisters all clustered around underneath: 'Isabelle! Come down, we beg you!' But I warned her. I said: 'One day you'll really fall! It's bound to happen.'"

Isabelle is now a dressmaker in Tours. She has three daughters, all "as lovely as the day is long." She has been through two divorces but is still "as merry as a girl," Mme Josette says. Once, when I was in Tours giving a lecture, I felt I'd like to go and visit her. But what for? She could hardly still be swinging her legs over wells.

"Oh, you might not have found her there anyway," Mme Josette informed me later. "She gets these funny ideas into her head, you know. Someone told me last year—a friend who just happened to be passing through Tours—that she had suddenly upped without telling a soul and left for Cuba."

"For Cuba?"

"Yes, Cuba. And when I wrote to her, asking for her views on the situation over there (you know how interested I am in these matters), the only answer I got was that she had visited some magnificent caves which you go down into from the middle of a pineapple field, and that she was very pleased to have seen that it is true about pineapples, that they do grow on the ground and not on trees, because she'd never believed it before. That's all she saw in Cuba, pineapples! Just think of it!"

Perhaps, after all, Isabelle the dressmaker from Tours does still swing to and fro over wells in the Landes?

"I mean really, just think of it," Mme Josette went on relentlessly, "to see nothing in Cuba but caves and pineapples, when there are all those problems . . ."

Yes indeed, yes of course. Mme Josette's thirst for knowledge, for impartial information, is a fine thing. But then so, undoubtedly, are pineapples. And caves. Which of us didn't dream of magic grottoes in his or her childhood? To see nothing but pineapples, yes, of course . . . But not to see them? One should see them *as well*. That's what's really difficult. And it's the thing I keep coming back to. We have used the beauty of the world so much as a justification for its injustice that we have begun to be ashamed of that beauty. How are we to make our children see—and if I harp on children it is because it is talking to my own that forces me to clarify everything for myself—that we belong to two worlds, this one and the other, and yet we belong to the other *through* this world, not separately from it? How are we to impart the transparency of this world without making it seem a way of escape, the joy of this world without it becoming uncaring? How are we to pass on to them a taste for the world's beauty and poetry, an awareness of how amazing it is that it exists, as well as the awareness that there is always so much suffering alongside that beauty?

For I, of course, find it both marvelous and funny that this woman I don't know, in a sudden impulse, should fly off like that to Cuba and come home filled with a lasting delight at having seen at last, with her own eyes, that pineapples are grown, as she had found it difficult to believe they were till then, in rows in fields, not much above ground level, almost like artichokes. Perhaps she had already seen this as a child in one of those educational illustrations chocolate bars used to have: "Pineapple harvest in Guadeloupe. Exotic Fruit Series," or in her geography book, and still she wasn't sure, there was a nagging doubt in her mind, they make children swallow so many things, and the landscapes of real life bear so little resemblance to those orderly worlds, reduced to three or four colors, presented by maps in geography classes . . . And now, at the age of forty-three, she knows, she has seen the miraculous stalactites underground and the pineapples above, and that seems somehow important to her, to Isabelle-who-swung-over-the-wells, to Isabelle-up-on-the-chapel-wall, more important than Cuba's agricultural statistics, Cuba's increasing literacy, Cuba's freedom from censorship, more important than all the things that would have fascinated Mme Josette, about which she would have returned duly informed, her suitcases bulging with lists and figures. Isabelle's attitude both enchants and saddens me. How can one hang on to the spirit of childhood without sinking into childishness, into the picturesque, into aestheticism? How is one to take an interest in the world's progress, keep informed, take sides, without losing the gift of wonder, of spontaneity, the ability to respond to the passing and precious instant?

I make an attempt to reconcile poetry and information by playing the children a borrowed record of the beautiful song, so epic and Victor Hugo-like, that the Cubans sing with the refrain "*Alfabetisar, alfabetisar* . . ." But Pauline has the gravest doubts about the common sense of a people that can sing with joy at learning to read.

"I could do without perfectly well," she says. "I can draw, and that's enough. And I didn't need to learn. Fancy having a revolution just so you can learn to write!"

"Perhaps if someone said you couldn't learn, then that would make you want to," Alberte says in her ear, proving that she is not unacquainted with the spirit of contradiction.

"Do they stop children from going to school, then, in other countries?"

"They don't stop them by force, but there aren't any schools, or else they're too far away from their homes, or else the children have to work in the fields, or . . ."

"So then there's a revolution?"

"Sometimes. There are a great many reasons for revolutions."

"What is a revolution?"

Whereupon Alberte, who has seen barricades going up just outside her school, breaks in with: "Is revolution a sin? And war—is that a sin?"

Vincent, who has a liking for textual authority and is always sure of himself in matters of theology: "Of course. It's in the Bible. Thou shalt not kill. And there's also a bit in St. Paul, I think, where it says you must obey kings and presidents."

"But if it's the president who says 'Go on' and you're forced to make war, then you can go on and the sin is on his head."

"You can refuse and become a conscientious objector," Vincent points out with a virtuous air.

Pauline, however, shrieks with laughter. "If the president makes you, then the sin is on his head, and you can kill all the people you don't like, bang, bang, bang, bang!"

"At that rate, all the presidents in the world would be in hell," Vincent points out.

"Perhaps they all are," Alberte says.

We meditate for a moment on this sad possibility.

"But, anyway, you can't start a revolution on a president's

orders, because revolutions are always made against the president," Vincent observes.

"So the poor students will all go to hell, will they?" Pauline asks.

"No, because they're not killing anyone."

"But what if you kill someone and you think you're right? And what if you kill someone very wicked? And what if . . ."

And on they go. Question after question. All children watch television today. Today their ears, if not their minds, are filled constantly with Vietnam and Biafra, the sound of grenades, the whistling of bullets. Perhaps they don't all ask these difficult questions. Should the fact that they do ask them perhaps be counted as a success?

"I don't know if war and revolution are sins. It's a question for one's personal conscience, I think. If you, for example, think that a certain war is unjust, then it would be a sin to fight in it even if you were ordered to."

"But if you refuse to go to war, you go to prison, don't you?" from Alberte.

"Not girls," Pauline puts in. "Girls can't go to war. And it's a pity because . . ."

"There were girls in the revolutions and there were some in the Resistance, too. And in Israel; they even have a uniform just like the men soldiers."

"Oh, good!" Pauline says, viewing the future with increased optimism.

I put in: "One can protest, and not necessarily go to prison. As Vincent says, you can become a conscientious objector, or ask to be in the Red Cross . . ."

Vincent: "Non-violence. I'm for it. But it doesn't often get results. Like those peasants you told us about in Sicily who built a road just to show they could do things and that they ought to be given work."

Alberte: "And were they given some?"

Vincent: "I don't think so, no."

Pauline: "So they started a revolution?"

Me: "No, not just then."

Pauline: "But they're going to? Is that it?"

Me: "I don't know."

Vincent: "In a case like that, where there's injustice, is it a sin to start a revolution and fight people?"

I am a little embarrassed by this question. But Alberte has the answer: "All you have to do is write to the Pope. You tell him: Look at all this, it's unjust, I really am being forced to start a revolution. And he'll send you a dispensation."

"Do you think so?"

Alberte is not prepared to admit any doubts on the subject: "Of course. In the old days, when it was wrong to eat meat on Fridays, the uncle of a friend of mine had an illness, and he had a dispensation saying he could eat meat, and so it wasn't a sin for him any more."

Her conviction is so absolute that Vincent and I are reduced to thoughtful silence. Eventually, however, Vincent cannot keep from voicing a certain skepticism.

"You know, the Pope's a very busy man," he sighs.

Progress

"And then, after the revolution," Alberte continues (safe in the shelter of Papal authority, that dispensation tucked in her pocket, seeing herself as reforming society from top to bottom), "after the revolution you have progress! Everything gets better."

"Sometimes. That's the idea, certainly."

"If things didn't get better, what would have been the point?"

"But you can never be absolutely sure in advance that they are going to get better."

"Then it's a very risky business," Alberte says, suddenly cooling off.

"But so is everything we do, you know."

"How do you mean? Everything?"

"Books, children . . . How can you be sure it's worth going to all that trouble writing books when you don't know how they'll turn out, or bringing up children without being certain they'll be happy?"

"Yes, but a revolution isn't trouble you go to so much as trouble you make for others," Alberte puts in pertinently.

"Sometimes." (I have the impression that the words I use most often with my children are: sometimes, perhaps, in a way . . . Is it commendable fair-mindedness, or dangerous indecision?)

"Yes, think of Louis XVI or Tsar Alexander," Vincent chimes in, delighted at the opportunity to display his knowledge.

"I think the revolutionaries on those occasions decided that it was worth sacrificing a few men for the happiness of the many."

"But were they right? If they couldn't be sure?"

"There's always that risk."

"Are you a revolutionary, Mother?"

"I don't know. I don't think so."

"Why not?"

"Perhaps I'm not brave enough. Or optimistic enough."

"Jesus said: If someone strikes you on the cheek . . ." Vincent murmurs.

"Yes, but he didn't say: If someone strikes someone else's cheek, walk away without saying anything."

"I wonder if it's possible to be a Christian and a revolutionary at the same time," Vincent concludes.

"A lot of people are asking themselves that."

"And yet they don't write to the Pope?" Alberte asks, still resolutely convinced that dispensations are the answer.

"The Pope can't decide everything for us, you know."

"Then what use is he, I'd like to know," Alberte asks truculently.

Money

"There are some girls at school," Pauline informs me, "who are more spoiled than us. At the beginning of every term they have a new book bag, even if the old one isn't worn out."

"Don't you think that's a bit stupid?"

"Course I do," Pauline says. "But *they* don't."

"You have piano lessons, dancing lessons, you go swimming . . ."

"Yes," Pauline says. "It's not that I'm asking for anything, you understand. It's just that what we have given us, well, it doesn't show."

"There are some girls who go to winter sports and have their own skis. We go to the mountains to summer camp, but it isn't the same, and we don't have skis."

"It would be rather expensive if I had to buy skis for all of you. There are some children who never have any holidays at all, you know."

"Yes, Negro children," Pauline says.

"No, not just Negro children. Children whose families are too poor."

"They can always go to camp," Alberte puts in. "Or if they can't, then it's because they're not good at managing."

"First, that's not always true. There are some people who don't even have enough money to send their children to camp. And second, even the fact that people are not good at managing may be the result of their being poor."

Alberte muses on this. Pauline bursts into passionate sobs. "Not even enough money to go to camp!" she wails. "We must send them some money, then! I'll stay home and let them have my place."

"You can only give them one place, and you can't send enough money for all the poor children there are," Vincent points out. "Think of the underdeveloped countries!"

"But we could send a little anyway," Pauline begs.

"It would be better to teach people to manage for themselves, rather than sending them money," Alberte says. "It would be longer-lasting and it would be more interesting for them. The only trouble is you'd have to know how yourself first. Not like you, Mother, you don't even understand the social-security forms."

And of course we take the easy way out. In the end we are going to send some money. But Pauline's phrase stays with me: "I'll stay at home and they can have my place." What family would agree to act on that childish impulse? The children must have "fresh air," and the winter has been so tiring; they have grown so pale this past term, our children, despite all the vitamins and the orange juice; and so one lets the impulse fade, one dismisses such childhood emotions, calls them "childishness," one lets it fade and die so that the child will have nice plump cheeks and get into the habit of thinking that its own needs come before everything . . . and we call this being sensible. Even in the most humdrum daily routine, we live in direct contradiction of the most fundamental Christian truths, the most basic Christian priorities, and we call it being socially adjusted. What mother would allow her daughter to give a friend her best doll, without a protest? She will say: "Why don't you give her that other one, the one you played with last year?" She will cut short the noble impulse, blur with a hint of duplicity the simple joy of giving, and believe all the time that she is being "sensible." How we sully these childish souls put in our care.

Hell

Alberte went through one rather difficult period. First she became lazy and disobedient, which she had never been before. Then she began stealing small sums of money, sometimes from my pockets, sometimes from Dolores, then from the purse of a temporary cleaning woman. Eventually it grew to disturbing proportions: thousand-franc notes, even a five-thousand-franc note, began disappearing. At the same time we discovered that she arrived late for school regularly, having had herself escorted by a policeman (!), whom she would persuade that she was lost—thus providing herself with an alibi. (She can find her way all over Paris perfectly well without getting lost.)

Our uneasiness mounted. I took the culprit to task.

"Now look, you must try to see this clearly. Cristina earns five hundred francs an hour when she works cleaning people's houses. You do realize, don't you, that when you take a thousand francs from her you're stealing two hours of her work? Two working hours is a long time!"

"Yes, but you paid her back," Alberte replies mulishly.

"I paid her back with money that represents my own work. You can't get out of it like that."

"No . . . But all the same it's fairer . . ."

"What is?"

"That you should give me your work . . ."

"That I should give it to you, yes, but not that you should steal it from me."

"Is money always work? There are lots of people who have money and never do anything."

"In that case it's what's called capital, it's money that works for them, when they've invested it. But it's too complicated to explain now."

"Ah, now I understand!" she cries, her face alight with mischief. "Those are the people I should steal from, is that it?"

I can't think of an answer. Inculcating a child with respect for capital is not my idea of an inspiring task; on the other hand, turning my own daughter into a Robin Hood in skirts . . . I am beginning to wonder whether the time has come to consult a psychologist, a psychoanalyst even, when suddenly one morning, remorse having made its secret inroads (in what mysterious fashion?), after five weeks of shameless crime Alberte abruptly manifests a violent contrition. "I'll never steal again! I promise I'll never steal again!" she cries, and thrusts into my lap the various fruits of her brigandage. A little small change, an incredible quantity of half-empty packets of sweets, half-eaten biscuits and bars of chocolate, a plastic butterfly, a pair of plastic earrings, a mechanical monkey that plays a drum, a set of watercolors, a geometry set in a mock crocodile case, and I can't remember what else. What can I do but console her, congratulate her, and deliver a little moral discourse on the power of conscience (Cain!) that makes me blush somewhat, even though Alberte greets it with grave approval.

"Oh yes, that's very true . . ."

"But how did you find out at last, darling?"

"It was yesterday evening in bed while I was eating my chocolate . . . I always wait till the light is out because of Pauline, because she tells everything . . . I was in the dark, in bed, and I said to myself: Now I'm in hell."

In hell! Whoever could have been telling her about hell? Never in her life have I referred to the life after death in any terrifying form, and I can remember several times having told them all of my conviction that after a greater or lesser period of time every soul, when it has been purified, returns to the "regions of light and peace."

"I'm not sure that there is a hell, you know, not in the form that people usually talk about. You know yourself that in the

New Testament Jesus very rarely talks of hell. I'm not sure that there is even one soul in hell. And, in any case, certainly no children's souls . . ."

Alberte doesn't seem convinced. Her nature is so somber and passionate that it is quite possible after all that she might actually want a hell to exist.

"It was dark, you see, and because I couldn't tell Pauline anything about it, and because I was afraid that someone would find the monkey and the geometry set, and all the other things I'd hidden behind the refrigerator . . ."

Yes, I suppose solitude of that kind, being shut in with the idea of sin like that, can very well give a sensitive child an intuition of evil, even of hell. Alberte is certainly the only one of my children capable of such an intuition.

Should I be concerned? Should I be glad? I have always had such a horror of a certain "sense of sin" that sees evil as residing in the creation and not in the creature that perhaps I am in danger of going too far in the direction of optimism?

However, Alberte's restless mind seems to be quitting those somber prospects without my help.

"But you did pay them back, didn't you, Cristina and Dolores?"

"Yes."

"Then if I give you all I bought with their money and you've given it back to them, then it's as though you'd bought what I'm giving you with your money? It's as though I hadn't stolen at all."

This argument seems to me very specious indeed, but Alberte is so happy to have shaken off her burden of remorse that I haven't the heart to refute it.

"In a way . . . But I'll remind you that I'm not in the habit of spending my money on mechanical monkeys and plastic butterflies."

"Don't you think they're pretty?"

"That's not the point."

"If you don't want them for yourself, you can put them aside till Christmas. Then you can give them to me as presents and they'll be rightfully mine."

A pause.

"It will save you money, too."

Later, returning to the subject: "It's true, you know, I won't steal any more," she says, nailing my eyes with her own blue, straight gaze. And her mobile face changes yet again, lights up from inside. "But all the same, if you only knew, when I was walking along like that, early in the morning, down streets I didn't even know, and buying myself anything I wanted, it was fabulous!"

Hell is a long way away.

What one most deplores, or what *I* most deplore, in a certain form of Christian upbringing is the inculcation of a sense of sin that disturbs and splits the child's mind at the very beginning of infancy, either inhibiting its instincts or else clothing Creation itself with a fearful (and somewhat suspect) supernatural glow. In a book that once had a great vogue I remember how Thomas Merton treated himself as a hell-doomed soul because he had had a few glasses of beer and read Marx as a young man. That would really be acquiring a Satanic halo at bargain-basement prices. How can nonbelievers take such remarks seriously? How can the mysterious figure of Evil Incarnate ever appear to them as anything but grotesque if it is present in the guise of a jolly young student downing wicked pints of beer? Not that I subscribe to the opposite excess, which consists in believing that only a very few rare criminals, one or two real monsters, have access to the realms of sin; but it is so important to differentiate between evil and the objects that temptation employs to present itself . . .

Yes, children, certain children, do have access to the realm of evil. Yes, "sin can be present even in a glass of water," even though the glass of water itself remains entirely innocent of it.

But how is one to instill such a standard in a child without its becoming an obsession? How is one to give a child a true sense of responsibility without its turning into a feeling of guilt that will poison the child's entire life? One would need to be perpetually inspired, and so free . . .

"Dolores is good really, isn't she?" Alberte asks.
"Of course."
"She shouts and she says swearwords, but she's really good."
"Yes."
"Then why can't I use swearwords, like her?"
"You can be good *without* swearing; they're not necessary."
"But it's not important?"
"It isn't enormously important in the eyes of God, no. But in the eyes of the world . . ."
"What does the world matter? God is all that counts," Alberte says.

"God forgives everything, doesn't he?" Pauline asks in a state of great agitation.
"He forgives everything in his love if we regret the evil we have done. But it is precisely because he is all love that we mustn't do anything to cause him grief."
Pauline bursts into a flood of tears. "I've committed a terrible sin!"
"What, my darling?"
"I took two hundred francs out of your pocket this morning!"
"Well, perhaps the best thing would be for you to put it back."
"But I've spent it all on candy bars!"
"Then that's just too bad, isn't it, my darling. But you mustn't ever do it again. Just look at how sorry you are now, how horrible it is to feel you've done wrong."
"Oh, yes," Pauline sighs, her long lashes wet with tears—the living image of contrition. "I've been feeling it all day long."

But then she adds, in her honesty: "After I finished eating all the candy bars."

Good Impression

Interregnum. Dolores has found a better-paying job in a bar, where her already tottering health is now being completely wrecked by a simple combination of excessive physical drudgery (eleven hours on her feet the other day without a break) and a no less excessive intake of strong spirits. From time to time she comes back to visit and presents us, very stiff and formal, like someone making a challenge, with a parcel of meat for the dog. She knows well enough that we would help her: was it that we lacked patience, or did she lack perseverance? The silence that lies between us during these reappearances of hers betrays our common impotence. "Life," that crushing weight, has been stronger than both of us . . .

So once more I go to *Le Figaro* to put in an advertisement. Once more that procession of faces from which, in ten short minutes, I must choose the one that will share our life (I was about to say our crossing).

Jacques takes me to task very seriously: "And don't go and accept the first one that comes along, because you just can't choose or she seemed sympathetic. Ask for *references*. Say you'll think it over. Ask for their addresses and telephone numbers."

"Yes, you're quite right."

But no sooner has the procession begun (call between 8 a.m. and noon) than I am crushed by an insurmountable sense of abasement and angst. So many people looking for a job, and I must give it to them or turn them down. With the greatest difficulty I manage to reject a Portuguese man with the most pitiful expression (after all, I did ask for a *woman* to live in and help in the house), and a rather more robust-looking Moroccan. But in doing so I use up all my remaining fund of respectability and social sense. The Portuguese man had such a big family! The Moroccan assured me that he really cooked so well! After those two refusals my energy is completely drained. It is beyond my powers to refuse anything to people who are trying so hard to make a *good impression* on me.

A good impression! But who am I to make such demands? To have my washing and my cleaning done by people who are just as good as I am? To have a wretched Spanish scullery maid with nails in deepest mourning and two teeth missing coming to abase herself before me to assure me through the gap in her teeth that she can do everything, absolutely everything, to perfection? The ones who can do everything are generally the most wretched of all, those unable to conceal from even the most cursory eye that the last abortion took place the day before yesterday and that the next bender is due the day after tomorrow (as soon as I have handed over the first "contribution"), sad, down-at-the-heel braggadoccio that one wishes one could embrace, piously, on its lean gray cheeks. There are those who don't know how to do anything, the young country wench with her red hands, a dime-store brooch pinned on her raincoat, innocent shoplifters ready to rush off with the first soldier who presents himself, having broken a kitchenful of crockery in six weeks. There is the woman living in the fantasy of the better days she once knew, the concierge whose back teeth are already awash with wine, the sixty-year-old "who is still very strong for her age"—the phrase rends your heart. Every kind of incompetence and human misfortune—how does one tell them no?

Jacques discovered me in tears in the kitchen. "You're just too sensitive," my tough man-about-the-house told me. "You go to your room, I'll answer the door."

Infinitely relieved, I retreated upstairs. But an hour later, intrigued by the silence, I came down to find him with a very old woman sobbing in his arms.

"She reminded me of my grandmother," he said after the woman (a Hungarian) had left, trying to explain away his moist eyes. "She was really too old for the work here, but she was so upset about it!"

"Hasn't she applied for other jobs?"

"Oh yes! Lots. But she didn't like the looks of them. She told me the French are all so dirty and so mean!"

Finally an energetic young girl took my fancy.

"I feel I could be happy here," she said. She could answer the telephone, cook, keep to a schedule; but she spoke with a rather disturbing distinction.

"Don't you think you really ought to be looking for a job as a secretary?" I asked her timidly. She seemed much too good for us, and I was uneasy.

"No, no, you're just what I'm looking for," she insisted.

It was decided that she should start on Monday morning, at eleven o'clock. She didn't arrive. That day went by, and the next . . . Once more we were deserted, surrounded by a sea of dirty dishes.

"Well, you said she was too good for us," Jacques commented resignedly. "You obviously convinced her too."

We went back to our daily cleaning women.

Allegra

"What a pretty dress that is," Allegra says. "I love the russet of Jeanne's skirt. What do you think of the Persian prints they're wearing this year?"

She notices all our skirts, our belts, our shoes. Passing a table, she will suddenly freeze, one leg still in the air, momentarily hypnotized by a picture in *Vogue*, in *Elle*, in *Marie-Claire*.

"Look at these two colors together, isn't it pretty! And those semicircular pockets, they're original, don't you think?"

"Allegra thinks about nothing but clothes," Jeanne says. "One begins to wonder if she's ever had a single thought about anything else."

Perhaps not. Allegra wants a baby; René, her husband, doesn't want one. "Bringing a child into the world . . . the responsibility . . . the political situation . . . the bomb . . ." "He's really afraid the noise will keep him from working," Allegra translates, her brow serene. "But once the baby arrives, he'll get used to it." She is preparing the layette. René rages against the split in the Left, the collusion on the Right, the fragmentation of the Church, the futility of the intellectuals, the triviality of everyone else . . .

"Every morning," Allegra murmurs tenderly, "I make him drink a glass of hot lemon juice. I think he's got a bad liver."

A mad author comes to visit me. Allegra is in the house. Jacques and I put our heads together. Won't our seeing him encourage him in his madness? If I refuse to see him, won't I be failing in my duty to the publisher who . . . We run through all the great authors of the past who were afflicted with neuroses; we consider the social aspect, the lack of state aid, the shortage of psychoanalysts. Time passes. Dolores puts her head in the door in panic. "*He* is pacing up and down like a bear in a cage. *He* is chewing his nails. *He* is twitching." The shadow of disaster hovers over us. The manuscript is not without merit.

"Can you imagine someone like that appearing on *Books for Everyman*?" I ask cravenly.

"You can't make decisions about manuscripts on the basis of their authors' possibilities on television," Jacques says.

"No, but he'll always be around. We'll have to listen to his tales of woe, he'll telephone us at midnight, he'll make fools of us . . ."

We already have enough trouble dealing with sane authors. I remember a mother who always used to telephone me at eleven in the evening, just as I had at last got to sleep, simply to shriek into my ear that her son was a genius. After a week of it I had ceased to think of it as touching. You can get tired of mad people very quickly.

Nevertheless, I go downstairs to gauge the extent of the disaster. In the dining room, calm again, smiling, displaying the suavest of good manners, the "madman" (suffering from nothing more than the slightest of twitches every fifteen seconds) is listening to Allegra sitting there beside him gently twittering. He leaves without demur, his book under his arm, turning at the bottom of the steps to give Allegra one last wave.

"You mean that's him?" she asks.

I know that Jeanne, despite all her goodheartedness, finds Allegra a little stupid. She isn't pretty either, but you never notice that.

Trini

For several weeks I believed in perfection. During another of Dolores's absences, the time she moved to the rue de Seine to take a job as a concierge, Trinidad, known as Trini, came to replace her. She was a woman of fifty or so, clean and neat, though without beauty, and of somewhat squat proportions. "A little tobacco jar," Daniel said she looked like. But she did seem to be endowed with numerous domestic virtues.

"What do you think of Trini?" I ask Jacques timidly.

"No plastic interest at all," he replies curtly.

Alberte displays the same lack of enthusiasm: "We can

never ask her to do anything in our Christmas play. You can
see she doesn't like plays, without even looking."

"Not funny," is Pauline's laconic verdict.

As for Vincent, precious and pedantic as usual: "The least
you can say is that she lacks nobility of bearing," he observes,
emphasizing every syllable.

I lose my temper. Though as always when one loses one's
temper, it is partly against my own weakness that I wax so
indignant.

"Now, children, I really want you to get it into your heads
that a home helper is not here to provide you with a model
or a source of inspiration [that is for Jacques], or to play the
flute to you, or to perfect her theatrical abilities and entertain you all, but to cook and to sew on buttons. And if she does
those things well, then I prefer her to all the canaries, the
flutists, all those other picturesque personalities on whose
account, until today, I have always been forced to do my own
washing!"

It is one of my house-proud, Flemish days. Trini in her
voluminous and impeccable apron (oh, Dolores and her down-
at-the-heel mules, her cigarette end at one corner of her mouth!
Consolación's suggestive pullovers! Louisette, whom I discovered one day scrubbing a plate with an old toothbrush!
Marie-Louise's corset left lying on the mantel!), Trini seems so
clean, so beautiful, dignified as a gleaming, much-used tool.
She is one of that class of small, plump women who are also
miraculously alert and nimble. She is silent. She never ceases
tidying up the disparate objects that clutter every surface of
our house. In the evening the smell of polish mingles in the
living-dining-studio room with that of pot-au-feu. I can scarcely
believe my nose. I am taken back to the land of my ancestors.
And Trini also cooks to perfection: eggplant baked in cheese,
escalopes of veal, crackling roasts, sardines garnished with
herbs, all succeed one another on our table. (Oh, the gluey
spaghetti Dolores used to give us! Franca's thick and tasteless

goulash! All those grayish slices of beef running with Spanish oil!) Uneasiness sets in.

"Trini, have you enough housekeeping money?"

"Trini always has enough. Trini knows how to manage a house," she proclaims in boastful tones. "Trini isn't like Dolores. She is thrifty. She is tidy. She knows how to use leftovers. She . . ."

Clearly she is very pleased with herself. Castilian pride, I tell myself. After all, even the greatest of mankind sometimes suffer from that defect. I let it pass. The sheets were mended, the children's clothes reappeared with all their buttons on, the cupboards became tidy for once and, once disencumbered of their layer of dust, even seemed to exhale a feeling of contentment. Trini replaced electric lightbulbs, emptied the ashtrays, the wastepaper baskets, the garbage can. The dog was fed regularly. I was in fairyland.

I became pregnant. Delicious treats appeared unendingly: thick steaks, delicate salads. One day she brought me my breakfast in bed. Angst mounted steadily inside me. But: "Don't you worry about a thing. Trini is taking care of everything. Trini isn't like Dolores. Trini . . ."

We nodded, though not without a fleeting feeling of remorse as we cast our thoughts back to Dolores and her flapping mules. "Can you hear the sparrows? They are singing my praises," Montherlant's Infanta says in *La Reine Morte*. Trini must have been a sort of Infanta, disguised in that coarse and graceless body. I lost the baby I was expecting. In the hospital, four days after the accident, Jacques came to see me and confessed to me, half laughing, half crestfallen: "You don't know yet. Trini . . ."

"Yes?"

"She left for Spain this morning, by plane, without warning, without leaving a note even . . . I only know from a neighbor who saw her taking a taxi to Orly."

"Trini?"

"Yes, Trini. And what's more . . ."

"Go on."

"Well, she's taken all my shirts, and all of Daniel's, and all our tablecloths and towels."

"!!"

"An hour later I happened to meet Violetta [another Spanish celebrity in the rue Jacob], who said: 'So, Trini's gone on holiday? You might at least have taken her to Orly in the car, she had so much to carry!' "

Despite my tiredness and our sadness, we both burst out laughing.

Warmhearted as ever, Dolores abandoned the rue de Seine and her concierge's lodge to return in triumph to the rue Jacob. To tell the truth, I think she was getting bored with being a concierge. Also she'd had a row with the agent.

"He tried to make me scrub the staircase walls. Is that a concierge's job? All I said was: 'I suppose you wouldn't like me to wash your feet for you as well, while I'm at it?' And he flew into a rage . . ."

Which did not prevent her from feeling from then on that she was indispensable. At the slightest adverse comment, we got: "All right, perhaps the meat is burned, but then *I* don't go off with your shirts!"

Nothing is simple. Before she left, Trini had confided to Violetta: "I can't stay. They're costing me too much."

And of course, when one thought back on it, all those steaks, all those sardines, all those culinary luxuries were inexplicable if the poor woman hadn't been eking out the housekeeping with money of her own. It gave me food for thought.

Dolores: "Now I understand. I didn't before. You used to tell me: 'She's wonderful,' and all the people she'd worked for before used to say: 'She's good for nothing.' "

Me: "Then why didn't you warn me, instead of recommending her to me?"

Dolores: "Oh, I knew you always had maids like that . . ."

Maybe, but at least now I understand, if people were always telling her she was "good for nothing," why Trini should have wanted revenge. Our amazement must have been a spur to her. I was almost grateful for the illusion she had woven around me during those few weeks.

She had said: "I shall stay in this house till your daughters are married."

And again: "Don't worry your head about anything, just write . . ."

And again: "I already love you like a daughter."

Was it a character she was making up? One day I slipped on a marble the children had left on the floor. The dish I was carrying broke and gashed my thigh rather badly. She fainted. She said: "You work too hard, you work like a woman from my own country. I feel sorry for you."

She used to sigh as she passed my typewriter, as though she were walking past some instrument of torture.

"And all that time the one thought in her head was how to steal your shirts," Dolores cried indignantly. "If I could lay my hands on her!"

All that time . . . No, I really don't think so. I think that all that time she was thinking how lovely it would be to be warm in the bosom of a real family, to be the one who is useful, who is indispensable, the one no one can do without, the one who is praised and blessed continuously . . . Don't we all dream of that? But it is a heaven that comes expensive, and like so many poor people she believed that giving means giving money. Then, quite suddenly, the day came when she had had enough. She could see her savings dwindling, feel her energies flagging perhaps . . . She couldn't face not being the perfect being, the miracle . . . So she fled. And since she was fleeing, since she was destroying, smashing that image of herself anyway, why not take our shirts as well, while she was about it?

Pauline

Pauline, eating her breakfast: "You know, Mother, you really have improved."

"Oh, have I?"

"Yes. When I was little, you were always getting cross, and you weren't so happy all the time, you were always trying to tidy things up. I do honestly think you've improved a lot."

"Thank you, my darling."

A Mother's Anguish

The doorbell. A dark-haired, pleasant, very embarrassed girl at the door.

"Could I just talk to you for a moment? Privately, I mean."

Somewhat taken aback, I lead her into my room.

"I am most awfully sorry . . . Your time is so precious . . . But I was afraid that a letter . . . I was told it would be better to come myself . . ."

I do my best to put her at ease. Delighted to see her . . . If there's anything I can do . . .

"My name's Sylvette, Sylvette Renard. I'm nineteen. My parents . . . in the country . . . Alone in Paris . . . Found a room near the Sorbonne, but my resources . . . looked for work . . . just beginning. I earn so many francs a month, and then there are the commissions . . ."

I still don't get it. A loan? I'm beginning to be used to this sort of thing after the legionary and the old lady who couldn't pay her rent.

"You're from Catholic Aid, perhaps?"

"Oh, no!" And then, without a pause: "I'm a very close friend of Daniel's."

Pause. I feel uneasiness stirring inside me.

"He didn't say anything . . ."

"No, I preferred . . . to introduce myself. More tactful . . ."

Another pause. My uneasiness mounts.

"Oh, honestly, if I weren't in difficulties, which . . . I wouldn't have dared to . . . I'd never have dreamed . . ."

"Of course, of course," I say mechanically.

"He told me—Daniel—that you're so kind . . . that you'd understand . . ."

For a long time now (ever since Daniel was fifteen) I've been half expecting something like this. The Lord giveth and the Lord taketh away. With resignation I raise my eyes and contemplate my future daughter-in-law. It could have been worse.

"Yes, go on. Of course I understand, only too well . . . You are young . . . you wanted to talk to me yourself before Daniel . . ."

"Yes. After all, I'm the one who gets the commission, aren't I? I must learn to fend for myself, but I'm so shy . . . I've only managed to get ten six-month subscriptions, and if I don't start producing better results . . ."

And that was how I came to take out a two-year subscription to *Magazine littéraire*.

Gilbert

Gilbert irritates me. I have to face up to it, Gilbert irritates me. Because he took coffee to the demonstrators at the Beaux-Arts in May he sees himself as endowed with great political awareness. Because his hair floats around him in a crimped cloud, because he dresses in Afghan waistcoats, flowered robes, and second-hand embroidery from junk shops, because he hasn't married the girl he lives with and roars obscene exclamations every time a miniskirt goes by, he believes he has an artist's soul. Because he paints, engraves, sculpts, gives it all up to devote himself to the dance, takes part in a happening, exhibits his work in a tent or a coach, because he demonstrates whenever the opportunity presents itself, because he lives a totally fragmented life, Gilbert thinks he leads an interesting life. Gilbert drives me crazy.

Gilbert has an opinion on everything. When you talk to him, he doesn't hear. He will ask a question, not listen to the answer, then give one himself and go on talking. In May 1968 Gilbert met me with a briefcase under my arm.

"What's this? You're working? At a time like this!"

Such remarks, forcing me against my will into a virtuous, prim-and-proper role that I hate, make me react by becoming a caricature of that role.

"I have responsibilities, you know," I answer in priggish tones.

"How middle-class!"

"Ah, your work is your life, is it? How Leftist!"

Gilbert drives me mad.

Gilbert comes to see Jacques's paintings. He tilts his head, criticizes, pontificates. He says to me: "How can you stand it, working every day like that, as though you were in an office?"

He has never worked more than two weeks in succession.

"I just don't see how you stand him," I tell Jacques.

Jacques: "Oh, he's got something, I'm sure . . ."

"He'll never do anything."

"Oh no, of course not. He'll never do anything. But that's just it . . ."

"Just it?"

Gilbert in the Flea Market, surrounded by old iron. Everything dazzles him. Glitter is gold. The conventions of the unconventional. He haggles determinedly. Would think himself dishonored if he bought anything at its asking price. In winter he wears shoes without socks, in summer a sheepskin coat.

"He's as affected in his way as one of those budding Prime Ministers at the E.N.A."

"Oh, absolutely . . . But that's just it . . ."

I go to see Gilbert in his studio. A dismal loft beneath a glass roof, freezing in winter, baking in summer; he lives there in meticulous chaos. He is still in a state of wonder and delight because he has just been given a hundred and fifty francs for some trompe-l'oeil landscapes to be used as fake windows: one of his own ideas.

"And how much do you get for them?"

"A hundred and twenty francs each. Oh, there's not much profit in it! But it's just an idea for getting myself known. Then if I could only turn them out in quantity . . ."

And he tells me how he is about to launch into the trompe-l'oeil business, buying plywood wholesale, standing the whole system of commercialized aesthetic standards on its head. He has so many ideas for making a fortune, so many ideas to make himself famous, ideas, ideas, ideas . . . Gilbert wears me out. Do I have ideas? One or two perhaps, and that's all I need. I can manage on that. I follow my ideas through, one by one, because that's the only way. How can he possibly follow anything through, living in that mental maelstrom?

"But that's just it," Jacques would say. Sometimes someone in one's family makes a little remark like that, and slowly it manages to insinuate itself, despite what you feel. Gilbert is poor, very poor, but he is aware of it only as a kind of dream. In his icy studio he is selling three tons of trompe-l'oeil windows, seducing a harem, demolishing Matthieu and Buffet with a single word. Gilbert is happy. He makes a mess of his palette, his talent, his life, his affairs, and lunches on a cup of coffee and an apple, all alone, a brave, dotty little man, alone, unbearable, feckless, egotistical, but filled with wonder at a blue, a green, a good turn, a grotesque piece of headgear . . .

My view begins to shift. Money isn't the only thing that can be hoarded: one can be a capitalist with one's talents too.

"Come and have dinner with us, Gilbert."

"I'd love to. But buy vodka, that's the only drink I really like, and Russian gherkins for starters, and . . ."

Gilbert eats nothing, drinks nothing. What he wants is the laid and lighted table, the full plate, the brimming glass; and then he takes one sip at the glass, pushes away the plate still three-quarters full, and hasn't even noticed the Russian gherkins. I think: "What a terrible waste!" Then I laugh at myself. How hard it is to kill one's housewifely reflexes!

Gilbert collapses in front of the television with Pauline on his lap. Not a word is to be got out of him the rest of the evening. Needless to say, we who are bourgeois enough to own a television never watch it (I wrote a television column for two years, and I saw enough of it in that time to last me all my life), but he, once he is in front of it . . .

I can't help taxing him with the irony of it: "I thought the two things you loathed most were the family and television?"

His monkeylike face, above Pauline's sleeping shoulder, assumes an almost human look for a second.

"Oh, it's all right here. No one will ever know."

For a moment a current of friendship flows. A moment, and that is enough. Am I not perfectly aware that he will smash it, spoil it with a word as soon as he can? Yes, but I see it all in a new light suddenly: one can also be capitalistic with one's friendships.

Friendships

We are always making investments. Memories, dinners, money and books lent and returned, the idiotic films one has laughed at, the convictions one has shared or respected, the moments of grace . . . We are always investing. A lifelong friend is a checkbook. The day you are in need, that memory locked away in the vaults, the attention, the commiseration, the admiration all paid up, is now due . . . We bear witness for one another. Nothing is more admirable than a twenty-year-old friendship. One is always on cue. Always sure of the outcome. There is a feeling of warmth, of tranquillity. In the end, one closes the door, one is "among friends," one draws one's pension of "do you remembers." A solid, family man's sort of investment in the "Friends come First" building society.

The flow of warmth freezes. Suddenly there are "the others." The friendship has become an exclusive, a specialized thing: political, or gastronomical, or social. Sometimes, alas, even Christian. We have become the elite of the local bowls players, of Paris society, of the parish Friendly Society, or the Veterans of Abstract Art, or Mme Verdurin's "little clan," or "the only true lovers of the wine of Corbières," a circle, a ring.

To break into the circle, to stop the dance—the antisocial act par excellence. The circle, by definition, must be closed, stay closed. However vast it is. "If all the lads in all the world would only clasp each other's hands . . ." I know the song. But there must be two hands ready to let go of one another, mustn't there, to let in the someone you weren't expecting? And the someone you weren't expecting, the poor wretch, the parasite, the one who upsets things, who bursts open the cozily shut door, isn't he always the same person?

Our friends, yes. We have friends who are very dear to us, who come to dinner with us over and over again, on Sunday evenings, and who share our hopes, our concerns, our projects. But at those dinners, because we never know how many of us there will be, perhaps those who don't come again are more important than those who do? Or at least the fact they don't come again.

I say to Jacques: "Later, when the children are married, when we're alone we'll be able to . . ."

And Jacques breaks in ironically: "Do you really imagine we shall ever be alone?"

The ones who have just come on the spur of the moment. Sometimes they never come again. I have tormented myself about it. Then I say: It isn't the friends that matter, it's friendship. "Thanks a lot," Jeanne says. Sometimes it's very difficult to make oneself understood.

Sometimes it's very difficult to understand. I think clumsily, slowly. I deduce, I analyze. And it is others, the ones who can talk without thinking about what they're going to say in advance, who suddenly hand me an answer. They come, they go, and sometimes they leave behind a word, a smile that to me is so precious that I would like to thank them for . . . But they've already gone, perhaps they'll come again, there's no knowing. I would like them to. I would like people to be able to wander in and out of our house the way one can wander in and out of cafés, railway stations, churches. No, those comparisons are too grandiose. The way one can wander in and out of a paper house, one of those Japanese houses that have so many openings, thistledown encampments scarcely resting on the earth, an idea of a house, and that's enough, because one is together inside it.

"Together, but sitting in a terrible draft," Jeanne commented when I tried to win her over to the idea of such an existence. My lyricism was deflated.

Drafts

Paper walls, after all, don't keep you warm. You have to provide all the warmth yourself. And if you can't . . .

If you can't, it's disaster time. You come home; your work has gone badly, worse than badly; you're torn with doubt about the ultimate usefulness of writing down lines of words, of reading all those sentences. The manuscript you were so enthusiastic about has been turned down by everyone. The book you genuinely found silly and insipid has been given two columns in *Le Figaro*. The day, as fresh and gleaming as fine porcelain, has been steadily tarnished by succeeding daily duties. Maria the Simple has got hamburgers on the menu once again. The smell of cooking onion in the air. Alberte is attacking her Czerny, but with distaste, I feel, without profit. A glance at the mail reveals too many buff envelopes, tax letters, a summons to the family-allowance office, forms to fill in, all quickly thrust away with the others in an already bulging drawer.

Why try to fool myself? I know that if I let them go on accumulating, the angst will go on growing inside me; it will just have to. Dining room: scales. Kitchen: Maria the Simple soliloquizing, Dani's room: music rehearsal, Bobby singing, Daniel scraping *my* guitar (today I feel very strongly that it is *my* guitar), while Pieri, a friend with weak tonsils, occupies the bed: he has a temperature. The other children's rooms: chaos and filth. A hamster emerges from Alberte's bedclothes. Vincent's pigeon fouls his desk (plop!) with serene disdain. Remembering the statues outside the Louvre, I imagine what Vincent's room will be like in a year's time. The hall is a pile of suitcases and tumbled garments, all different shapes and colors but sharing a look of having just been retrieved from a trash bin. "We need a coat room in this house."

Pauline, suffering from "blind" whooping cough (Why do my children always have "blind" illnesses that leave them in full possession of their energies? My mother says: "It's because of all those inoculations. They're not at all healthy"), has been cutting up *Pomme d'Api*, the Catholic magazine for little girls, on my bed. Cutting up magazines is a healthy and normal activity for a child confined to its room. But why on my bed? "I shall never get better except in your room." They have all said that, one after the other, at each attack of flu, tonsillitis, earache, measles, chicken pox, mumps, that God has sent us. And I have praised God for such a tender attachment to me, and I have lain down to rest, every night of those flus, those measles, those mumps, in a bed reeking of camphor rub, crunching with biscuit crumbs, scattered with scraps of cut-up paper, a big blob of cough syrup on the pillow that I always managed to locate with my cheek just too late, just as sleep is descending on me, when to go back downstairs and fetch a clean pillowslip is to lose it forever. And often I have laid my cheek down again, for good or ill, with love, with trust, and scarcely have I murmured the first words of my evening prayer: "Praise be to God in the highest and peace on earth . . ." than I am already asleep.

So why this emptiness and this satiety today? Why? This inner void, this distaste, this fading of life's colors, this sinking of its sap? The children's drawings on the walls are nothing but crumpled scraps of paper, a mess. Jacques's canvases piled up in the hall—just problems. When is the exhibition? Who will buy canvases that size and shape? And the piled-up clothes are nothing but rumpled clothes, the noise nothing but noise; those steps, those goodbyes on the stairs are those of strangers in a railway station. Everything has lost its meaning; nothing is left but a vast *clutter* inside and out . . .

I have to telephone Monsignor P., on the Bishop's Committee. I have to reply to that petition in favor of the O.R.T.F. I have to write to Editions du Seuil to recommend Georges's manuscript. I have to read Pascale's book, and fill in that form for Maria the Simple. I have to go to the bank. And it really is time we paid the dentist. And time to fill in another form for Alberte's piano competition. Then there's Pauline's X-ray. Must thank Simon for sending his book. I have to, I must . . .

Everything is sloshing around in my head like lumpy porridge. Shall I do exercises in the morning or shall I read the paper, "to keep myself in touch"? Healthy mother or good citizen? Which duty comes first? Shall I go to the hairdresser or accept the invitation to dinner from M. Loisel (a rejected author), or from Mme Dethiers (who is on the committee of a charitable society)? I read in *Elle* that at my age I have to begin to take more trouble over my appearance. Can one just "drop" writers who one day perhaps . . .? And that poor Mme Dethiers, a woman who means so well and who seems to set such store by having us to dinner . . .

Everything conflicting with everything else, a life of discord and clash. Is it possible to have children and be a writer as well? Is it possible to take an interest in politics and still preserve one's inner silence? Is it possible to make oneself available to everyone and also retreat at will into one's solitude? And, on a more mundane level, is it possible to open one's house to one's friends, to one's friends' friends, to casual callers, and also preserve a little order and decency in it? Is it possible to initiate one's children into poetry, into music, into the dance, to leave them free to draw, cut out, stick things together, sing, and not also turn them into dreadful dimwits, unfit for society, and with defective teeth?

Losing One's Powers

Contradiction: I am wandering like a stranger through my own house, through my own life.

Through my own work even. I once read a science-fiction story in which a man endowed with "powers" (I love that expression—you meet it so often in that kind of literature; you're in some critical situation, hanging from the edge of a roof, in a snake pit, dependent for life upon walking through a wall or reading your enemy's thoughts. What do you do? You just use your "powers"), while walking through an old neighborhood, discovered the entrance to a street that no longer existed. It had existed in the past but had been obliterated by fire to control an epidemic. But he (by means of his "powers") had stumbled upon the path into the invisible, into the past, and with the greatest of ease simply walked into the alley and met all its inhabitants. There is much wealth to be found in such simple tales. The path into the invisible can be found, can be lost. Yesterday's wonderful subject becomes today's banal story. The bright, clear revelation, that drop of water rainbowed with light . . . Suddenly the light has gone, and there is nothing there. And so it was with the hero of this tale: suddenly he could no longer find the entrance to his lost alley in the past. He had "lost his powers."

Color, music, everything that shimmered and had a meaning in this house and in this life has disappeared. Without a breeze, the paper house no longer hums. It is nothing but a paper building, fragile, inane. It is a desert I must cross. I must pretend. Smile. Sing even. Read, write, decipher or scribble down those empty signs. Show an interest in this drawing I am not even seeing, that song I am not even hearing. That terrible sentence passed on by Shakespeare's Julius Caesar now weighs with all its might on me: *He hears no music.* That's how all my terrible times begin—*I hear no music.*

No, I haven't "lost my faith." That's an absurd expression anyway. But I have, rounding a corner suddenly, "lost my powers."

Daniel

Then I must just do without them. Carry on as though nothing has happened. Which immediately confronts one with the question of sincerity. It's one of the false problems that we meet so often in the daily routine of Christian life. The sharp judgment that rises to the lips and that we bite back just in time, the wave of bad temper that doesn't reach the surface but continues to seethe below it, the patience at the end of its tether, the herculean charity that we grit our teeth to accomplish; in short, the absence of joy, of love, of spontaneity, of that childhood in God that constitutes our happiness. How are we to conceal all that? Ought we to conceal it?

Here I am, morose and empty, with a tendency to be possessive about everything. *My* time, *my* work, *my* bathtub. Wasting *my* time reading all those manuscripts, answering all those letters, making all those telephone calls; jeopardizing the quality of *my* work because Sara, an au-pair girl who has come to stay with us after a series of complicated quarrels with the people she's supposed to be living with, feels like chatting with me. Finding *my* bathtub full of socks that Daniel and Jacques of course expect me to wash . . . I conceal my irritation behind a vague smoke screen of "problems at the office." It's very convenient sometimes to have an office. And I carry on, making gestures, saying the right words, rather as one might do keeping-fit exercises. But others can sense it; that, there's no denying.

Daniel: "You're not going to tell me that Sara doesn't get on your nerves."

"Of course she gets on my nerves. But the more I think about it, the more irritated I'll become, so I prefer to concentrate on something else: the fact that she is unhappy, that she has a very sweet nature, really . . ."

The "very sweet nature" is perhaps rather less apparent to me today. Daniel undoubtedly senses it.

"The Coué method," he observes ironically.

There are days when I could answer that, but I am decidedly not in shape today.

"No, not at all . . ."

"Well, I find it hypocritical," he says with sudden fire, "this determination to behave as though everyone is nice, as if you loved everyone; it lessens what you really feel. It's affected, I think. We ought to tell the truth, show what we really feel."

"But it isn't always what we feel that is the truth," I say listlessly.

His surprise at this answer does revive me a little, however.

"When I'm working, for example, and one of my children disturbs me, what I feel is impatience; my work seems to me much more important than the child; but if I let the child see that, then it will believe that it is *always* so, whereas in fact I couldn't work, or even think, if a child of mine was in any danger."

"Yes, perhaps," he concedes. "But where others are involved, people you have no feeling for . . ."

"The same is true. They wouldn't be 'others' in our eyes, they wouldn't be people we had no feeling for if we saw them in danger or if we really understood them. So by being nice to them, by banking on what's best in them, one isn't being hypocritical, one is simply relying on what one *knows*, on what one *believes*, rather than on what one feels."

I can see that I won't succeed in convincing him today. Nowadays there is a sort of veneration for instinct, for the spontaneous, that has its liberating, even its creative side, but it also jars me sometimes because it is promoting our most fleeting, most subjective element to the rank of supreme and intangible verity.

"If what we believe isn't what we feel . . ."

"It isn't what we feel all the time. Not with the same intensity, anyway. You love someone, but you're bowling, so you aren't feeling that you love him. You're told that person has just been hit by a car; it isn't that you love him more, you just feel your love more. Does that mean that, at the moment you are feeling your love less, you ought to behave coldly or rudely? Sincerity isn't bad manners."

"It isn't good manners, either," Daniel replies, not without a point.

No. Of course not. If that's all it is. It's not just that. But how am I to explain?

Daniel goes on, with that lovely gravity: "If you don't feel what you believe, how can you be sure that you are right to believe it?"

A pertinent question, but not one I want to face today.

A Christian daily life is indeed a double life. Colors, joy, gaiety, affirmations, emotions, and then, abruptly, that void that isn't quite a doubt, not yet . . .

The political struggle that is sometimes so discouraging, friendship sometimes betrayed, work suddenly turned into drudgery, the joys of motherhood becoming wearisome labors . . . "But from him that has not shall be taken even the little that he hath." When grace has once quickened a life, and then withdraws, what is left isn't even life. Despondency.

Suddenly the desert irrigated by this thought: let us praise God for having a life in which, when he is not there, there is nothing.

Another Way Out

Another way out of this void: a sense of humor. I particularly remember one desolating return home when the two hundred bottles (more or less) piled up in the kitchen, the towel used in my absence to polish the brass, the bathtub coated with black varnish (I could only suppose that the strangers who had dipped into it were all workers in a tar factory), the pigeon quite evidently back in the best of health, the piles of bills and summonses, were all unable to wring even a smile from me. It was a Monday morning. I had spent Easter with my sister Miquette: shining floors, neat linen cupboards, children all spotless, *yet* charming. My eyes must have been opened by all that perfection. Our own incompetence was suddenly a blinding and painful fact.

I had lost my sense of humor.

Monday dragged by in dismal discouragement. Jacques, helping me with the dreary task of doing all the accumulated, congealed washing up, lent warm approval to my pessimistic tirades. I called his attention to the overdue tax bills, the angry dentists, the schools about to throw all our children out, the danger to my health, our precarious occupations. Then Daniel's untidiness, Vincent's laziness, Alberte's stubbornness, Pauline's rowdiness: shouldn't we send our children away to school, economize, do without wine and the telephone, go to live in the country where there wouldn't even be the cinema to tempt us? Far from contradicting me, Jacques was only too pleased to add his contribution to the mood I was creating. However, having a more abstract mind, he was also concerned about the dire political situation, the instability of the franc, the debasement of the very concept of art. Then, after a short digression (a virtuoso cadenza on our collapsing nervous systems), he went on to deliver a general denunciation of youthful selfishness, pronounced an immediate sentence of deportation upon all members of the animal kingdom (cat, dog, hamster, tortoises, pigeon), with a possible reprieve for the goldfish by virtue of its longevity, a sentence then extended to all non-family members (see under DANIEL), and ended by expressing the conviction that even with such desperate measures total disaster could not be averted. We would have to give up smoking, too, and having our sheets done by a laundry.

Sitting at the kitchen table, we shared a can of beer, almost pleased in a way at the extent of the catastrophe looming over us; who wrote the poem about the Lisbon earthquake? But I hadn't got back my sense of humor.

Tuesday dawned no less gloomy. Not a single bed was made. The end of the world was at hand. I gave the children bread and butter for their breakfast instead of the chocolate digestives with which I usually indulge their sweet tooth and my laziness. Reserved silence. Then Pauline announced that she had lost her watch at camp. Despondent silence. (I'll give them lunch out of tins. I won't write to thank Simon for sending me a copy of his book; he'll be very put out.) Pauline sensed which way the wind was blowing. "I'm not going to brush my teeth," she announced. "That's your lookout," I said. She was so disappointed by the reaction that she wasn't singing as she left for school.

I take the sheets to the laundry. For the last time. The cleaning woman doesn't come. Ah, well. The fish I serve for dinner that evening is ice cold. No one complains. The whole house is becoming pale and lusterless, like an unwatered plant. Alberte attacks her Czerny with despairing determination.

Wednesday. I sit on Daniel's bed. He looks like a Roman warrior now that he has lopped off his luxuriant locks. I point out that all this has gone on too long. Those clothes lying in the hall must go. And all those calls to the South of France. *Who* is making them? If they all think I never look at my telephone bills, they're mistaken! The state of the bath, the perpetual disappearances of our combs and toothbrushes, of my umbrella . . . Everything just vanishes! Daniel, like the good son he is, murmurs reassuringly. He can see that I'm not my normal self. Would I like a cigarette? Should he make me some tea? (He kept equipment in his room for the purpose and was constantly blocking the washbasin by emptying his teapot into it.) But I refuse to be softened. Today there shall be no idle chats, no joss-stick fumigations (his passion), no relaxed discussions on the comparative merits of our favorite thrillers. Life is serious!

The afternoon crawls on. Toward three o'clock, emerging from a manuscript I am plowing through with the bitter pleasure of a duty accomplished (the only pleasure that particular book could possibly afford me), in the narrow passage outside my room I pass a stranger emerging from the bathroom. He is a rather well-dressed gentleman, yes, a gentleman, the sort of man you might expect to see on a city street, twenty-five, neat tie, dark suit . . . He flattens himself against the wall to let me pass, with the polite indifference one associates with cafés, with railway stations. "Pardon, madame . . ." I turn back to look at him in stupefaction, I watch him continuing that tranquil progress toward the front door, opening it, vanishing. Perhaps he just came in to use the lavatory?

A hysterical and liberating fit of laughter nails me to the wall for a long while. My visitor's sober dignity, the total unconcern with which he has made use of my apartment, his air of a city gent leaving a public convenience—they are beyond any possibility of indignation. When I have stopped laughing, I realize that my sense of humor has returned.

After Daniel's return, later in the afternoon, we try to work out who the mysterious stranger could have been. "It wasn't Jean-Michel? Or Richard? Perhaps it was . . ." But we have to give up. Never mind, I shall cook escalopes milanaises for dinner tonight, to celebrate the return of my sense of humor. That polite, proper gentleman, perhaps he was an angel?

More Dolores

"I'm going with a chap of sixty-seven," Dolores tells me. "He's very kind. I mean, really kind. He's a coal merchant. He wants to marry me."

"Perhaps it wouldn't be a bad idea."

"That's what everyone says. But I don't think so. I can't be nice to men for money."

"He doesn't give you money?"

"Why should he? I'm not nice to him," Dolores says with a laugh that reveals a brand-new gold tooth.

And Allegra

Allegra looks down at her son. The baby smiles, gurgles, plays with a woolly pom-pom, stretches out its arms.

"Aren't you going to pick him up?" Jeanne asks.

"No. Why?"

Allegra, always true to her name.

And Nicolas

He thinks he's so astute, Nicolas. He's been trying to borrow money from D., whom he got to know in the hospital.

"Lend me fifty thousand francs. I'll give it back to you in a fortnight, when I've been paid for this job I'm doing."

"I'd rather give you twenty thousand than lend you fifty," she answers.

"Because you don't trust me."

"Perhaps you won't be able to finish the job, perhaps you'll run into a snag, how do I know . . . Here, take the twenty thousand as a present."

"You'd rather give me twenty thousand francs than risk trusting me, is that it?" he sneers.

She has had enough. "I'd rather not have to think about you and the follies you will be committing nonstop for the next two weeks, yes!"

Nicolas is triumphant. "She admits it! She claims to be my friend, but she's prepared to pay to get rid of me, so she won't have to think about me for two wretched weeks!"

Yes, she admits it. And what does Nicolas get out of it? One more piece of evidence in his case against the world, against the world's injustice toward him, against the absurdity of the people who claim to be friendly and helpful. "I made her see . . ." But does it bother them to see, my poor Nicolas? In this suit you're so intent on bringing against the world, against mankind, evidence is of no use at all in the end. You can win it twice, three times, ten times over, but the important thing is that the victory itself is meaningless.

He is a stickler with God too, this self-righteous parasite. To him he says, in effect: "Just look, I have given them the opportunity to be good, to be kindly, to honor you in my person, twice, three times, ten times over, and every time, at the crucial moment, they have failed you. What do you say to that?" He sets his traps with an easy conscience. After all, the more unbearable he makes himself, the more he is doing God's work for him, right? The more opportunity he gives all these wretches to demonstrate their patience, their equanimity —then comes the moment when their resistance weakens and they throw him out with such "appalling injustice."

"You just don't interest me! You BORE me!" a friend of his, B., a columnist on *Le Figaro*, shouts at him, finally reaching the end of his patience.

Nicolas, superb in his dignity, and good faith, says to me: "Now, Françoise, how could he say a thing like that to me? Isn't every human being on earth interesting to a writer?"

When D. or I get him jobs with publishers, he immediately sets about stealing vast numbers of press copies and selling them. We reprimand him, but he says: "Now look at it this way: is society being just toward me? Am I mad? Then let it provide treatment for me. Am I unemployable? Then let it put me in a home. Am I ill? Then let it put me in the hospital. But if I am none of those things, and society refuses me a secure job, then aren't I within my rights to defend myself?"

And were society one day to dispute those rights and fit him out with a police record, that would be the supreme triumph, the ultimate proof of his view of the world. "This world is beyond the shadow of a doubt unjust," he would say. Q.E.D.

But, for the moment, people just feel vaguely sorry for him; they scold him, lock their doors, and take him out to dinner, take precautions . . . Nothing is definitely settled, ever. Nothing is clear cut. Good or bad? Guilty or innocent? Nicolas can never quite manage to win his case against God and the world. And it grieves him.

Messenger of the devil! Sometimes he gets tired, weakens, stops his indefatigable accusations against a world that rejects outsiders like him, he stops because he wants to live—even if it means shutting his eyes.

"Do you think so? Perhaps I was wrong; yes, perhaps I was . . . Underneath it all, D.'s very kind . . ."

For an instant he does close those reddened, sleepwalker's eyes. Momentarily he would like to do what all the others do, he would like to fool himself, to hope, if only for an instant— yes, he would so like to . . .

"And yet I'm not sure, wasn't there something in the hurried way she did it, the way she *stuffed* that money into my hands, wasn't there a sort of contempt there, a sort of fear, I don't know . . ."

He would like to, but he can't. He is what we call a neurotic.

Jacques Writes

Jacques writes: "It is through the consumer product that the way now lies to the world and knowledge. To grasp this singular deviation is to return to, to go beyond, the truth of Dada that lies at the very heart of given reality. It is now a tin of jam or a jacket that leads to the absolute. In other words, God is a tin of jam."

Jacques pushes this note across the table to me at Les Deux Magots, where I am working.

"What is it?" I ask.

"It's my preface to your book," he replies proudly.

Your Work: No Anecdotes

"I don't want any anecdotes," she tells me. She is a serious, not unpretty, slightly dried-up young woman who is collecting material for a big article about me, but not a "woman's magazine" article, not an "atmosphere" article, no, a proper literary article, the themes running through my work, my favorite authors, influences, ultimate goals, etc.

"You can rest assured," she tells me with a superior smile, "I don't work for *France-Dimanche*! Your children, your private life, I couldn't care less about all that."

I could, though.

"That's not what I'm after. What I'm looking for is the writer in you."

All well and good. But who is that "writer" separated from all that surrounds her, conditions her, nourishes her? A wretched school child being asked to hand in a test paper that she already feels will not be saisfactory or will be too satisfactory. Of course it's no good being disingenuous about it. I know perfectly well, I know only *too* well what to answer, with fifteen years of professional writing behind me. Perhaps that's what is so tedious about it all.

Welling up inside me I can feel the same somnolence that used to flood through me at school; there was always, on those long, white, warm days, a fly buzzing somewhere, a pneumatic drill out in the street, a bell far, far away in the distance, and time stretching, stretching on and on without end, the sun soaking warm through the blinds, or the rain underlining that colorless eternity . . . And that passionless antipathy I used to feel then for anyone who dragged me back out of my soft non-being now revived for this young bespectacled woman so firmly determined that I shall be sensible, that I shall classify, that I shall label, that I shall vivisect these things that for me are not books so much as little moments of my life, little messages, at once ridiculous and extremely serious, which I have dispatched almost haphazardly, like paper boats floating down a stream—and I hope, of course I do, that they will arrive, that they have arrived at some destination, but since I myself am still going on, even that isn't really of enormous importance either.

She is going to say: "Why do you write?" She is going to say: "What influences have had an effect on you?" She is going to say: "In your first, your third, your sixth book you were trying to . . ."

I overcome my lassitude. I force my eyes, already wandering here and there, already disappearing behind a veil of gloom, back to that really quite pretty face, those quite lively eyes, that quite pleasing figure. This physical presence beside me seems to be denying itself, insisting on the fact that it is purely accessory to its functions, that I must not set any store by it, that though it is in fact there, surrounded by those paper masks, seated on my bed-raft and discreetly put out by such a riot of colors, it is only in the office of a symbol, because it is solely the big round spectacles, and the notebook the young woman is so firmly holding, that have any real existence; it is with them that I shall be dealing. She, then, where is she?

I try to think about the little girl she must once have been, with her spectacles and her serious air. Perhaps we have read the same poets? But it is impossible today to work up any soul-sympathy. No fuel. I feel I am the class dunce. I feel an urge to tell fibs, to tell her that my favorite food is smoked bacon, that I am writing a detective story, that my favorite author is

Paul Féval. But one can't do things like that. One can't because the tiniest attempt at humor will immediately set solid,
the smallest word will become a stone and imprison me in a
cell that is simply just that much narrower, that much more
different from any other . . . Because no one can understand
that it's possible to be serious without taking oneself seriously,
because everything commits you and nothing really means anything, because . . . There is no other way out but patience,
good faith, and a sympathy that today will be a little forced, a
little deliberate. What would Daniel say if he could see the
overbright smile I am wearing, the diligent good will with
which I am asking my visitor's first name . . . It does help.

"Gabrielle," she says, with a slight shrinking of her narrow
shoulders. "Tell me, why is it that you write?"

"The first time I felt the desire to write, it was because I'd
read a story I didn't like. I was nine. The story was in *La
Semaine de Suzette*, I think. It was called "The Singapore
Diamond." Some English scientists were on their way to India
to wrench a precious green diamond out of the forehead of a
mysterious Buddha hidden in the depths of a cave. Their
guide, a 'wily native,' a 'fanatic,' betrayed them, though, and
it was only after endless ordeals (being thrown to the crocodiles and then saved *in extremis* by an understanding young
Hindu girl; being lost in a jungle and fed poisoned curry by
the treacherous guide—a touch of local color—but again
saved, this time by a devoted servant boy, who perished after
eating most of the fatal curry, etc.), and after presumably
meting out a just punishment to the traitor, that they succeeded in returning to England with the diamond and, I
think, presenting it to the British Museum. The trouble with
the story was that I liked the traitor. I refused to accept the
author's description of him as a wily fanatic. It seemed to me
that he was perfectly within his rights to lead astray a lot of
Englishmen who could just as well have stayed at home, that
he was completely justified in defending his 'idol.' I decided,

therefore, as though it were a true story I had read (and all stories are true stories), that the author had *distorted the facts.* Lakdar Mokri (to this day I remember the 'traitor's' exotic name) was neither cowardly nor wily. He was very handsome, a little barbaric perhaps, and in the end he would win. He would take the diamond back from the British Museum, while the scientists, struck down by a sort of magic spell, would die one after the other, under Tutankhamen's curse (I was a little confused about things East of Suez, you understand).

"Later, profoundly moved by the mental effort expended in rehabilitating my hero, I fell in love with him. I thought about him at night before I fell asleep. I murmured 'Lakdar Mokri,' and they were magic syllables. I saw a handsome brown man lean down toward me, thanking me in a slightly guttural voice for having understood him."

Gabrielle Lenoir pushed her spectacles back on her nose (a small, pretty nose, rather frivolous even on her serious face) and informed me, firmly, severely: "That is what I mean by an anecdote."

"Oh. Is it?"

"Yes."

"I have no favorite authors. I have a catalogue of images, of words, of colors. A passage in Paul Féval—yes, that's right—in *Les Habits noirs,* made a great impression on me. He describes an art that is wholly forgotten today: that of the newsstory painters. They were artisans, almost fairgrounds people, and they painted, in sort of giant comic strips, realistic depictions of the most dramatic incidents in nineteenth-century news stories: the murder of Fualdès, for example. Then the news tellers went around all the villages, taking the illustrations with them, and they delivered their accounts of these blood-and-thunder stories with the paintings held up on poles to help them. I'd love to go around the country like that, and Jacques could paint the placards for me. But with all that competition from the evening newspapers, I don't know, really . . ."

"That's an anecdote too," Gabrielle Lenoir says.

"Oh. Is it?"

"Yes."

I like the name Lenoir. It's the name Marius gives Cosette when he sees her before he's in love with her. M. Leblanc is Jean Valjean, and Mlle Lenoir is Cosette. I've spent a lot of my life among those Victor Hugo characters.

"Yes, but I don't think we can really call that an influence."

"What's an influence, then? Is it a page, a sentence, a minor character that makes you sit and dream?"

"No. That's what I would call anecdotal."

How strict this Gabrielle is with herself. She doesn't wear her hair pulled back into a bun, because she is a modern young woman, twenty-eight years old, who works for modern newspapers, for the radio, for television, but the perfection of her hair set, the simplicity and fit of her dress, her figure itself, all make it clear that she never lets herself go, that she is always on the alert, that she lives in an environment that is foreign, almost hostile to her, and that undone buttons, bohemia, the picturesque, all that kind of thing, well, it cuts no ice with her, it scarcely touches her, runs off her like water off a duck's back. She meets all these writers, these painters, but she always goes straight to the point, to the heart of the question, to the creative center . . . But is there a center to creativity? Or is it everywhere, scattered, proliferating, monstrous, meaningful yet meaningless, the very jungle through which we battle on without a compass? Both, probably. I can't think of the words I ought to be saying to her. Or else I just can't say them.

"Gabrielle, tell me about yourself. Perhaps that will help us get somewhere."

She smiles a tiny smile that twists one corner of her mouth a little—not unbecomingly; a tiny smile that betrays a sense of humor, a trace of repressed bitterness, a charming, unshowy kind of courage.

"Oh, me . . . There's not much to tell. I'm an intellectual."

I like her for having said that. I have discovered that there is a certain courage in saying it. I discovered it . . . And I tell her about it.

The Shame of Writing

A combination political-literary meeting. Going into the room is rather like walking into a cold shower.

"What specialized knowledge do you possess? Would you like to give a talk on something? What branch of publishing have you studied specifically? What can you do?"

"Me? . . . Nothing."

"I see. Ideological committee."

On it I meet other writers. All very likable. It's possible that there's nothing they can do, like me, but if so, they're clever at hiding it.

". . . to us writers," someone says.

"Oh, no! Not 'writers'! Why don't we say, oh, I don't know, 'literary workers' or something."

"Why?" from me.

"The profession needs desanctifying."

"Well, I can't see that there's much that's sacrosanct about writers. Writers, intellectuals, they're everyone's Aunt Sally these days. And that even goes for other intellectuals. I've always felt one might well adapt Figaro to this particular situation: 'Considering all the virtues expected of intellectuals (disinterestedness, immutability, infallibility), how many leaders of industry would get the job . . .'"

"It doesn't alter the fact that we are privileged . . ."

"To a certain extent. But . . ."

". . . and bourgeois . . ."

The final insult has been spoken. Once you've said bourgeois, there's nothing left.

"Don't you sometimes feel that we use the word 'bourgeois' the way the Nazis used the word 'Jew'?"

I hadn't intended to express myself quite that strongly. But still, I dislike any racial concept, and being ashamed of what one is, whether bourgeois or writer, doesn't seem to me the best road to self-improvement. And these writers, so embarrassed by a profession that is just as good as any other, end up by embarrassing me in turn. I much prefer the little section meetings where it's just a question of putting up posters or handing out pamphlets, and where the fact of your being or not being a writer is of little interest.

"So in fact you keep political action and writing in two completely separate compartments?" a bespectacled young man with beautiful velvety eyes asks me.

"In compartments? . . . No, nothing is in compartments. My political opinions, my religious beliefs, they're bound to be reflected in what I write, inevitably, because I'm trying to express a totality. But I'm not so completely mistress of what I write that I can calculate its practical efficacy in the realms of politics or religion."

"In short, you think of being a writer as a personal responsibility?" the handsome young man insists, sadness in his eyes.

". . . Yes . . . of course . . ."

Scarcely able to credit his ears, he gives up.

I encounter this feeling of shame in so many manuscripts, so many books. I have been amazed, time and again, at all the excuses, all the zigzagging, the complicated somersaults, all to avoid that most shameful of admissions: I am writing a book. For my part, I tell a story, I describe a landscape, natural or psychological, I juxtapose colors and words, I talk, I am inside or outside, I communicate, and occasionally I give an opinion on what I am seeing, on what I am telling, and sometimes I don't have an opinion, I am not even clear what it is I have done, gaze at it rather as one gazes at one's children, at once so close and so far away: I have done what I can, and now it is up to the book to do its bit. And to others to form opinions, draw conclusions. I've done my share. Whether it turns out to be a large share or a small share isn't my business, and I give it very little thought. But blush for having done it, no, never.

That is why I like Gabrielle when she lowers her short, stubborn forehead slightly and says: "No, I'm not married. No, I have no children. I am—and she raises her head, aware that she is exposing herself to opprobrium—"an intellectual . . ."

But I don't like Gabrielle so much when she says: "I should like to see your library."

Because I don't have a library. It is a fact that makes me ashamed on those occasions—very rare ones—when I visit other writers' homes, when I see ranged in orderly rows on their shelves all the books one ought to have: the volumes of Stendhal, Sade, Leiris, the copies of the *Nouvelle Revue Française* all so neat and yet so well used (their pages turned often, but by lamplight, with clean hands, never once dunked in foam baths), and then in other homes the tomes of Montaigne, Henry James, all the books that "make the man," that create a favorable impression . . . But I have no library. I have books, of course; but they are rarely the ones I love, because the ones I love I lend, and then they don't come back.

"Well . . . Have you any favorite authors?"

Everyone has favorite authors. And you would think the past fifteen years would have given me more than enough time to sort them out, to review them, to prepare for this examination. But in fact, to be honest, my favorite authors are rather like my bookshelves, where an odd volume from a set of Montaigne that's losing its pages is tucked in with a volume of Milosz poems, a detective story, a bound Balzac that has been dunked in the bath half a dozen times, and a beautiful complete Baudelaire won by Vincent in a raffle. There are also little groupings, here and there, of notably unfingered novels that I have been sent to review, have reviewed, and shall never

read again. And my memory is the same. In addition to Paul
Féval, I can fish out of it a stanza of Villon, a song three centuries or three days old, a Bernanos sentence that I have been
turning over and over in my mind like a precious stone these
many years. Out of a sort of fog there looms the plaster elephant in which Gavroche slept, and the gentle darkness ad-
vancing under the arcades of the rue de Rivoli, or in a deserted
Biarritz, winter reigning supreme over those somber Second
Empire façades. Or again, across the Croisic salt beds, in
Béatrix's Guérande, it seems to me I can see the ensign
Christoph Rilke making his sad, melodious way.

But when you try to say all that, it becomes: Your first influences were predominantly Nordic, I notice, and then the discovery of Balzac . . . In the end you say yes. Because you are
tired, and also because, of course, we must have no anecdotes
. . . I'm not dealing with *France-Dimanche*, remember, and
haven't I myself just denounced the trap of the picturesque?

"Yes," I say, "but doesn't poetry come into being precisely
in that zone of conflict between the picturesque and the deeper
meaning . . ."

"The deep keening?"

"All right, if you like, the deep keening of the world that
serves as its context. Seen contrasted in that way, in a sociological, or political, or psychoanalytical context, which may
explain almost everything and yet, and this is just it, not *quite*
everything, not that little spark of grace, of freedom, that tiny,
tiny mote of chance, to use less grandiose words, that fraction
of play—in the mechanical sense—that can never be lapped
out of existence: aren't those sociological, or political, or psychoanalytical 'explanations,' by the very fact of their almost-
accuracy, with all there is room for in that minute almost,
aren't they all poetry too, and . . ."

I thought at last I was clambering up to her level, but
Gabrielle, raising her hands, begs me for mercy.

I apologize: "All I wanted to say was that there's nothing in anecdotes, but that if one has a unity, then an anecdote contains it all."

"I'm not a poet," Gabrielle says, with modest and becoming arrogance.

Oscar Brik or Blek

I don't know whether I'm a "poet" or not. I like telling stories. Stories with no purpose, no problems, no message. And yet, simply because it is me as a totality, my whole self expressing itself in the story, in those images going slightly to my head, I would be pleased if a purpose, a hope, a message somehow found its way in.

There is no evading the fact that I enjoy myself most telling stories when I am thinking least. Talking one day to my niece Thérèse (thirteen, a tiny Egyptian face, and the sharp, probing curiosity of a Sherlock Holmes), I said: ". . . and he was hairy, so hairy . . . like Oscar Brik, who was descended from a bear."

Where did he appear from, the unexpected Oscar? I can't say for sure. From a mischievous urge to intrigue Thérèse, who is always putting me off the track with the most fiendish questions. But also from a vague memory I had of Mérimée (Lokis), a desire to inject a little humor into it with the Christian name Oscar, a little Nordic mist with the *k* of Brik. Then, once the *k* was there, I had a glimpse of sledges, of bears, of snow, and after one last glance in the direction of Milosz, of the beautiful name of Lithuania, there in my mind, fluttering like a modest but jaunty ship all ready for its maiden voyage, the character of Oscar Brik had appeared.

"Brik with a *k*?" Thérèse asked severely, piercing me with her almond eyes.

A smoke screen, I decided, was the best method of escaping further interrogation.

"Brik with a *k* or Blek with a *k*. No one has ever been able to find out. He came from a very old Lithuanian family and one of his grandmothers had been kidnapped by a bear, so that in all the old chronicles it's never certain whether the Briks—or Bleks—were men or whether they were partly bears. Any more than it is certain whether they were Bleks given the nickname Brik or Briks given the nickname Blek."

"I think the real name is Brik," said Suzanne, who is Thérèse's twin sister, despite the fact that she is unlike her in every way.

"I think it's Blek," said Louise, the twins' younger sister, who has an angel's face framed by long gold hair, and a great deal of mischief under that angelic appearance.

Françoise, the youngest of all, didn't take sides, as always preferring to remain free and shift her allegiance according to circumstances.

"And was he good or bad?" the straightforward Suzanne demanded.

"Both at the same time, perhaps," Thérèse said, already familiar, from her reading, with the ambiguity of human nature.

"Exactly. He was double. Just as no one was ever certain whether his name was Brik or Blek, so no one was ever certain whether he was good or bad. They called him Oscar Two-face."

That was how Oscar came into being, together with his interminable life story, which has been going on now for four years. Every time we are all together, my nieces, my children, and I, Oscar's saga acquires a few more episodes. Sometimes a flashback into his dark past brings the revelation of some hitherto unknown piece of skulduggery. Sometimes a lightning dash into the future takes us on a visit to an Oscar who has, for example, become a hermit (but is he sincere?) and has found his long-lost children, Hildegarde and Ildefonse, in the depths of an Austrian convent. But throughout his complicated adventures Oscar's appalling literary taste has always been in evidence. After having started life as a plagiarism from Mérimée, he then lived through a childhood inspired by Hector Malot, Rouletabille, and Hans Christian Andersen. At the age of four he saw his parents devoured by wolves while on a sleigh ride, piously rescued their heads, had them embalmed, and since then carries them with him everywhere in plastic bags. Then he was despoiled of his Lithuanian estate and his title of count by wicked uncles, became a shoeshine boy, caught the fancy of a sausage millionaire, and was adopted by him. His ineradicable and deplorable taste for Rocambole and Fantomas then led him to murder his benefactor and at the same time to form a gang of malefactors whose power is felt throughout the length and breadth of Paris. A return to the pious strain evident in his early childhood then causes him to fall in love with an angelic orphan girl who is regularly visited by angels and is also in love with him. A brief period of remorse overtakes him, he hears the distant pealing of Lithuanian bells and bows to medieval tradition by dedicating the baby Angélina is carrying in her womb—the future Abbess Hildegarde—to the Virgin Mary.

Alas, he then returns to the deplorable literature from which he has only just escaped, and falls into the habit (derived from *Tintin*) of throwing people he doesn't like into a pool crammed with man-eating eels and piranhas. Angélina leaves him in a moment of revulsion and, to earn a living, signs on in a not un-Dickensian soap factory, thus enabling me to deliver a passing broadside at social and industrial conditions in the past century. She dies of hunger while Oscar is busy elsewhere, sawing a trap door in the stage of the Opéra to kidnap a famous singer—also called Angélina—during the course of an entertainment entitled *The Somnambulist*, which I am able to sing from beginning to end, if requested, and which ends with an unforgettable chorus: "Somnambulist! Somnambulist! Asleep she lived and faded in a mist!" (Thérèse, who still occasionally feels slight stirrings of mistrust, asked me when

exactly this opera was put on, and after how many perform-
ances Angélina Marmaduke was kidnapped. I replied with
great assurance: "She was kidnapped on May 4, 1904, during
the dress rehearsal." Thérèse then asked: "What is a dress
rehearsal, exactly?" I explained. I never shrink from parentheses.)

It would be tedious for the reader—since once I start I
never know how to stop—if I were to continue this résumé
of Oscar's adventures to the end, especially since they have
no end. But I would never find it tedious myself. This summer,
when the television broke down, I sat for hours, circled by
seven attentive little faces, passionately and interminably
pursuing my Oscar through all the mystical or criminal, comical or tragical ups and downs of his eventful life. I kept on
and on, without plan, without specific goal, guided solely by
the questions, the objections, the reactions of my audience. I
made them laugh, I even made them weep. I felt I was totally
fulfilling my function.

I say to Jacques: "One day, when I'm old . . . when I have
more experience . . . when I dare . . . I'd like to write an
enormous book, a thousand pages long, with a thousand
characters all doing exactly what they want."

"Why not do it now?" he asks.

"It wouldn't be right at the moment."

"You just don't dare."

"I just don't dare."

I don't dare be as serious as I really am. I don't dare be as
unserious as I really am. I don't dare pray as much as I would
like, sing as much as I would like, fly into rages as much as I
would like, send people packing as much as I would like, love
people as much as I would like, write with as much power and
bad taste as I would like, with as much simplicity—or for as
many pages—as I would like. In my optimistic moments I tell
myself: I don't dare *yet*. After all, I'm still under forty.

And why don't I dare? I want to be fair, I want to weigh my

words, I want to make allowances for everything, I want faith, justice, beauty—but if I were living fully, I wouldn't need to want them. There would be no more anecdotes. And the most trivial of news items would take its place in the history of the world. And Oscar Brik—or Blek—would express all the things that I wouldn't even need to express any more.

Mme Josette has a story: Braque was working next to Van Dongen. After a while he said to him: "Pass me your eraser." Van Dongen said: "What's an eraser?"

Mme Josette interprets this as the reply of a proud man. I interpret it as the reply of a humble man.

"He thought he was perfect."

"He accepted his imperfection as part of the plan of the universe."

The same thing, perhaps? At all events, I'm still using an eraser.

Authors and Manuscripts

As a writer I think about myself. As a reader I am on the other side of the fence. And I feel ill at ease there.

I have already mentioned the old lady who once persecuted me, shaking me out of my first sleep at eleven every night to reproach me for having rejected a manuscript sent by her son, "a true genius." For several weeks now I have been pursued again, this time by an elderly antique dealer who is anxious to show me the work—"so full of promise"—of his "protégée," a young girl called Dominique. A classic case. I reply evasively. Let her send the manuscript and I will read it. But what she wants, what they both want, is to *see* me. I'm not very famous, you might say; but even my small measure of celebrity is sufficient to make certain people long simply to gaze at me, like a monument, without any wish to carry the encounter further.

I remember one quite ordinary-looking woman who stopped me once in a Prisunic and said: "You're Françoise Mallet-Joris, aren't you?" "Yes, madame." "Ah!" and she gazed at me for a long while, examining me from head (unfortunately a bird's nest that particular day) to toe, without saying another word, yet without embarrassment or shyness, taking her time. The irritation I felt was titanic. The insistence displayed by Dominique and her aged protector came at a bad time. I was swamped with work; Pauline's "blind" whooping cough, that scourge of parents, had now transferred itself to Alberte; my book wasn't getting anywhere, and the pile of manuscripts and bills beside my bed grew taller every day. The telephone rang nonstop (half the time it was the antique dealer, and I would assure him in shrill and faltering tones that Mother wasn't in). Then the express letters began arriving, each more urgent, more tragic almost, than the last. He begged me, he beseeched me! An hour! Just an hour of my time! It was a matter of *crucial importance* to him. He had underlined the words twice, in red. He began sending me hydrangeas.

I felt ashamed. I am not normally all that inaccessible. In fact, I am really quite happy to have writers visit me. There was an old White Russian who came several times to explain his religious views, which were based on something called caodaism. There was an Armenian philosopher who once read me an interminable pamphlet that I assured him was absolutely remarkable, even though I hadn't understood a word. Daniel's friends all make it their duty to hand in their essays to me—so true is it that in France literature is the cornerstone of the nation—and I take great pleasure in reading them. A certain curiosity, combined with my natural and sometimes rewarded optimism, always makes me reply to the various letters I receive on pages torn from exercise books informing me that the author of these lines has important revelations to make to me. There was a young Marxist who taught me a great deal: we exchanged several letters on various metaphysical subjects. One girl in the Ardèche wrote asking me for spells because her love was not being returned. Country clergymen have sent me charming discourses on the forgotten virtues of various plants and the pleasures of mountain climbing. Missionaries have asked for books. And a madman convinced he was being persecuted by the local police inspector once wrote asking what to do.   ,

I would glance up at Isabelle—a friend who is kind enough to act as my secretary sometimes—with mingled amusement and amazement. "Do we answer?"

And Isabelle, who is kindness itself, would say with a pitiful, tender look: "It doesn't take a minute . . ."

So we replied. Sometimes the heterogeneity of my correspondents made me feel more like a fortune-teller than a writer. And the thought occurs that perhaps fortune-telling might prove a good second string to my bow, something I could take up when I retire. Perhaps it is a sign.

Then there was the woman who insisted on seeing me in person. It was "of the utmost importance" that she should do so, needless to say. Yes, she had a serious revelation that could only be made face to face.

"You've simply got to help me."

"I should like to, of course, but . . ."

"Well, I know it sounds idiotic, but . . . I'm bored."

"Ah!"

That was all I could think of to say. Though I was rather angry, all the same. I am not, after all, a theatrical booking agency, or a circus. My caller, thirty-five, elegant but very ordinary, then felt it incumbent upon her to explain that her boredom—without which she would never have come to disturb me like this, just think!—was not just a boredom like anybody else's. Boredom in the seventeenth-century sense, almost. Nothing, absolutely nothing had ever succeeded in pulling her out of it. And then, while attending a lecture I was giving for a charity, she had got it into her head that I and I alone could rescue her from her boredom. And there

she was, waiting for the ultimate oracle from my lips. As I said
—a fortune-teller.

". . . because I said to myself, she has four children, so they
must bore her a lot . . ."

"Oh no, I assure you . . ."

"And you said you read manuscripts for publishers, that
must be very tiresome for you . . ."

"Oh no, really not . . ."

". . . Then you must certainly have some method, some
system . . ."

Why not a magic potion? But a bad workman blames his
tools. I questioned this woman. I ended up fascinated by her
insoluble problem. Because she had no lack of money, her
husband was "quite bearable," her children "all perfectly
healthy," she had received "quite a good education" . . . She
would have liked to find something to do, but she didn't want
to get involved in anything that had a religious or political cast
to it. The arts did not attract her. She was repelled by the idea
of charity work: children tired her, teenagers terrified her, old
people disgusted her. There was no kind of occupation for
which she had any particular competence or any particular
taste. She did not need money. I confess that my interest was
in fact caught by inner penury on such a scale. She hadn't any
vices either. But after a few meetings it became clear to her
that her hope in me had been misplaced, and in the end she
said goodbye, with these disillusioned words: "Never mind,
it's all helped me to pass a little time, at least."

Well, although it was true that the "all" she was referring
to (the futile, empty interviews during which I tried to com-
prehend the gray non-being from which she *only just* suffered,
that *only just* being the one and only living point in her non-
existence, the single quivering dot on the flat, formless, colorless pond of her life) had in fact caused me not simply to pass
all that time but to waste it, it was also true that I had begun
to feel a certain interest in the woman, as I might for a rare

specimen, for some dull, unlovely, dead fragment of mineral whose one claim to my attention was that it was the only one out of countless millions that was in fact dull, unlovely, dead to quite that extent.

So why not the aged antique dealer? Why am I suddenly slamming the door, suddenly rebelling against the constant intrusions of society and other people, suddenly feeling so bereft of generosity and patience, so proprietorial about my inner life? Perhaps it was the vulgar writing, the pretentious paper, the bombastic style that were putting me off. The man's method, which consisted in inundating me with flowers and exclamation marks, struck me as distasteful. I dug in my heels. He dug in his heels. Then abruptly I gave way.

The truth was that I had wasted a great deal more time in refusing to grant the interview than I would have wasted by saying yes the first time. Not to mention the trouble I had been forced to go to on the telephone, disguising my voice successively as that of a simple-minded Spanish maid, a twelve-year-old girl, an efficient secretary, and finally, when desperate, as that of a husky-throated youth: "No, I'm just friend o' Dan's. No, I dunno where they've gone." But I was defending a principle. Am I a psychiatrist? ("It will do her so much good to see you," the enemy wrote.) Am I the Labor Exchange? A career-guidance officer? ("She" was not sure which way to go, needed to consult me before committing herself to a career that, a career which . . .) Am I the Eiffel Tower? (It would give them so much pleasure to "see" me; on television it's just not the same.) And then, in the face of yet another assault, appalled by the lengths to which my antique dealer was obviously prepared to go, feeling that he was about to appear any moment and pour petrol over himself on my doorstep (the children did in fact claim to have seen him waiting outside the front door more than once), I gave way. In any case, it had only been an "attack" of principles, as it were. It is only when I'm without principles that I feel that I'm really myself. I made an appointment to see them.

"I was sure you would," Jacques commented philosophically.
"Why?"

"Oh . . . refusing something, it's just not like you," he said
without turning away from his canvas.

Well, maybe it isn't like me, but the trouble is, of course,
that we are all like ourselves so very little of the time.

I go to keep the appointment feeling as if a knife is being
held at my throat. The dread of confronting human beings
that one senses are going to be a bore and banal, the effort of
seeming to listen and understand, the disappointment that
almost inevitably must be inflicted, and then the rancor that
these "admirers" display just as you begin to feel a little
sympathy for them.

At first glance my antique dealer looks even worse than I'd
imagined. At least seventy, with that suggestion of the Mon-
goloid child that you get in people who've had their faces
lifted—though it must have been quite a while ago. The skin,
too dry and too fine, falling into tiny creases all over the forehead, bagging a little under the eyes . . . "Go have yourself
made new again," Pauline would say. He wears a signet ring
on his left hand, a polka-dot tie, and smiles constantly, showing
his teeth and tipping back his head, like a politician who has
turned into a machine for demonstrating universal breeziness
and cordiality. He is in fact made up of two distinct characters
that are constantly fighting to occupy the center of the stage,
perpetually alternating in the most amazing fashion: a coquettish old maid of good family, anxious to be thought well con-
nected, simpering a lot, and doubtless writing poems on the
sly; and a shady, crafty politician determined no one shall
put anything over on him and convinced that everything can
be bought. These two personalities succeed one another with
an almost dizzying rapidity.

"I did so long to meet you! So many things in common! A
quality of soul, you know. But I'm practically certain we've
already met, at the X——s, at a cocktail party for Y." (Here
the transition between coquettish old maid and the politician

is accomplished with a smile skilfully modulating from simpering to jovial and an abrupt lowering of the voice by several octaves.) "Of course! Of course! Two Parisians like us, living here all these years, we must know one another, we do know one another! I was telling Dominique: leave it to me; if you want to meet her, then meet her you shall. I know her, and she is such a sweet woman. She loves young people, she will love your book. But I had lost sight of you a little since the days when you had that little apartment near . . . near . . ."

"The Panthéon," I say automatically.

"Yes, of course, near the Panthéon." (The voice rising in pitch, the smile moving back toward the simper.) "What a delightful part of Paris that is! That youthful, bohemian atmosphere, and of course I myself, I think I told you about it once, I write too. Oh, in the most modest way of course, for the *Normandy Courier*, the *Birn-Lichtli Gazette*, in Switzerland, literary criticism, I try to make it worth reading, to put things across, and poems as well, and interviews, in the footsteps of Sainte-Beuve, d'you see—oh, it's all terribly, terribly provincial of course, needlework, petit-point I do for a little circle, a Verdurin's little clan, as it were. Ah, ha! Ah, ha!"

At which, with prima-donna virtuosity, the fluting laugh once more sinks an octave, passing from mincing affectation down to coarse vulgarity by successive stages: charming irony of his own erudition (soprano); complicity with me as writer (mezzo); we can come to an understanding, there is always a way (baritone down to bass); moreover, I can assure you that you are very much read there (in Birn-Lichtli?), very highly thought of. "I am working on two articles about you now in which I pulverize all those other women writers—no, really, literally pulverize them. To me you are a man, absolutely, a man!" (Slight rise back toward the soprano.)

Given the sort of man he appears to be, I am in no way reassured by this last statement. I begin to wonder, in fact, whether I heard him right and whether it is not quite simply a young author he is concerned with rather than a young authoress.

"And I always say so! I write it! I am one of your most ardent supporters. In my next article on you, a whole page, six columns, I defend you against the people who claim that Françoise Sagan is a better stylist than you, though she hasn't your imagination. I've really hauled them over the coals about that, you'll see!"

"That's very kind of you," I say with what little breath hasn't been knocked out of me, stupefied as I so often have been by the way you can end up seemingly in debt to people you've neither wanted nor asked anything from.

"Don't worry," the politician goes on. "You have your loyal followers—I count myself among them. A small band of devoted friends can sometimes support a writer more effectively than . . ."

I think I am on the point of saying something really unpleasant to my devoted friend when, by chance, my eyes come to rest on his shoes (somewhat scuffed, very carefully polished), then climb slowly up the navy-blue trousers, so brightly shining all along the crease that he obviously irons himself. And the well-pressed, rather too tight jacket, the tightly knotted tie suddenly take on a quite different meaning. It doesn't look as if the antique trade can be exactly booming at the moment. I promise myself to eat very little. And here is "Dominique" coming to join us. She is not at all what I expected. What I see is a frail, wan young girl with huge forget-me-not blue eyes that remind me of Lillian Gish, Broken Blossom of the silent screen. But when Blossom opens her mouth, the voice that emerges is that of a Paris taxi driver, very racy but something of a shock. I have two surprise merchants on my hands, I think.

"Hi, how's it going? You found one another all right, eh?" Lillian Gish roars as she approaches.

"Of course, of course, as you see, and we have renewed an old acquaintance that . . . an acquaintance which . . ." our antique dealer simpers, his refinement of manner even more pronounced by contrast. "Take off your bolero, darling, and just let us have another moment or two. I was asking our friend some questions, one or two scraps of information for the *Birn-Lichtli Gazette* . . ."

"Oh, I won't stick my nose in," the child replies, visibly impressed, twiddling her ringlets with the end of one finger . . . "I'm not the literary type, chouchou, I don't care what you say . . ."

I have had my bellyful of Birn-Lichtli and this pitiful farce. All those questions: "What do you think of the position of women today?" "Is there a modern spirituality?" "Do you really like the novels of Françoise Sagan [or Simone de Beauvoir]?" And many many more—on how to bring up children, on whether the Mass should be in Latin, on the new novel and political commitment. The whole thing ceased to amuse me long ago, even to annoy me. Lassitude, a vast, despairing lassitude descends on me when I am faced with all those questions that no one believes in, that no one is interested in (not even my admirers in Birn-Lichtli), and to which I am really only expected to answer quite mechanically. Anything at all will do, as long as it can be recorded or printed, can provide three minutes or three columns to add to the flood of noise or the torrent of paper that must of course be kept flowing, because so many people's livelihoods depend on it . . . So I answer. I answer. I even answer quite seriously, weighing my words. I make my answer to someone who isn't there, who would have understood, because when all is said and done, in the end it is less sad and less boring to do things seriously.

And the childlike eyes, blue as some old-fashioned flower— their color could only be qualified with old cottage-garden names: columbine, forget-me-not, periwinkle—rest on this affected old man, camp and crumbling, with filial admiration and affection.

"You're fabulous, chouchou!"

The evidence is there before me suddenly, beyond the shiny jacket, the affected speech, this third-rate farce we are in: these two beings love one another, lean on one another, need one another.

And as though they had immediately perceived it, that glimmer of sympathy flashing through me, they begin telling me their story, which is as banal and touching as some old novelette. She is the daughter of his concierge. Her drunken father abandoned her. She was obliged to leave school, become a hairdresser, provide for her invalid mother, who eventually died. Left alone in the world, she is taken under his wing by her "old friend," who looks after her "education," finds in her the home and family he has, alas, never had, a consolation for all his troubles. And yes, an "unfortunate forgery business" obliged him to sell his elegant little shop in the Palais-Royal and to start again, after two years "in the wilderness" (a euphemism which I presume I have understood), in a less well-favored location on the Faubourg-Poissonière. But he has kept his connections, his old friends—it's a great consolation to him.

"Oh, yes," the girl breaks in. "It's really done him so much good, your saying you'd see him again. He didn't dare, he kept saying: 'Now she's so famous and all, maybe she won't remember . . .'"

A sudden gaiety seizes me; my sympathy for him has been growing steadily since his revelation of the "unfortunate forgery business." Swindlers always exert a kind of fascination on me.

"But you ought to have dared!" I cry, inspired with a sudden spirit of mischief. "Don't you remember those visits to us in the rue Royer-Collard, when you used to bounce Daniel on your knee?"

The glance he gives me, piteous, full of understanding and thanks, spiced with a hint of wry humor, is a masterpiece. I no longer regret the time I am giving him. What does that matter, compared with my being able to bring some pleasure into these two lives? The old man so desirous of dazzling the girl, the girl so ready to be dazzled by this luxury, the only one he is in a position to offer her: the company of someone who has had her name in the paper, her face on the television screen.

The book . . . It is a collection of poems in whose composition the "old friend" must certainly have had a hand. These insipid and disembodied stanzas resemble Dominique's eyes more than her speech. Needless to say, it is unpublishable.

"I have some savings, salvaged from the wreck," he says. "Do you think it could be done, at the author's expense . . ."

"Well, that's not so easy these days, you know . . . But at any rate I'll see, I'll try . . ."

The child's face lights up with a joy that makes her almost beautiful. To be published! And thanks to him! They gaze at one another, they clasp hands.

"I was sure of it . . . I know what Dominique is worth . . . Ah, she's not one of your modern young girls who . . . A pure mountain stream, so clear, so fresh . . . It will cut right across all this writing we are getting at the moment that . . ."

How we need to believe in purity! The voice, breaking under its load of inane emotion, is abruptly the voice of an old man, yet it contains not the slightest note of irony. And yet this old man with his overtitivated appearance is also, I would swear to it, one of those who haunt the public lavatories of Saint-Germain-des-Prés with hangdog humility . . .

"I'll do what I can. Whatever I can."

It won't be much though. What can I be expected to do for such lachrymose, old-fashioned poems crammed with subjunctives (and the little hairdresser is so proud of them: they are "prestige" subjunctives, as we say today) that might well have been written by my grandmother? I shall suggest a few corrections, try to keep them from forking out a large sum . . . The usual sort of thing . . .

Walking back home from my rendezvous, I reproached my-self for my hardness of heart. Why had I been so stubborn about not seeing them all that time? Am I so precious that I have to keep myself under the counter, like some choice food reserved only for people who deserve me? And by what right was I to say that Chouchou and his Antigone were unworthy? Again, as always, the thrifty housewife pokes her nose in. But one must learn how to throw away one's time, one's presence. If it is gold, so much the better for other people. If it's dross, so much the better for me since I am able to give an illusion of largesse at so small a cost.

Moreover, Chouchou's story is a sad one. The little hair-dresser is in a sanatorium now. Chouchou, on account of an "unfortunate business" with a television set bought on credit and resold for cash, is back "in the wilderness" for eight months. The little book of poems, published by Editions du Scorpion, is in front of me.

Someone says: "I wonder why you keep such inanities."

"In memory of an old friend."

Dominique: Oh, Chouchou taught me everything, spelling, politics . . . We're Royalists, *hein*, Chouchou?
Chouchou: One says *"n'est ce pas."*

Me: Four years ago, at the time when I was so depressed . . .
Writer Friend: What pulled you out of it?
Me: I was helped enormously by reading Marcelle Auclair's *Le Livre du bonheur.*
Writer Friend: Don't say things like that! Just don't say things like that, for heaven's sake!

[It is a wonder he desn't look behind him to make sure no literary spy could possibly have overheard my admission.]

Sometimes you just don't seem to realize how quick people

are to label a person. Writers can't just go around saying whatever they like, you know.
Me: What a pity.

Television

They are doing a whole program on her. Jacqueline, thirty years old, six children. Lives in a "spick-and-span" flat in low-cost housing block surrounded by rather less spick-and-span waste ground. How does she manage? A woman's program. Another woman's presence is therefore necessary: mine. I ask the questions. Gently, with respect. And she deserves respect, this slight, gallant, even gay Jacqueline who manages, who keeps her head above water—modest expressions indeed to describe the herculean labors she undertakes and accomplishes in her brightly polished three-room flat with its spotless linoleum, its spotless sink, its spotless children.

I think it was a good program. We were all of us (cameraman, director, electrician, sound engineer) kind and gentle with her. She wasn't displeased to have us there; it made a change. The children loved having us; we brought them sweets, and a dictionary for the eldest girl, something she'd always dreamed of. It didn't matter how cluttered we made the tiny flat with our cables; we were still welcome. And Jacqueline, never pausing in her washing, her rubbing, her polishing, her ironing, answered our questions, quite relaxed, pleased, but not excessively so, at the idea of being filmed. Natural. Simple. Everyone to his trade.

For a time after the program was on the air, Jacqueline received letters of sympathy, presents for the children, little things that gave her pleasure and that she accepted with the same simplicity, the same natural ease.

Claude, the director, would have liked her to refuse them,

to be indignant. But why should she have done any such thing? She wasn't outraged because she hadn't the time to be. She was too busy doing her life's work, unable to see further than that cleanliness, that spotless domestic routine that was her form of honor, her creation.

"But she *ought* to be outraged," Claude said.

"No, *we* ought to be."

She wasn't unhappy. Worried, yes, but only to the extent that you worry when the whole course of your future life already lies clearly, immutably before you. And she herself didn't figure in her worries at all. It was this one's schooling, that one's health, and always those floors, the washing, the brass . . . Not mean-minded, either. A little hard on other women, the ones who can't manage, who can't keep their heads above water, who drink, who go out on the town, who want to have lives of their own. I was told the program was depressing. But Jacqueline herself certainly wasn't depressing. She had peace of mind, like all who live for something other than themselves. That program was double-edged, in fact: comforting in that Jacqueline was able to live that hard life of hers in peace and almost unconscious sacrifice; depressing because there is not one human being in a hundred who is capable of living that life in that way and yet there are so many hundreds who are faced with her situation exactly. Awareness of joy, then, becomes inseparable from awareness of misfortune. It is intolerable that there should be situations from which the only escape is renunciation.

"She's a saint," said Roger, our cameraman.

No. To be a saint she would have to be aware of the injustice of her situation as well as accepting it as she does. But she isn't aware of injustice. True misfortune keeps you from even laying claim to your own virtues. When Jacqueline criticizes those other women, the ones who feel they can't breathe in that block of concrete municipal flats, so lonely out there in its acres of waste ground, who are suffocating between the ironing board and the stove, who try so pitifully to find a way out, by drinking, by running away (and they all come back, six months later, a year later, with another child—another link in the chain that binds them—in their arms or in their bellies), when she criticizes those women, Jacqueline is aiding and abetting the society that is her oppressor. And yet, when Claude denies the validity of that serene success, is that not a sin against the human spirit?

Someone says: "Now ask her if she uses makeup, if makeup is important to her."

"Oh, now listen, no, it would be indecent."

"Nonsense, I can assure you it won't embarrass her in the slightest."

It doesn't embarrass her. She answers, serene as ever. But it embarrasses me.

Jacqueline is not without a sense of humor. She tells us how she came to get married:

"He [her husband-to-be] was an orphan, and his sister wasn't much of a cook. So he used to come and eat at my parents' place every night. After six months of that, my parents said to me: 'As long as we're feeding him anyway, why not marry him, it won't work out any dearer.' So we got married."

Despite the constant drudgery, despite the meager wage and intolerable headaches her husband brings back from the factory, Jacqueline still indulges herself in one extravagance: she dresses her youngest children in white, a spotless, eye-catching, shocking white. She has no washing machine, and people exclaim: "White! You must be mad!"

She smiles. Her first proper woman's smile, sly, with a pretty sparkle of defiance in her eyes.

"But there it is. That's how I like to see them."

It is her luxury, her signature, the flourish with which she finishes off her work, as an artist does a canvas, for no good reason, for its own sake. "Everyone has to go overboard a bit now and then," she adds.

Television II

We are moving. Pauline is lamenting the fact that she will be losing her little playmate, Pierre, who lives down on the courtyard.

Pauline (wringing her hands with anguished intensity): Pierre! My Pierre! My little Pierre, I adore him so much! I won't be able to go on living!

Me (reading, or rather trying to read, a manuscript in bed): Pauline, you're being ridiculous.

Pauline: I love him. If I leave him, we shall both die of grief!

Me: Who puts those ridiculous ideas into your head?

Pauline (suddenly wholly matter-of-fact): It's the television. It's terribly bad for children.

Comics

I had come out of Grasset, the publishers, and was standing at Sèvres-Babylone waiting for a bus and reading *Spirou*, the comic I buy every Tuesday for my children. An old lady came up to me: "Oh, my dear! When there are so many good books!"

The New House

When we are in the new house, Pauline is going to be tidy and Alberte will be able to practice her piano in peace. When we are in the new house, Dolores, so she assures us, will at last have enough cupboards to "get herself organized." The animals will be kept under control, some of them even eliminated. There will be a severe weeding out of all knickknacks. I shall catch up with my mail and I shall never misplace another manuscript. Daniel will have his own room and will be able to entertain his friends without disturbing us. Vincent will have a new desk and won't blotch up his clothes and his homework as much. We shall have normal people coming to see us— people who won't set up camp in the hall, people who don't even play one musical instrument. We shall have two bathrooms.

"I shall have a proper home at last, and so will you," Dolores generously informs me. "We can really settle down now."

And with that expectation she goes out and buys a television set on the installment plan, and a mauve velvet dressing gown.

"From now on, I shall only go out with men who are really serious about me. And I won't invite them to my room."

When we are in the new house, Jacques will never again be seen drawing at midnight at the foot of the bed, in just a shirt, by the light of a flashlight. I shall have a complete, brand-new dinner service. There will be curtains at the windows, towel railings beside the washbasins, and I shall sort out my books. I shall issue invitations to all those "useful connections" I never dared ask to share our rather too eventful meals in the Panthéon flat. We shall have loads of laundry baskets and we won't ever absent-mindedly get into paint-splattered trousers or skirts with unraveled hems. We . . .

"You do realize," Jacques broke in as I lay dreaming aloud one day, "that we are already *in* the new house?"

At least we can still say to people who don't know us very well: "Do excuse the mess, we've just moved in." We've been saying it now for two years. I think we can keep on pulling that one for about another six months. After that, we're in real trouble.

The Strainer

Dolores picks up the strainer, whose curve (designed by the manufacturer to receive the liquid that one wishes, presumably, to strain) has been flattened because the drawer she keeps it in is not high enough. With a swift blow of her fist, biff! she restores the aluminum circle to its correct shape. She uses it. Then, with a swift blow of her fist, bop! she flattens it again so she can put it away. After a dozen or so biffs and bops, the maltreated metal snaps. The strainer has to be replaced.

"It's just incredible how flimsy they make them," Dolores comments. "Though I must admit, if they were stronger I'd never be able to put them away."

Habitual crockery smasher, incapable of helping herself to any liquid without spilling at least half of it, forever covered in cuts and bumps, in glue, in ink and paint, scattering meals in all directions, running, shrieking, stumbling, falling, yelling, singing, laughing and crying at the same time, to such an extent that it's impossible ever to tell whether she is laughing hysterically or sobbing her heart out, Pauline has been honored by the boys with a new nickname: "Po-po Catastrophe." She is utterly delighted with it.

"If I become a singer, I shall use it as my stage name," she tells us.

Youth

Why shouldn't Daniel lend, or indeed give, all his pullovers, his trousers, his records, his books to vague friends of friends who happen to need them? Why shouldn't Daniel rough it, sleeping on a rug while his bed is occupied by a friend who's "going through a bad spell"? Why shouldn't Daniel's room serve as a refuge, a smoking room, a canteen, a discothèque for passers-by of all ages and colors? Why shouldn't he give the freedom of our refrigerator, at midnight, to anyone who happens to be in his room feeling a little peckish? "Clothe the naked, feed those that hunger." "They're all like that these days," I am told by a woman with a son the same age. "Though, all the same, it's a bit trying when you've bought your son a cashmere pullover and two days later you find it's been re-placed by a faded old U.S. Army surplus jacket!" But "is the man not more than the apparel"? And is a cashmere pullover really the best thing we can find to give our children? Some-times my head swims a little with it all. Are we living by a set of rules that are exactly opposite to the Gospels? Ought Daniel and his peers not be our models rather than a source of con-cern to us? "They toil not, neither do they spin. And yet I say unto you, that even Solomon in all his glory was not arrayed like one of these."

One afternoon, in a little café in the rue de Buci, I sit waiting for a friend and thinking about these things. Nearby, a group of young people had collected, some with bare feet, others jangling with pendants and beads; faded jeans mingling with flowered shirts and Oriental robes. They were criticizing a priest from nearby Saint-Séverin in rather harsh terms because they had seen him in a restaurant, "stuffing his gut."

"Do you think Jesus ate meat? In the first place, he visited India, that's been proved. He was a kind of guru, Jesus. A priest ought to hide if he wants to stuff his face like that— that's what I figure."

"If you hide things, you get repressed," chimes in a learned Portia, perhaps fourteen, pretty as a dainty flower painting.

"There ought to be fasts, like in the old days, like the Moslems, man, forty days . . ."

"Like you're fasting all the time, huh?"

"Well, I don't make a pig of myself, anyway."

"You drink, though."

"It's not the same. I drink to find that other dimension, just like I smoke."

"If Jesus had lived now, would he have taken LSD?" an Oriental priestess with a silver dot between her darkened eyes muses.

"Of course he would!"

"Of course he wouldn't!"

Two beards in confrontation.

"He didn't need it. The Word . . ."

"But when he talks about the lilies of the field, he means . . ."

There they are again, my lilies of the field. One must admit that they can be turned to any number of uses. And all the old commonplaces are about to be brought out: Jesus was a guru, a beatnik, he didn't bother earning a living, the Apostles were just a group of friends like us, and Ramakrishna said . . . A hodgepodge, an Australian salad of half-digested Orientalism and ignorance, of presumption and enthusiasm, of rebellion and idleness. The hairdresser's son dreams of ashram, the businessman's of permanent revolution. At least, for the moment, they are rubbing shoulders. Perhaps this moment of their lives is one of the most "valid"? Who can say? Doubtless their dream of all going off to India together, of founding a community of brothers, is in fact no more than a dream, and based ultimately on the certain knowledge that they can all return, any evening they please, to a family home only too glad to welcome them back. But who is to measure the power of children's dreams? Perhaps one of them will go, abandoning his studies or the family shop . . . Only to return in disappointment perhaps, or ill, or burdened with an Oriental wife (I have seen it happen) whose exotic charms will evaporate as quickly as the scent of a spice box left open to the air. And he will live, he will get by "in the village" on the strength of his past adventures, something of a yogi, something of a spiritualist, hovering on the fringe of bohemia along with the painter who does not sell and the faith healer who has no patients, all of them referred to as "failures."

The scorn that that term implies has always amazed me. Painter without buyers, writer without readers, composer without an orchestra, inventor without patents, mystic without a church—the "failures" are precisely those who were fired by great ambition. Who calls a successful businessman a "failure"? Who speaks of some rich and idle person, some dull and high-ranking civil servant as being a failure? And yet who is to say what any of those men might have become in the sphere of knowledge, of beauty, of love? A failure, as the word is commonly used, is simply someone who has attempted something and been unable to find a niche in society. Inner wealth, the necessary courage, none of that is taken into consideration in this supposedly cultured, idealistic, and Christian society of ours. So is it so surprising that an ardent and disgusted younger generation should be attracted to saris, gurus, yoga, and meditation? Jesus was just someone who failed as King of the Jews. If he had seized power and lived a little longer, his life would really have been worth something. Even the Romans would have respected him.

We say that we are Roman Catholics, but in fact we are more Roman than Catholic. Baudelaire was a pretentious failure. Van Gogh and St. Benoît Labre were tramp-type failures. Edison and Denis Papin, Bernard Palissy and the man next door who has never been able to get anyone to play his symphony or publish his book, they are all failures—for a while at least. Judgment is made, and the line is drawn, with the help of a golden rule that boils down to the bank account, the photo in *Paris-Match*, or the good graces of a Louis XIV. Fénelon, who was a political and mystical writer of great range and power, a dedicated archbishop, a wonderful friend, a lover of children, gardens, justice, and his faith, is regarded by most critics as a failure. Why? Because Louis XIV disgraced him in a fit of authoritarianism. He enlightened the Church and found salvation, but that doesn't count. He joined with his friends to form a circle that radiated faith and love, and whose correspondence can still touch our hearts today, but that doesn't count. His mystical writings possess a beauty and nobility worthy of Chateaubriand, and his political writings were read all over Europe, but that doesn't count, doesn't count in the slightest, I tell you. He wasn't permitted to attend the court lotteries over which Bossuet so jovially presided. He wasn't invited to those infinitely tedious and futile "Marlys" at which the Sun-King attempted to warm up his old age with a little blaze of senile sadism. He could not defeat Bossuet's intrigues, or Louis XIV's influence in Rome. He was forced to content himself with the esteem of the most respected minds of the nation; but what is that, compared to being received at Marly? One sees immediately what side his critics would have been on. And note, moreover, that we are speaking here about a priest, for whom, it is generally accepted, "success" is not exactly the same thing as for an ordinary mortal. Is that a "Christian civilization"? Would we not dream of leaving for India too, if we were twenty years old and had a calculating-machine future ahead of us?

So let there be saris that are such lovely colors and don't cost that much; let there be good friends who swap their crazy ideas and their pullovers. And even if Jesus was a guru, and even if Jesus was a beatnik, let us proclaim that Jesus was also, above all else, a failure.

"All the same," X. points out, "if you weren't a success yourself, you couldn't say these things. You knew how to play your cards, all right."

"That doesn't make me a professional gambler."

In Teilhard de Chardin's letters I find this: ". . . Having reached this peak, you will realize that nothing is separated from anything else, that nothing is petty or profane, since the least of consciences bears the destinies of the Universe partially within itself, and cannot become better without making all that is around it better, too."

That nothing is petty, that nothing is profane . . . That is what I should have liked to say to Gabrielle Lenoir. But I didn't find the quotation until afterwards, when it was too late.

I was leaning against a wall in the rue Saint-André-des-Arts, not at my best-dressed, waiting for Jacques, who was at the wine merchant's, returning some empty bottles, when a tall and very tattered young man came up to me.

"You wouldn't have a hundred francs?"

And I answered, feeling facetious that day: "I was just going to ask you the same thing."

Whereupon he said: "Oh? Here you are, then." And he placed a small coin in my palm, while I stood there dumfounded.

I kept it a long time, until one of the children pinched it and changed it into toffee. I used to look at it and muse. I am neither so simple nor so full of illusions as to try to endow that little coin with any earth-shattering virtues. It wasn't the "widow's mite" we read about in the Gospel, the thrice-blessed alms given by the poor to those poorer than themselves. There was no sacrifice, no mortification in that gesture. It merely expressed an easy gaiety, a carefree way of life, a contempt for the goods of this world that is pretty sure of falling on its feet. In default of the great virtues, are the little, pleasant qualities to be disdained? One may sometimes progress from the latter to the former. And even if they had no other merit than that of contributing a little charm to life, that's something too.

Mme Josette and the Younger Generation

Mme Josette had a visit last Sunday from an old friend of hers who lives in the suburbs.

"He has a really very pretty little house. I've seen it in a photo, with a barn at the end of a little meadow, really quite countrified. Rather a lot of noise lately, but it's making him look quite young again."

"Traffic noise, Madame Josette?"

"Oh no, not that sort. It's just that last May he put up some young fellows who were in trouble with the police over some sort of posters—I don't know exactly if they were beatniks or hippies." Mme Josette is always very scrupulous about such historical points. "And they spread the word, of course. So he always has three or four of them there these days. They're company for him. Well, I've asked him to send me one."

"A hippie?"

"Or a beatnik, I don't care which. I should be very pleased to hear one of these young men's views on everything that's happening today. I feel that they don't let them express themselves sufficiently on the radio or in *Le Monde*."

I am more than somewhat taken aback at the idea of a hippie in Mme Josette's minuscule dining room, under her orange lampshade, in front of her Breton dresser.

"And is he going to come, Madame Josette?"

"Certainly he is. On Sunday. I'm going to make him my gratin de crevettes and my chocolate cake. Do you think that will be suitable? What do hippies eat? Are they vegetarians?"

"Oh, that depends."

"It's just that I wouldn't want to shock him . . ."

Mme Josette prepares for the arrival of her hippie as though for an ambassador. She has all the ingredients for her gratin de crevettes and has written out a list of questions. What exactly is the meaning of the slogan: *Take your desires for realities?* Why do young people chant: "Elections, betrayals." What is your opinion on the electoral system? Etc.

"You know, Madame Josette, this boy may not necessarily be up on everything that's going on in the world! He isn't a government minister!"

"Do you think government ministers are up on everything that's going on?" she says, effectively shutting me up.

I was a bit apprehensive about the meeting. Would the hippie appear? Might we not find Mme Josette murdered? Or might there not be sad disappointment on both sides? But apparently all is well. The hippie's name is Mark. He is an American who has fled his country to avoid having to fight in Vietnam. He has a big beard and long hair.

"He's really very interesting," Mme Josette tells me with great simplicity. "He was perfectly willing to answer all my questions. He brought a friend with him, and I can tell you my gratin didn't last long."

"Didn't you mind that he brought a friend?"

"Not at all. After the meal they sang a little, some very interesting songs about last May, about the social question. At bottom, you know, these young people are really very serious about things."

To my great surprise, Mme Josette continues to receive visits from her hippies occasionally on Sundays. Do they come for the gratin de crevettes? Perhaps. But that's too simple an explanation. What these young people desperately need, as much perhaps, as a roof over their heads and food in their bellies, is someone to listen to them. How many fathers, how many mothers listen as attentively to their own children—without condescension, and not just trying to humor them—as Mme Josette does to those young men? I admire her for it, and tell her so.

"I am keeping myself informed, that's all," she replies with dignity. "I don't share their opinions, but I am pleased to hear them."

Mme Josette has the gift of egalitarianism. As for wondering whether any maternal feelings insinuate themselves into her relations with Mark and Jean-Pierre, whether she has any interest in their love affairs, their sufferings, their well-being—that is something that Mme Josette would find it most out of place to mention.

A Really Very Curious Remark of Daniel's

We are watching a film on television: one sequence depicts a gypsy wedding that has been arranged by the two families.

Daniel: "Perhaps, in the end, those arranged marriages were really no worse. Seeing a girl for as long as you can remember and thinking: that's the girl who's going to be my wife, and that's that. Maybe that's no worse than being crazy about someone, getting married at twenty, and then regretting it afterwards."

You could knock me down with a feather. What about Love, and Instinct, and Spontaneity, which I had thought inviolably installed as the new triple divinity? I sit musing, without answering.

A few months before, Daniel said to me: "I'm not sure I shan't end up as a Trappist."

"But . . . You mean you've recovered your faith?"

"How is one to tell . . . I don't know . . . It's more the way of life that attracts me."

A Trappist's way of life? And yet I do understand him. The shocks administered to our sensibilities and our imaginations by modern life are so violent, so frequent, and so incoherent that, incapable as we are (partly from sheer fatigue) of regaining our lost unity, we are tempted to seek it in a rule, a ritual, an authentic tradition that will restore our overworked subjectivity to its rightful place as an instrument instead of a guide.

". . . you don't believe?"

"Yes," Daniel answers. "I'm sure I do. We ought to find a way of reconciling that inner liberty and the necessary tradition. The gypsies . . . But we have our own folklore."

Everything is passed off with a smile, it's no good talking about it. But at such moments I find I still have my conviction (sometimes tarnished by so many bills, dentists, dirty dishes) that to make a family is to make a work of art.

Allegra as Always

Jeanne talks about the work she is doing with handicapped children.

Allegra (*also present*): "Oh, I'd love to come and visit them! How sweet they must be!"

Jeanne, put out: "They're not sweet at all!"

Watching Jeanne, I understand how it is possible to be unpleasant out of kindness, to be angry out of kindness.

Allegra does go to see the children. She puts on a yellow-and-pink dress, one of those mad dresses she looks so good in, with a belt covered in intricate metal plates. The children adore playing with the belt. She leaves it for them.

Jeanne: "They'll hurt themselves."

Allegra: "But they'll have had a good time."

Jeanne says to me: "She's coming, then she doesn't come, she brings them ridiculous presents, or nothing at all. She isn't serious, she just does it for fun."

Watching Allegra, I understand that kindness is not necessarily serious.

Bobby

"We were quite friendly. Well, we used to eat lunch together, I used to lend him money, you know, so one day I said to him, I'd like to be a writer, I feel I could be. He began to laugh, I mean really laugh, and he said: 'You're too dim, honestly you're just too dim.' Well, I didn't like that, as you can imagine —put yourself in my place—so I said to him: 'Explain that remark.' And he punched me in the nose!"

"And then?"

"Well, naturally, I didn't see him as much."

Bobby II

". . . and two or three months later a friend said to me, you know, Charles is broke, I mean really broke, he can't even go out and look for work, he needs a suit, so naturally I gave him the suit, but I didn't give it gladly."

"You bear grudges."

"Oh, horribly."

Monseigneur and the Modern World

I have to go and see Monseigneur. I am on a committee of serious-minded people concerned about our information service. They asked me and I said yes. One can't say no to everything. Perhaps it is a duty to take part in these things. One complains about this, about that, about the way parish affairs are run, about the way the nation's affairs are run, so one can't refuse to take part from time to time when something is actually being done. So I am going to see Monseigneur. Later I shall sit on the committee—and have nothing to say.

I am on my way to see Monseigneur. Somewhat nervous. I'm not actually stupid, but between the deepest part of my mind —which is, I think, serious, or even grave—and my surface humor—which is very lively, even childish perhaps—there is a gap. I don't have that in-between layer, the layer that enables you to be serious without being really serious, to talk about subjects you know nothing about, or subjects you're not particularly clear on, or subjects you just don't care about, even though they may be very important. Some people have a gift, as soon as "serious" subjects are broached in their presence, of putting on an appropriate expression, so that you know how profoundly they have grasped the importance of the problem even though they're so busy with other things, so that you know they're seeing it in a world context and if they only had the time they could even solve it. But it is a gift I lack. If ever I do manage to produce such an impression, it is by expending such a tremendous amount of energy that I am exhausted for the next two days and quite unable to write.

I am going to see Monseigneur, armed with just one conviction: I would like to do something for my faith. But am I capable of doing anything else but pray, sing, write, welcome anyone who chances along, and endure all the rest? People will tell me that that's enough, and I grant that it could be worse. But it's a bit too *innocuous*. It's only too easy to become a reassuring excuse for other people along those lines. They say: now, *she* doesn't feel it's necessary to go to such lengths, and she's a writer, after all. She's quite content to be a good wife and mother, she cooks well and invents delightful stories for her children, she . . . And that is all too close to a certain image of myself that I loathe, that makes me long for spectacular martyrdom or itch to create a scandal. One must be simple in spirit, not simple-minded. Childlike, not childish. I will do what I can. So I'm on my way to see Monseigneur.

Modern building, filing cabinets everywhere, soundproof rooms; typewriters, secretaries, charts on the walls. I take myself to task. All this is necessary in the modern world. Monseigneur is young, dynamic, likable. He explains what is required of me. My point of view on the problems of communication, my point of view as a non-cleric, may be of great value. I work for a publishing house, so I must know . . . Figures. My mind is already playing truant. Monseigneur looks just a little like a bank manager. But very nice about it, and a bank manager who believes deeply in the usefulness of what he is doing. I wonder if it is possible to feel that one is truly fulfilling God's purposes to the letter when one works in a bank. Yet banks are necessary. A Catholic bank? There is a certain repugnance in facing up to the fact that Church affairs are to a large extent money affairs. You cannot serve God and Mammon. Holy Spirit and Jesus Christ Joint-Stock Bank? Shocking. I'd prefer something like "Catholic Bank Because It's Our Duty," which would make C.B.B.D.—no less impressive than B.N.C.I., it seems to me. And precisely because it's so boring, so lacking in glory and pleasure, the job of bank clerk in the service of Our Lord Jesus Christ would perhaps be very meritorious.

But is it certain that people don't take pleasure in being bank clerks?

In any case, it does seem to me that we ought to squash a certain over-individualistic, family- and tradition-oriented conception of Christianity that in the end is nothing more than ghetto or group morality. Let us be good to our neighbors, to our children, to our friends, to our co-workers (and there I am throwing the net a little wide, when you think of the tiny circles some people live in), and let us close our eyes tight, so that we won't see the world around us, where all the wicked people are slitting one another's throats! Oh, I myself tend only too strongly in that direction. I love my children, my friends, my work. Those things are quite enough to fill a life. I loathe forms, articles that have just been dashed off, fragmentation, people having numbers instead of names. These things tend to estrange me from the modern world and from any action on that world (a world in which Stone Age barbarity mingles so bizarrely with mandarin bueaucracy). Any form of action today is a matter of formulas, publicity, speed, sloppy workmanship (one must take a stand on all manner of problems that would take a lifetime to study in depth); and all meetings—parish meetings, union meetings, party meetings—take place in the evening. In parentheses, I wonder how it is that militants, whatever their persuasion, never feel sleepy?

But I live in this world, and I complain about it, and others complain about it, too. Yet progress is not only relative and slowly achieved; its advantages are quickly lost. And liberty, though it is relative and implies other forms of servitude, is in many ways comparable to disease, which as soon as it is conquered in one form (leprosy or cholera) reappears in another (cancer). Should we give up treating any illness simply because we will one day die? Do we invoke the relativity of things to justify having our adenoids removed? Because we are bound to have other headaches, do we refuse to take an aspirin for this one? In all things there is a question of hope.

I listen to Monseigneur. There is a problem of communication. In my very small way I may perhaps be able to help to some degree. One should take the same attitude toward events as toward people: hope for everything and expect nothing. But, oh, how I dislike statistics!

And yet, if one loved, hoped, believed enough, even statistics would be a song.

There Are No Seasons Any More

In fact, except for children, almost everyone loathes the modern world. We live in the seventies with 1870 ideas. Wonder is a thing of the past, and from moon shots to "status clothing" advertisements we are sickened by this never-ending ballyhoo, these never-ending surprises, these never-ending discoveries. Shall I find happiness because I am at last using a deodorant soap, or shall I sit and grieve over Biafra, about which I can do nothing? There are no proportions any more. I am being scientifically pumped full of guilt at every level: my washing isn't really white and the United States is racist. The Russians have invaded Czechoslovakia and I ought to "economize by buying *more.*" A little hairdresser's assistant, nineteen years old, arrives late for work because the métro was so crowded she had to let three trains go by . . . "Quickly, to the barricades!" she cries. There are no standards any more: we are all at sea. "There are no seasons these days," the wise old folk say. And it's so true.

How is one supposed to bring up children in this chaos? Pauline: "You'll have to buy me a new satchel. My old one's gone out of fashion." And Alberte, later: "*All* the other girls at my school attend winter sports." Daniel refuses to eat at home any more and eats nothing but sausages bought in cafés or chips from a street stall, because "all the other kids do it." It's not enough just to say to them: In my day we had only one satchel all through school, and we worked harder too. In my day no one went to winter sports and we were all the better for it.

They are living in *this* world, in its chaos and its publicity mania, so if you try to bring them up outside it you are merely postponing the moment when it hits them, simply preparing them to be twenty-year-old social misfits. We must re-invent the seasons. And that's not easy.

One can, of course, just buy them the latest satchel and this week's number-one record, send them to skiing classes and imagine that that's enough. You can also sing Bach, inspire them with a contempt for rock 'n' roll, with a taste for good books, wood fires, evenings at home. But who is going to provide the link between the two? The way from Bach to Boulez, from the family out into the world—what can make that clear except a living faith?

Concepts root so deeply in early childhood. A little boy of twelve with whom I am appearing on television watches a cartoon film in which flowers, watered with a magic potion, suddenly shoot up as tall as a house. "That's all modern stuff," he says disdainfully. Modern meaning crazy, idiotic, absurd. Everything that isn't flatly realistic is the work of those "moderns" with long hair who do abstract paintings, write books no one can understand, and put up barricades in the streets because they can't think of anything better to do. There is a whole spiritual world lurking behind that "that's all modern stuff." One can sense a sensibility already warped, a curiosity and a perceptiveness stunted in their development. It's modern because it has sinned, be it ever so slightly, against the rules of realism . . . But what about the German fantastic tradition? The medieval supernatural tradition? *The Golden Legend*, the talking flower of the Knights of the Round Table?

Yet it would be difficult for me to start a discussion of the German fantastic tradition with Gilles . . .

"That sort of thing used to be done in the past too, you know. In stories, in poems . . ."

"Yes, but for babies," Gilles replies with assurance.

"Not always. Cyrano de Bergerac . . ."

"Yes, there have always been madmen, but today the whole world is mad," comes the child's self-assured answer.

Gilles is a nice-looking little boy with nice white teeth, a round face, a bottle-green velvet outfit that suits him very well. He has a very blond, very dainty little sister called Dominique. "Dominique and Gilles . . . Gilles and Dominique . . ." *Les Visiteurs du Soir*, that masterpiece of folklore, of the fake past, of papier-mâché poetry, of pastel tints (I loved it once, before I understood what that idealization of the past was being used for).

"Why do you think the whole world is mad?"

"You only have to look! The clothes, the pictures, the . . . Everything."

"The rockets, too?" I ask treacherously. I have hit a weak spot. There are not many little boys who aren't impressed by rockets.

"All the same, it would be better to build more schools with the money," he says virtuously, putting temptation behind him.

It would, indeed, be better. But are we doing particularly well to teach Gilles, who is only twelve, to dislike and despise the world he has been called upon to live in? Let him learn to defend himself against advertising, vulgarity, the consumer society, certainly. But we should not imprison him in a ghetto of outmoded harmonies.

There is harmony everywhere.

And yet . . . paint a still-life of apples and flowers and guitars: everyone will find that quite natural. Then do a still-life of Coca-Cola bottles and detergent packets, and no matter how serious you are about it, to others that painting will seem

to have an air of deliberate provocation about it. Give a con-
cert of classical Chinese music, and its dissonances, its difficulties will be greeted with attention and serious appraisal;
but the same audience faced with the dissonances and difficulties of a serial or dodecaphonic piece will snigger, because
it is "modern," because it has no guarantee mark of age on it,
because they risk having given their attention for nothing . . .
But attention is not a treasure that will decay. Everything is
always a question of hope.

The Church, the Church, Always the Church

Renée, a Catholic: "Christ, yes! Christ is more beautiful than
Buddha. Christ is more beautiful than anything! But the
Church!"

"But if there hadn't been a Church, you wouldn't even know
your Christ existed! In the beginning the Church was quite
simply all those who had received His word and were trying
to spread it and put it into practice."

"Ah, yes! In the beginning! But afterwards!"

"There were the saints . . ."

"Oh, the saints—I'm not saying anything against them, but
the Church!"

"You wouldn't know anything about the saints either, without the Church. The saints are also the Church. And then
dogma—the Incarnation—the purity of dogma that had to be
preserved, just as monotheism was preserved by the Jews . . ."

"Oh, yes! Dogma! Yes. But the Church!"

"Without the Church you wouldn't have the sacraments,
you wouldn't have the strength the sacraments give you, the
carnal link with God . . ."

"Ah, yes! The Sacraments! Yes. But the Church!"

Running out of arguments: "But wouldn't your faith be too easy without the Church's imperfections? And the cross?"

"Yes, that's true, of course."

Private Joke

"I'm glad Monseigneur B. has been made a cardinal," says Father N., a very close friend. "He's a man of remarkable intelligence, extremely enlightened . . ."

"Oh, indeed . . ."

We each sense a reservation in the other. A spark of malice glitters in Father N.'s eye.

"Of course, one couldn't exactly accuse him of being a social misfit, could one?"

We collapse in helpless laughter. Perhaps people will guess what we're laughing at. No, it's no good, we can't stop laughing.

Another Joke

"The one I just can't understand is St. Simeon Stylites," Vincent says, looking up from *The Desert Fathers*. "He must have been so bored up on that pillar. And what was the point of it?"

"I suppose he wanted to show people that if you have God you don't really need anything else."

"It's such a pity he didn't have television," Pauline puts in. "He'd have got such good reception, even on channel 2, because the pillar would have been like an aerial."

"I suppose he wanted to show people that you can even do

without television—except that it was books, in fact, in those days; that you can do without everything, in fact."

"A cottage and a loving heart," Alberte says, with that gentle irony only she has the secret of.

It couldn't be better put. Why is it generally accepted that human love is a sufficient recompense for any sacrifice, whereas a lot of people would think it, if not mad, at least very eccentric to reduce your standard of living even a little for the love of God. Unless, of course, you have an "official" reason for it—are a monk, or wear a uniform of some sort. Is there a uniform for the Christian life? If so, I have the feeling that ours must certainly have a few buttons missing.

The Construction Worker

For the past year they have been repainting our building. They scrape holes everywhere, plaster them up, leave us for a month or two stewing in our own rubble, only to come back and start again, as far as we can see, from scratch. One builder has a cough. "What a cough that builder has!" Alberte says. Vincent, always sociable, goes over to talk to him: "You ought to try some cough syrup . . . That's what Mother gives us. And then in the evening you ought to rub your chest with Vick's." The builder gives a quick look all around; then he puts a finger to his lips and goes "Sssh!"

Vincent is deeply puzzled. "Why did he go 'Ssssh!' to me like that? I was giving him good advice."

"Perhaps he doesn't want people to know he's ill."

"Why not?"

"They might dismiss him."

"But what about social security? What's it for?" asks Alberte, who believes in all institutions on principle.

My prognosis proved accurate, however. A few days later the tearful children were forced to witness the firing of the unfortunate Portuguese construction worker, who was decidedly coughing far too much.

"Can't you take him on, maman?" Pauline implores.

"He told me he hasn't got any social security yet," Alberte says with a worried frown.

"He said: 'The forms aren't filled in yet.'"

"Can't we have a demonstration?" asks Vincent, never one to shrink from extreme measures.

"We can't demonstrate on account of just one man, I'm afraid. You can have a demonstration over the treatment of Portuguese or foreign workers in general, but not just for one alone."

"So no one has a right to be alone?" Vincent retorts bitterly.

"Yes, we all have the right. But if you decide to go your own way, well, other people will go their own way and not help you. It's the job of the unions to get all the people who work at the same trade together, so that they can help one another."

"Perhaps he couldn't find the building . . ."

"What building?"

"The union building."

"Or perhaps it was the forms. You know. You're always saying: 'Oh, these forms, all these forms . . .'"

"Perhaps he's not too bright," from Alberte.

Vincent, vehemently: "Just because someone isn't bright doesn't mean he hasn't got the right to be ill!"

Pauline: "Is there a union for people who aren't very bright?"

"Not exactly. But there's a building workers' union. I expect he will become a member in the end."

"You expect, but are you sure?"

"No. Because there are some people who always take a long while to straighten themselves out."

A short, meditative pause.

"It doesn't exactly work like clockwork then?"

"It's no good claiming . . ."

"Well, thank goodness there's heaven," Alberte says firmly. It occurs to me that she is envisaging heaven as a sort of better organized super social security.

"Yes. But you can't simply place all your reliance on heaven and not do anything while you're on earth just because you know everything's going to be made right later on."

"Place all your what on heaven?"

"Reliance. Use the idea of heaven as an excuse for not committing yourself here on earth."

"For not what yourself?"

"Oh . . . Forget it!"

There are times when one has had enough of explaining. Especially when one isn't too sure what the answer should be. How is one to chart a course between the simple faith in progress that they are prepared to swallow like a two-penny ice ("We are better off than in the Middle Ages because in the Middle Ages people were *serfs*," Pauline recites like a model pupil) and the stultifying effect of a promise so precise that it absolves them from thinking? Resignation? Rebellion? And what about joy? And the sense of grace? And action, and commitment, and hope without illusions, and the endless battle, and the little instants of eternity that are scattered throughout all that, inexplicable sparks of proof? How is one to convey that sense of grace to them and yet not encourage them to use it as an excuse?

"So it's not true, then, that everything comes out all right in heaven?" my secretive, sensitive Alberte asks, grief in her eyes.

"Yes, it's true. But we ought to behave as though it weren't true. Or rather . . ."

"I see. You mean you find it a bit complicated too?"

"Sometimes."

Floods

During our years in the Panthéon flat we flooded our down-stairs neighbor, Mme Kesselbach, ten times. Mme Kesselbach was from Alsace, staid, plump, wholesome, an expert hand at pastry, with a scent of apple tart always floating about her. Our floor, to be honest, was defective. In fact, it was more of a colander. And Mme Kesselbach must have thought we were using it as one. One day Pauline tipped over a bowl of water we were using for the washing. The next day Catherine was so busy playing her flute she forgot she'd left the kitchen tap running. Mme Kesselbach came up.

"Madame, I don't wish to be unpleasant about it, but there is water dripping through again. And when I say dripping, what I should say is pouring! I can't live my whole life under an umbrella, you know. You must do something."

She spoke with the accents of the Baron de Nucingen in Balzac's *Splendeurs et misères des courtisanes.* We bowed our heads in shame, and we did something. We subjected Cathie and Pauline to a long and edifying reprimand, during the de-livery of which—as a result of their haste to come enjoy our eloquence—the sink overflowed again.

Once when he was very little, Daniel decided to try out a new submarine in the bath. He turned the hot-water tap full on. His friend, Hot-nose, did the same with the cold-water tap. And then, finding they couldn't turn them off again, they tiptoed out into the street to play marbles. Before long, there was a foot of water in the bathroom.

I walked in. "Oh, my God! Mme Kesselbach!"

She was already ringing the bell. She stood there imper-turbable, both hands in the pockets of her apron, gray plaits neatly in place around her head, resigned, with the suspicion of a tiny, albeit discouraged smile.

"I don't want to persecute you, but there is water dripping through . . ."

She was such a nice woman, Mme Kesselbach. In fact, we had to replace an entire ceiling for her.

One Fourteenth of July, when we had gone out dancing, the bathroom pipes exploded and ten gallons of boiling water went cascading down onto Mme Kesselbach's bed, mercifully unoccupied at that moment. But this time, when we were in no way responsible, she could not forgive us. Hair all askew, eyes full of horror, she stood in her blue satinette dressing gown, and went on and on telling the neighbors in a toneless, sleepwalker's voice: "I came out of the lavatory, madame, and what did I see? My bed *smoking*, madame. A smoking bed!"

Far more than the damage, than the close call she had had, it was that insane vision, that moment of madness, the arbitrary, the illogical, the impossible smashing its way into her pastry-making, Alsatian countrywoman's life that she could not accept. "A smoking bed!" She moved.

In the new flat we occupy two floors, so when the basin in the bathroom does overflow, the water runs straight down into Alberte's piano. There are no repercussions.

Why Dolores is Dishonored

Dolores often says in the most matter-of-fact tone of voice: "The man who dishonored me . . ."

"Now why do you say that, Lo? You're not dishonored at all."

"Yes, I am. I have a child and I'm not married," she replies in a self-satisfied tone that brooks no reply. And at other times, when I suggest that she could perhaps drink a little less, or show a little more patience in certain situations rather than behaving like a crazed tornado, Dolores replies: "Oh, what's the good when you're dishonored!"

"Where do you get these idiotic remarks?"

"We all know that. In the picture romances."

It is very strange, the world of picture romances. There was one rainy summer in Normandy when I really buried myself in them. I read a pile of them as tall as Pauline, and went through them with mounting avidity. Then Jacques started too, and finally Daniel. At the end of a week we stopped, completely sated. Why are picture romances worse than the popular novels that preceded them? What makes Paul Féval more readable than *Aimée on Capri*? Simply because there is more actual reading to be done, perhaps? The extreme formality of the picture romance creates comic effects that the ordinary romance or novelette manages to avoid. "I am a burglar, you are a society girl. We have nothing in common." "Nothing except love," the society girl replies, almost bursting out of her tantalizing low-cut nightdress. The world of the picture romance is a strange one. Fathers still curse their children, girls are dishonored, the rich are very very rich, the poor very very poor, and honest too—unless of course they have been led astray by bad company or some wicked seductress and they steal a piece of jewelry and then have to go into a monastery. That last development, which recurs quite frequently, betrays the origin of the picture romance, which is for the most part either Italian or Spanish.

What the form lacks, and what makes the popular novel or romance far superior, is those fantastic episodes that discard superficial reality to plunge into a deeper reality, that of the dream, of the unconscious, thereby providing a link between the popular novel and the fairy tale. Those children abandoned on church steps who turn out to be "none other than" the heirs to Black Castles; those mysterious bands of robbers with their secret language, their passwords, their dungeons; those bloodied ghosts; those mysterious avengers—all have far greater authenticity than the middle-class love stories of the picture romance.

But what finally turns the stomach about picture romances is the fact that they so rarely express any deep and universal impulses of any kind, the fact that, on the contrary, they offer their readers a hodgepodge of things utterly foreign to them, utterly removed from their daily lives and even their deepest aspirations. In short, they offer a means, if only by increasing one's vocabulary, of rising in the social scale. The popular novel provides dreams. The picture romance offers education, and that is why it is abominable.

The popular novel is rooted in the truest needs of the heart. In that, it is worthy of respect. The worker reading Paul Féval knows perfectly well that it is only in his heart that the Sicilian fisherman is "none other than" the rich Prince Ruspoli, that it is in the world of dreams that the foundling is raised to the highest dignities of the Kingdom (that ideal Kingdom so close to Kafka's world) and that the avenger outwits the villains' machinations. The servant girl reading her picture romance has no awareness of any such duality, of any world other than this one, of any dimension that may lead her back to the true origin of things. It isn't the finding of lost treasure, or a birthmark on the shoulder, that enables the workman to marry the boss's daughter; it isn't in any mythical dimension reflecting the deeper truths of the heart. It's hard work and honesty, thrift and evening classes, it's in a world that is proffered as real, with Ideal Home Furniture and spick-and-span council flats.

That's where the humbug lies.

Dolores knows perfectly well, of course, that workers do not marry cover girls, that these days unmarried mothers are not "dishonored," that children from orphanages, even hardworking ones, very rarely end up on the board of directors. But she thinks one ought to believe in all this. It is the thing to believe in it. To blame herself (because she has a child, because she doesn't attend evening classes—the only thing, as far as one can see, that keeps her from running a fashion house—because she "has a good time," which is of course very wicked indeed when you have no money), to blame herself for all these things is in her eyes a way of finding a place in society instead of criticizing it. So she adopts a "middle-class" vocabulary, "middle-class" standards, and in so doing acquires the right to throw away the little freedom she does possess. Having been "dishonored" once and for all, she is relieved of the burden of safeguarding her "honor." By accepting the vocabulary of a particular society, she is relieved of the duty of examining it and—perhaps—protesting against it.

That is why Dolores, an avid reader of picture romances, says of the popular novel: "It's childish." She is thereby emphasizing its incredible, its fabulous nature. The popular novel is a parable; the picture romance is a conjuring trick. The popular novel transposes; the picture romance travesties. It is a piece of social humbug, whereas the popular novel is an affirmation (a desperate one) of the rights of man.

Dolores says: "Things don't happen like that." And indeed the popular novel, by its use of fantastic paraphernalia, admits openly that things don't happen like that. But it is affirming at the same time that things ought to happen like that, that things do effectively happen like that on another level, or in another world. The picture romance, on the other hand, affirms that things do happen as it shows them, or at least that they would happen in that way if certain conditions were met: piety, virtue, sobriety, and perfect resignation on the part of the disinherited. I would go so far as to say that the popular novel is religious, the picture romance social. And I must stress this: it was in the nineteenth century, at the moment when the moral oppression of the people was at its peak, that the popular novel flowered, because it was a desperate transmutation of that people's aspirations to equality and justice, a picturesque and disguised protest (the popular novel, abounding in codes and secret languages, is itself a secret language) against the triumph of money and hypocrisy. And without going beyond the bounds of reason, one could even interpret the avenging hero who at last makes it possible for the true values of life to surface again—his archetype is Eugène Sue's Prince Rodolphe—as a Messiah figure.

The Dual Personality

One of the themes that recur most often in the popular novel, apart from secret language, is the theme of the dual personality. The orphan girl in her rags is "none other than" the daughter of a duchess. The coarse blaspheming bandit has in reality sworn to avenge his father or succor the poor. The magistrate is a convict, the convict an innocent man, the innocent man a prince. The existence of a hierarchy of values other than that of appearances, different from the "official" hierarchy (the characters of bankers, judges, and priests are treated particularly harshly), is affirmed throughout. It was from the need to express this other set of values that the now hackneyed character of the "whore with the heart of gold" first sprang, though she has since undergone a subtle transformation. A living proof, like the outlaw, of the supremacy of the heart over appearances and over the reputedly vile activity to which she devotes herself, the "whore with the heart of gold" has now become, in an age when eroticism is ever more acclaimed but less and less felt, the champion of the instincts—she is the "real" woman, as opposed to reputedly frigid virtue— against what has become social purity. When the middle-class man demands "a real girl" the way one asks for a vintage wine, scorning the simple and primary need of just drinking or making love, it is in the realm of the instincts, not of the heart, that the prized and differentiating value lies. The character has been simplified, impoverished. It has moved from the sacred sphere (La Louve, in Eugène Sue, reveals a heroic firmness and a saintly devotion beneath her prostitute's appearance) into the realm of psychoanalysis (possessing opulent advantages that a castrating fashion forbids to the "socially acceptable" woman). This is because repression is exerted in different areas and in different ways today.

The nineteenth century treated social ambition almost as a vice—it was culpable not to "know your place"—and this barefaced repression led to rebellion or escapism. The twentieth century makes social ambition a virtue, almost a duty. "Knowing one's place," "having no ambition"—this is deplored. If you remain a maid of all work or an office boy all your life, *you have only yourself to blame.* You are told often enough to join the Club Méditerranée and buy clothes with more *status!* An underhand form of repression that turns your rebellion back against you in the form of self-accusation. "Women no longer have any excuse not to be pretty" runs the heading of an article in a woman's magazine. Why haven't you done your exercises every morning? (After an abortion the evening before, they hurt a bit.) Why haven't you scoured the stores to find this little dress at so many francs that can be had in eight sizes and five colors? (After eight hours in the office and with the children waiting, it's a little difficult, you answer weakly.) Why aren't you reading such and such a newspaper, when it's so cheap and will "keep you informed"? (Because I am utterly exhausted and prefer *Tarzan* is obviously no answer.) Very well, a triumphant Society answers, if you don't become a company director or a top fashion model, don't come complaining to us. We threw all the opportunities in your lap.

The amazing thing is that people believe it. And since driving yourself out of your mind finding the money to meet the payments on your car is more absorbing and more tiring than reading Paul Féval or telling your beads (which are opiates if you like, but opiates do nothing worse than calm you down, whereas amphetamines drive you mad, and installment buying, slavery to fashion, overwritten newspapers, and status-seeking are all amphetamines), you have no energy left, absolutely no energy at all, to demand a little real liberty, real equality, real fraternity. That's progress, as they say.

Guilt has shifted ground. Dolores's social guilt today is no longer guilt at being an unmarried mother; it is guilt at not being elegant, ambitious, self-seeking, at not trying to improve her status. Being an unmarried mother is a convenient curse, because "the harm is done" and therefore dispenses you, once you have been "outlawed from society," from making any effort to fight your way back in.

Dolores, the unmarried mother, is, according to her ancestral Spanish taboos, a condemned outcast. But from the point of view of the modern world's demands and modern morality, she is liberated. Those perpetual tom-toms telling us to be beautiful, to be up-to-date, to keep ourselves "in tune," that anxious race for possessions—all this Dolores can royally ignore. In her old slippers, her face barbarically daubed after some antique fashion (black, red, white) like the statue of Pallas-Athene which the ancient Greeks painted so brightly and which we prefer with its insipid pallor, Dolores, thanks to her "dishonor," possesses the superb indifference of the nomad. She laughs to herself at the advice offered by *Elle*, at the assiduous efforts of a friend to "rehabilitate" her as a nurse or social worker's assistant, and burns with impatience since May for the ideal revolution, the revolution that will shatter all false scales of value, that will pulverize all hypocrisies and turn all silly and guilt-making advertising to derision. Such is Dolores's liberty (Dolores: "If I wear a miniskirt, it's not out of vanity, it's because I'm not afraid to show my legs . . .")

But it is a despairing liberty. For living a wholly gratuitous life—her kindness is brutal, her independence is of no use to her, and if she fritters away her intelligence, her heart, her body, and her health without a moment's respite, it is out of an absurd pride that has nothing to sustain it—Dolores does not recognize herself as having any right to liberty. To recognize that she does in fact have a total right to it would be to recognize that she must also accept the responsibility of it. She prefers simply to enjoy it, making believe that it has been imposed upon her by her own unworthiness, and by her words honors a society that she repudiates with her behavior. And that is why Dolores is dishonored.

Eroticism

It is talked about a great deal, it is said to be all-powerful nowadays. I'm all for that. But when I read the books that come to me for reviewing, some of which do deal with the subject of physical love, I get the impression that sex isn't really going too well for writers today. Unlike the awakening of Victor Hugo's Booz, their awakenings seem to me more sickened than triumphant, and their feats, or what we are permitted to glimpse of them, more deserving than actually heroic—in view of the depression that seems to follow. People are ashamed of making love, just as they are ashamed of writing; though it is also true, of course, that people have never before written so much, and I am perfectly willing to believe that they have also never before made love as much. But there is no doubt that these efforts, accomplished with such lassitude, sad ingenuity, and discouraged self-knowledge, no longer have much connection with eroticism or literature.

A new poster appears, vaunting the merits of a new brand of tights. A gigantic female behind is suddenly blazoned on walls all over the neighborhood. Confronted with this sight,

Pauline laughs, Vincent doesn't notice (he is more interested in Superman), Daniel is disdainful, Alberte says: "It's rude." Confronted with the sight of some nude dummies being painted with bright flowers in a store window, Pauline says: "What fun!" Vincent says: "That's pretty." Alberte says: "It's ridiculous." Why such different reactions? At the sight of television embraces, Pauline shrieks with joy: "There! They love each other!" Vincent shows little interest, unless there is a rival on the way with a gun in his hand. Alberte lowers her eyes. However, they are children of their age. Alberte, at the age of eleven, announces that she is "a little in favor of the pill" in certain very clearly defined cases. Vincent isn't sure about it; he'll have to think. Pauline, meanwhile, has been rummaging through the pile of books that have been sent to me to review and comes up with a sex manual which she is now perusing by the lamp, forming a charming Bergman (Ingmar) picture, diligently following the lines with her fingers: "The sper-ma-to-zo-a come out of the father and . . ." Should I snatch the book away from her? Be outraged? Or start in on all that stuff about the pollen and the bees and the flowers?

"Can you understand that book you're reading, Pauline?"

"Oh, yes!"

"You don't want me to explain it to you?"

"Oh, no! I understand it all."

"Good. How . . ."

"I've seen all the animals on M. Brosse's farm in the country. I saw how the calf was born. I saw how the cats make other cats, and the dogs, and the horses. But you know, chickens do it all quite differently; so do snails. Do you want me to explain it to you?"

"No, thank you."

(Though I must admit that, as far as the chickens are concerned, I don't really know. I just bless the country for having spared me the pollen and etc.)

Alberte is reading an old copy of *Elle* in which the stages of pregnancy and birth are explained with diagrams. I prepare to fill my office as a mother: "Do you understand it? Do you find it interesting?"

"I love it," she replies, hunched over those really most unpoetic diagrams. "It's more beautiful than anything."

True enough. But what exactly is there left for me to do? Or perhaps whatever had to be done has already been done. Or perhaps it was really a question of things not to do, like making a fuss, blushing, getting embarrassed, refusing to answer misplaced but innocent questions? Nevertheless, I am sometimes astonished at the frankness and ease with which they approach these questions.

Alberte: Jean and Jacqueline, they're going to have a baby, aren't they?

Pauline: Anyone can see that!

Alberte: Why don't they get married?

Me: That's their business.

Alberte: But they love each other?

Me: Yes, I think so.

Vincent (hopefully): That's the important thing, isn't it?

Me (cautious): It's very important, certainly.

Alberte: Then why aren't they doing what everyone else does?

Me: It isn't necessarily right to do what everyone else does. It's just more practical.

Pauline (all merriment): Of course! What does it matter, being married or not?

Me: It could be a nuisance where the children are concerned, where money is concerned, if a time comes when you don't get along any more . . .

Vincent (dreamily): Yes, but when you do get along . . .

Me: The sacrament of marriage, in the Church, gives us . . . ought to give us the strength to get along with each other always, to make concessions . . .

Vincent: I see. You mean outside the Church it's not worth the bother?

Me: . . . Well . . . I mean that, er, from the point of view of society . . .

Pauline: You mean, if people aren't married, and if they have a baby and they get along well, then it's wrong to make a great fuss about it, is that right?

Vincent: Sexual relations, they don't necessarily mean people love each other, do they, Mother?

Me: No. It would be more beautiful, but it isn't necessarily that . . .

Vincent: And when it's without loving each other, what's the point of it?

Me: It's fulfilling a natural need.

Vincent: And that's bad?

Me: It's not bad in itself, it's only bad in the sense that it's less beautiful. Because we must always strive toward the greatest beauty, the greatest good. We should be able to wait for the most beautiful.

Vincent: It must take a lot of patience.

[Vincent is preoccupied by this question and returns to it later.]

Vincent: But if people don't wait and have sexual relations *[he has a liking for this abstract expression]* with people they don't love, is it *bad*?

Me: I'd say that it's a sort of sin by omission, because they're acting simply out of instinct, like an animal, whereas they're not in fact animals, because they've been called upon by God to understand more things and to experience a more complete form of love.

Vincent: But there are even animals that love each other. I read about them in *The Animal Kingdom*. And they let themselves just die if they are separated.

Me (rather against my will): That proves that there are some
animals more sensitive and with more feelings than some
men.

Vincent: That's what I've always thought.

[I feel a little cross with myself for having let him come to
that conclusion. But how was I to avoid it?]

Sex and Femmes Fatales

My mind returns to the subject of eroticism as I read the
"human interest" stories in the papers, as I look at the faces
of the women who for a few days achieve the status of
front-page "heroines."

One has a fat, stupid-looking face, cowlike eyes, a permanent. Two men have killed one another over her. A second is
a thin brunette, obviously by no means shy, exhibiting the
most distressing saltcellars and a pair of etiolated calves in a
bathing-beauty pose. Nine lovers, one of whom lost his temper.
The third is very blond, very pale, quite washed-out-looking,
the sort of doll you win at the fair with a bar of nougat thrown
in for good measure: her father-in-law has raped her, her husband has killed the father-in-law. Dark passions. Ghislaine
with her pig's snout "was still attractive to men at the age of
sixty"; Jeannine, who weighed 190 pounds, "said no once too
often"; Josyane, despite that humble, undernourished child's
face, her broken front tooth, her hands stuck in the pocket of
her checked apron, was "a wanton"; and Renée, "the game-
keeper's mistress," got into her Citroen 2CV and tried to run
her rival down.

These are the true seductresses, the real femmes fatales,
the ones in the newspapers, in the magenta-tinted photographs
of *Detective,* those faded, poetic photographs of the women

who stand in state on country sideboards, on folding tables in dreary flats until one day . . .

I read the newspapers. I read *Detective*. And what do I find? That the great tragedies take place in front of cheap reproduction sideboards, the great passions flame into life between Formica-topped tables and stoves, the world's truly passionate hearts don't have running water. It is not lecturers in philosophy who kill fashion models for the sake of their beautiful eyes; it is the postman who loves the baker's wife, the hairdresser who kills herself on the milkman's grave. It is in the suburban dance halls and in co-ops that people still fall in love at first sight and forever, in bungalows that they dream and poison one another, in roadside cafés that they die of love.

I can't help laughing at the people who complain about the wave of eroticism in our advertising, in the novel, in the cinema. The gulf that separates these so-called "femme fatales" from our miniskirted beauties in their wigs and mesh tights is staggering proof of the opposite. This so-called eroticism is a desperate attempt to revive a dying and once sacred fire so that it can be packaged and sold—just as the fake veneration for instinct, for barbarism, for the unmodulated yell is an attempt to conceal the growing impotence of an art that is ashamed of itself. People talk about violence: our age is not violent; it is cruel, as all periods of transition and degeneration are. Violence implies enthusiasm on the other side of the coin; the barbaric implies faith and simplicity. There is no other side to cruelty but mediocrity, gloom, boredom.

What is today called eroticism seems to me regrettable, not because it threatens to awaken or strengthen the sexual instinct but because it falsifies it, turns it from its true goal, and changes it from an instinctual drive into a social value.

After all, is it really to please, in the immediate, sensual sense of the word, that women dress, bleach their hair, slim, expend such anxiety in keeping their figures, being well dressed, staying young, looking gay? One look tells us it is not. The women that arouse great passion, that have many lovers, the women who are looking for a husband, for the love-of-their-lives, or merely for a great many partners in bed, do not necessarily correspond—in fact, rarely correspond—to the stereotype in the women's magazines. No, the woman who wants to look like a film star, who dresses like a model and longs to be slim or have triangular eyes the way the fashion writers tell her she should have, seeks to embody an image rather than attract a man or men. And as a result, for there is some justice in this world, she will succeed in catching only men who love images, not women.

The man who goes out with a model he doesn't even fancy is proving that he is attractive and the possessor of an officially accredited desire-object. To denounce "the eroticism found everywhere today," then, is to walk straight into the trap of a piece of purely social humbug.

This doesn't mean, though, that the social element can be excluded from eroticism. It finds its way into whatever we do, like any other distortion, and eventually succeeds in acquiring reality by becoming a vice. The desire is directed not at the woman but at the prestige she provides. But it is for all that a desire, and eventually expresses itself in the physical mode, lending to an eroticism that has now become real but fetishistic (the desire felt for a woman who has been lent prestige or "value" by fashion is comparable to that felt for a prostitute dressed up in a First Communion dress) a morbid gloom, a specifically modern disenchantment.

What I fear for my children when I see them exposed to posters, magazines, films, is not that this so-called eroticism will awaken precocious sexual desire in them. It is that when the time comes for them to feel desire and, I hope, love, they will not recognize it.

A Modern Prude

"You mean you love him?"

Sylvie, an emancipated twenty-eight-year-old who is working at being a journalist and venerates all the modern taboos, blushes as she answers with Victorian modesty: "Oh, no . . . It's purely sexual . . ."

Sex has become the excuse for sentiment instead of sentiment being the excuse for sex. The prudery is the same, and Sylvie's graceful shrinking movement as she realizes with horror what I have asked—one doesn't talk about such things —is exactly the same reaction her grandmother would have shown had anyone insinuated that she loved anything in her young polytechnic student other than his soul.

The Brassière Party

I am taking Alberte to the Bon Marché to choose her first brassière. Rather tense, but very dignified, Alberte tries on, then chooses. We leave.

Alberte, in a slightly strained voice: "Maman, when you go out and buy your first brassière like that, isn't it usual . . . I mean, doesn't one give a little party?"

A Masseuse

"Oh, the bodies I've seen," sighs Mme Paule, an old, shriveled-up masseuse, covered in wrinkles, an old maid if ever there was one. "And do you know what? There are some women of fifty, with varicose veins and lumps of cellulitis everywhere, and yet they vibrate, they're alive there under your hands. And then there are young kids, models, mannequins, I get the feeling I'm massaging so much cotton wool."

Then, contemplative, distant: "It must be a curious thing, love . . ."

Virtue

Recently I glanced through a report in a women's magazine of a survey in which well-known men had been asked to say exactly what attracted them or repelled them in a woman. On the attraction side, the criteria chosen were fairly diverse: beauty, gentleness, even intelligence were the qualities those seducers were looking for most. But when it came to the things that repelled them, one word recurred time and time again: virtue. Above all, no virtue. Did they want wives or mistresses who would be sharp-tongued, miserly, envious, or even systematically unfaithful to them? I imagine not. I am led to suppose, by pure deduction, that in the mind of the modern man virtue is identified with ill-temper and frigidity. A curious development.

What, when all is said and done, do we have left of a Christian civilization that has lasted so many centuries? All that is worst in it. A cult of sacrifice without joy, of virtue without purpose, a sense of sin without a sense of forgiveness, a cult of pain that seems to be merely the austere antithesis of pleasure, a horror of nature, of vitality, that offends the very dogma of incarnation itself every moment of every day. Jesus tells us to sell all our belongings in order to acquire a pearl of great price. He tells us to amass treasures that thieves cannot steal or rust corrode. He doesn't tell us to sell all our belongings and get nothing for them, or to renounce all treasures of any kind and sink into a joyless poverty of spirit. It's true, of course, that we cannot possess that pearl except in the way that we possess beauty or love: by contemplation alone. But to throw away joys in order to go on to a greater joy, is that a sacrifice?

It is as though no sacrifice can appear meritorious in our eyes unless it includes no compensating advantage, even of a spiritual nature. The widow who has not remarried "because of her children" and now resembles a plant needing water, and the old maid who has always lived "just for her mother" and given up all idea of a career or "a home of her own," are two typical examples constantly cited. Even then, it must be clearly evident that the renunciation has dried up its victim and reduced him to despair, before the spiritual value of the sacrifice can be accepted. Jeanne, who works in a clinic and has in fact never married because she prefers to look after her invalid mother—Jeanne, who is so gay, so gentle, so luminous —is one of these "cases" that people commonly feel sorry for.

Seeing her so gentle and so motherly with her patients, I say to Jean: "What a pity Jeanne has never married! She would have made such a good mother."

"Yes, she sacrificed herself for . . . But you musn't forget that Mme X. . . . is a very charming old lady. A very lively mind still, good-tempered, cultured. And Jeanne has a job she's interested in, too. One needn't feel sorry for Jeanne."

Of course, I agree. Jeanne, who is on her feet eight hours a day at the clinic, running here, running there, from injection to back rub, from bed bath to pulse reading, in order to have some time to do her shopping, a little washing, take care of her mother, chat with her a while—of course Jeanne is not someone we need feel sorry for. If she really wanted to satisfy people's demands, she would also have to have a mother who was cantankerous and sharp-tongued—though Jeanne would probably be able to cope even with that—and she herself would have to be embittered, disappointed, repressed, suffering every moment of the day and night because of a choice she herself made. The Jansenist poison must have infected us deeply indeed if virtue has come to seem compatible solely with gloom and misery.

Jeanne's joy exists, it can be felt, as can the pain that grips her womb when she is confronted with other women's children. Can virtue have a womb, then? We must presume so.

But people's mistrust in the face of joy is such that even suffering cannot redeem it. One day I smiled at an old lady in church. It was Easter: the Alleluia of the Resurrection (that Resurrection too often overshadowed by a cult of pain built up around a Passion that in fact exists only *for* the joy of Easter), which they sing so well in the Orthodox Church, was ringing through me. I smiled at her simply because it was for her too, that Alleluia, wasn't it? She gave a sort of outraged shrug. It's unheard of, smiling in church. But if not in church, then where? Where?

I Want to Speak

I should like to speak of the rare smile that Dolores smiles, a smile that blooms only once every three years, like certain cactus flowers, but then, barbaric and violent though Dolores herself is, so delicate, so subtle, so total in its response to a kind word or a compliment someone makes her, tinged with such an exquisitely girlish confusion that it veils that rough-hewn Norman Christ's or Empire Amazon's face with a dawn, a cloud of impalpable light: there are no words light enough to describe it. It would take colors: the pink of a tea rose, pearl gray, the pale yellow of the sun . . .

I want to talk of a stranger taking his little boy to school, both of them unhappy and awkward.

I want to speak of M. Van Thong the bicycle seller, ex-officer in the Vietnamese army, calm amid his gleaming bikes, his red cycles, his blue racers, marvelous insects buzzing through little boys' dreams, M. Van Thong sighing briefly: "One can't put up with war forever."

He lived a quiet life, and his children, half-French, well-fed, so clean and neat with their cropped hair, used to go to school with Daniel. And M. Van Thong sold his bicycles; a sage, though one day he did let slip an admission: "When I walk around this neighborhood in the evening with my dog, and I see the trash bins . . . the things that people throw away here . . ." His eyes were still seeing famine, war. The weariness in his look, the silence in his look, eyes no longer concerned with dignity. I should like . . . Not to explain, not to show . . . I should like to tell you.

I should like to tell you about my former neighbor M. Massès, eighty-two years old, ex-Garde Républicain, wounded by a saber thrust in Morocco in 1904, always gay, always lively, always in good health, who used to take my children to the Garde Républicain barracks to see the horses parading and being trained. I should like to recount that life full of clinking metal, of tiny glitters of sun on polished harness, of healthy horse smells, of puns and fine uniforms, of admirable, red-white-and-blue, warmhearted stupidity, and how, when M. Massès uttered that banality, that triviality: "Are we downhearted? No! Up and at 'em!" it rang out clear as a clarion call, even echoing that instrument's heart-rending, slightly ridiculous gallantry. I should like to tell how it was not courage, yet it was the childhood of courage.

I should like to tell of the amazement of a vast green-and-orange hat in the middle of a stilted and frigid reception, the unseemly irruption of jollity in the midst of that social ritual, my impulsive movement toward that lady, who said to me: "I am Mme A." What did that matter? For an instant she was dissonance, lack of taste, poetry. I should like to say thank you to her.

I should like to say: I know a man called M. Roanne. He began his career as a tap dancer. He married a bareback rider. He amassed a small fortune and acquired a honey-colored Louis XIII château. There he lives with his wife, who is gentle; his daughter, who is beautiful; his son, who is brave; and lions, tigers, macaws, and beavers. He trains young lions and tigers, and his son also exercises the noble profession of animal tamer. Covered in glorious scars, M. Roanne is a poet. He is a Christian. He writes no verses and practices his religion in his own way: he glorifies the Creation in its most natural and most grotesque forms—the animal kingdom. He is ready to admit, indulgently, that man too sometimes takes strange shapes, and he does not judge him on that account. M. Roanne does not judge himself either: he is everyone's equal.

Let me tell you about Sunday evenings—so many drawings done by the children during the day, now lying crumpled and forgotten on the floor; so many poems lightheartedly composed and never written down, already far away; hours as bright as pictures in a storybook; a casual visitor who dropped in and will never come again. I want to tell all that cannot be told: a line from a song you hear everywhere before you ever hear it in any one particular place; the infinitely gentle gesture of a gray man in the métro turning to protect an old lady when the door starts to slam shut. I want to say the silences of love, the silences of misery, the silences of prayer—all that is transitory, all that is already over, that means nothing, is good for nothing, is already forgotten—unless nothing has any meaning, unless nothing has any use, unless nothing ever dies.

I should like to tell you about everything that is made of paper.

Sylvie, ten years old, was made a present of one of those "children's" books in which everything, story and vocabulary, seems to have been worked out by computer. Her reaction was profounder than it seems at first glance: "I don't like books where there aren't any words you can't understand."

Bibliothèque Nationale

In about A.D. 1300 a host of children decided to take up the cross. The noblest of the Crusades were already over. The knights of the Holy Sepulcher, the kings of Jerusalem, were all lying at rest with their hands flattened on their swords and their dogs at their feet, or trading in historic souvenirs and spices, or were "going native" and busily building up their harems. There was no one left to go, no one left to believe that "delivering the Tomb of Christ" was still a thing worth doing, no one except children . . . It is a sad story, and one about which we know very little. What innocent, what village priest ignorant of all politics, for whom Saladin, the emir with the gorgeous tents and the civilized manners, was quite simply the devil; what fanatic or fool encouraged those shabby little bands? Villages were so closed in on themselves in those days, the shutters all up, the doors all closed, and fear was everywhere. Fear of wolves, of bandits, of the devil. Was it a longing to see beyond the furthest field in the parish? Was it hunger? Was it boredom?

After all, children knew a lot more about life and death in those days. Famine, plague, and war were like relatives, familiar as grandparents poking their livid red or spectral faces, their kindly or terrible faces down into the very cradle— and in the evening, by the fire, the stories were all of the terrible misdeeds of those same forefathers (Old Father Cholera!). Perhaps those children, who all had little brothers, little sisters in the graveyard, were all aware how little a

twelve-year-old, a fifteen-year-old life weighed in those days?
Going on a crusade was an act of defiance, perhaps?

Or was it the call of the sun? Why not? The Christ of the
Monstrance, radiating his warm beams. And life shut up in a
village can be so cold. Or was it the call of the desert, of the
sea, of the boundless? Or even the call of death, though not
the faceless death, not the death they were used to seeing, its
horrible wrinkled face (another mouth less to feed) lolling
above the soiled bedclothes or sitting waiting in the old quiet
garden, already surrounded by a little family. Even the dead
were prisoners in that enclosed life! And perhaps there was
one school boy or peasant lad who said to himself: "I'll be all
right," and another who was looking for the Angels, and a
third, just like the song, who took his whistle, his knife, his
bread and butter, without a thought for anything, neither
forward nor behind, and whose only regret was that he had
no shoes?

It is a sad song, with many verses. Most of it I have forgotten now, but a little remains, a few words . . . The first
boy, the one who sang, was eaten by the wolves. The second,
the one who prayed, was sold as a slave. And the third, the
one that followed with his knife, with his whistle . . .

And the third . . . I can't remember. It's a lost song that I
found once in the Bibliothèque nationale, under the dust, one
day of deep depression. It is sad, that graveyard of stories and
songs. I visit it often, telling myself that perhaps that old
gentleman with the scurffy shoulders, and that imposing cler-
gyman, and that fidgety, ample-bosomed lady have all heard
a song like that, as they sat with their bundles of paper,
once . . . We all have a day, an hour of sensitivity, of grace,
when an image comes through to us, when a note, a word
rings out inside us . . . For me it was those children who
decided to leave home one day, who left, and then, around a
bend in the road, just disappeared.

There is a beautiful Breughel depicting the Massacre of the

Innocents. The snow is painted with a velvet brush. And the blood. And the clothes and cuirasses of the peasants and soldiers all churning together in that confused brawl. But the causes of the struggle, those pitiful and naked bodies, those little blind faces, you hardly see at all. They are interchangeable. They have no names, like the children in my song, like those in the lament, the three little children who went wandering in the fields. And they have no thoughts, those innocents whose massacre is an inauguration in blood of the birth of Jesus Christ. They too are Lambs of God, blind lambs, newborn lambs: theirs is the innocence; sainthood is for those that bore them. If they knew. Did they know, those mothers, that their children were dying for someone else? Did they, in the inspiration of thought or in the obscurity of instinct, accept it?

I know, it is only a song, only a legend, only a picture. Like the story of the first-born of Egypt, who died so that Israel, under their leader Moses, could set out, freed from bondage, toward Canaan. The first-born of men, all innocent, and the first-born of the animals, more innocent still. And it is not for nothing that the legend includes the animals; it is as though it wants to do everything it can to make us see the animal innocence, blindness, incomprehension of the sacrificed victims. And sacrificed for whom, for what? So that some Jews, a band of slaves, could go off into the desert to worship bronze serpents or golden calves, could journey to Canaan to cultivate a narrow nationalism and make intricate and hair-splitting laws to dull the brains of a race that was to engender and then deny its own saviour? To die so that salvation may be given us is also to die that sin may be given us. That is the mystery of the innocence that with us, or in us, *must* die. "It's convenient, having a religion," one is always being told.

In the Café

In the café there is a fifteen-year-old apprentice, looking eternally bewildered, voice not yet broken, always being told off by everyone for everything.

"No, no! Why are you taking those sunshades out onto the terrace? Can't you see it's going to pour in an hour's time, eh, dimwit?"

"No, no! Don't open up the snack bar before eleven. We need the room for the coffee customers!"

"What? Haven't you set up the snack bar yet? Can't you see there are people who need the hint to get moving?" A glance toward me. "We shall be losing lunch customers soon."

Then, turning toward me, to soften the allusion: "He has no sense of responsibility, you see. But what can you expect! He's young, innocent . . ." Then to the boy, who is standing there looking dazed: "Enjoy it while you can! You get all the fun . . ."

At the Seaside

A woman having lunch, to the café owner: "I was down on the beach, I swam a few strokes out to sea, I turned around, and what do I see? A young woman—well-dressed, though, you understand; you wouldn't think, to look at her . . ."

"Think what?" the café owner interrupts.

"Why, I'm telling you! A young woman rummaging in my bag! As calm as you please, like someone just going through her own things. And then out comes her hand with my wallet! I swam, I ran, I can't tell you how. When she saw I wasn't going to let her go, at the edge of the beach, she threw the wallet down on the ground, on the sand. Oh, it gave me such a shock! Such a shock! I was trembling all over. To see someone with one's own eyes, actually *see* someone rummaging through your own things! What do you say to that?"

The café owner, sympathetically: "I'd say that life being what it is, you're lucky you've never seen anything worse!"

Yes, innocence is robbed, jeered at, persecuted. That is what it's for. And when the day comes that it realizes as much, though its merit may be increased by consenting to that truth, its efficacy will be no greater.

Serge, eight years old, a friend of Vincent, the son of one of my friends, and brought up in total ignorance of any religion, sees a big modern silver cross around my neck on which the figure of Christ is depicted by a very flat, stylized cutout.

"What's that squashed man?"

"That's Jesus Christ."

"Oh, yes . . . What happened to him, exactly?"

"He was hung on a cross."

"And run over by a car?"

"No, just put on a cross."

"Poor man! It's much the same; with all the accidents these days, I wonder why everyone still talks about him."

Then later: "Are all the children who go to First Communion hung up on crosses one day?"

I answer: "No, Serge, of course not."

But in my mind's eye I see those Spanish babies: Juan, who even at the earliest age must have been able to sense that inextricable knot of fury and love twisted in Dolores's heart; Manolo, who from being with one woman first, then with another, then left alone for hours on end, eventually got into the habit of calling all women "mama"; Sara, who had scarcely been placed in her mother's arms when she was being sent off like a parcel as far away as possible . . . Not the massacre but the crippling of the Innocents; perhaps the most mysterious feast on the calendar.

We refer to those Innocents as "saints." Saints? Those blind and mewling newborn babes that we see in the Breughel painting, snatched up by the sneering soldier they might perhaps have become? Saints? Those tender and unaware little bodies that had yet to smile or speak? How are they saints, any more than the wretched fowls I have seen being carried to market in the country, head down, feet broken, wings folded with unconscious sadism by a farmer's wife who sees her absence of pity as a just source of pride? In what way more saintly than those aborted fetuses that are swilled down in the hundreds into the sewers of our cities, torn from betrayed bellies, from frightened, revolted bodies? (Conchita informs Lo and me, after one more of the "miscarriages" she takes such pride in: "It was a boy." "Oh, Concha, be quiet!" "Why?" she says. "One unhappy creature less!") Saints? Are they any more so than the children in underdeveloped countries, born to die of famine, with emaciated faces and ballooning bellies? It is the mothers who are saints, bringing their sons into the world simply to be crucified.

I once read an attack on the use of the pill and sterilization in underdeveloped countries. It was written by a monk and seemed to me the cruelest thing I had ever read. "It is no doubt true," this Father wrote in so many words, "that many of these children are doomed to a premature death by disease, by famine, by the lack of hygiene and work. But have we the right, on the basis of purely material statistics, to deprive all these mothers of the act of hope their continuing to give birth constitutes?"

Nothing harsher, more shocking, more contrary even to the pragmatic morality of our world could be uttered. When I read those words, I felt the blow in the entrails that any mother, even a Christian mother, above all a Christian mother, is bound to feel when she is reminded that in giving life she is also giving death. The Virgin Mary's *Fiat* to the birth of Christ is a *Fiat* to his Passion, to his death. To his resurrection. But in order for that finality to justify the birth, it is necessary for it to be viewed outside the realm of earthly life. It is the mothers who are the saints, if they are not blind—or despairing.

I remembered that Father, whom I have such difficulty calling that, when recently I lost a child toward the fourth month.

Vincent was grief-stricken. "Why?" he kept saying.

My daughters, already wise, already women, had rejoiced more in prospect but were less cast down at the loss.

"You mustn't be sad for him, he didn't know anything about it," Alberte said, melancholy and tender.

And Pauline, in the words of Jarry: "You're still young, goodness, you'll have lots more."

But Vincent goes on saying "why?" to suffering and evil.

"Why did the little baby die?"

"He didn't die; he just wasn't born, that's all. It's like a lot of things in this world, you know. Nature wastes a lot of seeds before she succeeds in producing a plant, an animal, a human being that will achieve its full development."

"If I died now, would I have achieved my full development?"

"I don't think so. Although there are some human beings that reach a sort of perfection very young, I think."

"And then they die?"

"Not necessarily."

"If I died now, you'd be sad, because I wouldn't have ach . . ."

"Yes."

"And if I had achieved it, you wouldn't be quite so sad?"

"In a way, yes."

"And if I died without having achieved my full development, would you rather I hadn't ever existed?"

The trouble with Vincent is that he understands too quickly. Straight to the bull's-eye, straight to the heart. I have to answer him, but not as we answer, too lightly, at baptisms: "I renounce, I believe . . ." I have to answer him with all my summoned strength and all my faith: "No."

"And you wouldn't rather not have been expecting the poor baby . . .?"

"No."

"Maman . . ." he sighs, his head on my breast as though I had just given birth to him a second time. My thoughts go back to Father X. and to his acts of hope.

I should like to be certain that before writing those words, before letting fall those savage and saintly blows, he had devoted his whole life to struggling against those "purely material statistics," that he had paused only for an instant to write those lines, an instant taken from an incessant fight against famine and epidemics and unemployment. Then, perhaps, that instant would be acceptable, those words would be acceptable. Perhaps.

Suffering

I was expecting a fifth child. I lost it before it was born. I had an operation: I shall never have any more children. A hard moment in my life. I had prayed a great deal that the child might live. I had prayed with great faith, with a profound intensity. God *could* make my child live. I was sure of that.

And when I knew that it hadn't, that it was finished, for several days, perhaps weeks, my heart was hard, closed, uncomprehending. I had been so sure. Not because I felt I had merited a grace, a miracle. *On the contrary.* Precisely because my prayer was a request without any offer made in return; I had held up no merits in exchange, made no promises, no superhuman vows. In short, I was giving God the opportunity to manifest the absolute gratuity of his gifts, which no man could ever earn.

I laughed at all pessimistic predictions.

I knew.

Afterwards several days, several weeks passed in that state of stupid incomprehension. Stupid in its primary sense: smitten with stupor. Then, slowly, as a plant unfolds, this thought: if God *could*, if I had had that trust in him, perhaps he was putting trust in me too, perhaps "it was written" that I *could*, in the same way, bear this suffering, offer up this suffering that was as unearned as the joy would have been. Everything was falling into place again in the mysterious universe of grace.

Without that mystery, everything is absurd.

The worst came later. "It's so much better for you! You already have four!" "How wise of you!" (I have never been able to bring myself, not to forgive, but to face, the woman who said that to me.) "You'll have so much more time now." "It wasn't a very practical idea anyway."

How can they know what is "better for me"? Or decide what is "practical"? And what about all the practical considerations that spring into my mind? Just when we had a suitable flat! Just when our affairs were beginning to work out! Just when I was about to get my American royalties!

But everything has returned to normal. What I feel now is *only* grief.

Innocence Again

Carol singing, "poetry evenings," plays written for Christmas: they're all what we call innocent pleasures. Accordion, braised beef, plants and pets; and the children, one thinks, the labors of learning, homework, the "evenings by lamplight" so tellingly evoked by prize books, red tomes, Jules Verne or the Comtesse de Ségur, and sung with such nostalgia by tormented souls, Baudelaire or Verlaine ("Ah, how big the world is by the light of lamps")—we have all that. "There's no harm in it," as good honest people say. But that's just it. Are we sure there's no harm? The family circle, the circle of friends, is so quick to snap shut. "Wherever two or three are gathered together in my name . . ." There must always be room for a third. Let us keep ourselves warm, keep ourselves snug in our joy, but with the door open. Keep the poor man's place always laid at our table, in other words. It doesn't matter who comes to sit at that place, or doesn't come. The place is there; the wound is there.

Innocent pleasures are only half innocent. One would have to have very tightly shut eyes, very tightly stopped ears, not to be aware that they last only an instant. That they are hemmed round not only by the suffering, the evil, the chaos out in the street, in the world, but also by the same things in us. The harmony, the friendship, the grace of that luminous instant will pass; we shall have to wait for them to come back, and we can never be sure that they will; the poor man's place will remain empty; perhaps so long that we may forget that a presence did once, long ago, make itself felt there. The center of the heart will remain empty, poor, barren, until that grace comes again, that grace without reason, without justification, for which our expectation, and not our merits, will have made room. Joy knows all that. Innocence doesn't know it. Innocence is unscarred, a shut door, a pure but armored heart. Joy bears a wound.

"There's a girl at my school," Pauline announces with delight at the superiority it gives her, "who says that God doesn't exist!"

"There are a lot of people who think that, you know."

"Oh, yes, I know." Still radiant: "They're *pagans!*"

"But you'd better not call her that. It's not polite."

234 / Françoise Mallet-Joris

"But it's true."

"Yes, if you're going to insist on everything being called by its right name. But that isn't always enough. Perhaps in her heart of hearts that little girl loves God without calling him by that name. Perhaps there are even 'pagans' that love God—without calling him that—more than a lot of the believers that go to Mass."

"I see. Then why are they called 'pagans'?"

"So that we know where we are."

"But all the same, it's better if you do go to Mass, isn't it?"

I knew she'd say that. Our whole educational system is based on merit, on the best and the less good; the fact that Pauline's school (to her great disgust) recently changed from marks (numbers) to evaluations such as *Good* or *Excellent* has done nothing to modify this. (Excellent, that means 9, she explains.) Who will rescue us from this accountancy of merit?

"It's not better. It's simpler. It's truer."

And after all that, when she's fifteen, will she refuse to go to Mass because it is too simple, and take to reading the Bodhisattva or some other hermetic and obscure work instead? Well, I prefer that to the spiritual ghetto. The idea of a spiritual elite is even more repugnant to me than any other social group claiming to be in some way chosen. The elite of the Perfect, who wonder whether it is permissible to accept divorced people, Jews, foreigners . . . The elite of the *Pure* (and the vocabulary of the Cathari comes naturally to the pen here), who fear unhealthy company, unhealthy books, the bacteria of the world and the impurities of the creation. They are so fragile and so hard, those innocents! The best are like porcelain eggs, ornaments, beautiful pebbles. One loves them, one contemplates them, and then, in the end, seeing them so untouched, one feels pity.

Mme Guyon, the seventeenth-century mystic, lived her whole life in innocence. She was what her biographer, Father Cognet, so aptly called "a rich nature." She loved children, animals, the poor. She despised money, ambition, prudence. She was slandered, imprisoned, and freed, all without flinching. She became fashionable and rejoiced at the fact because she longed ardently, passionately, to make converts. She was silenced and heard her sentence without bitterness, for if God wished her to be useless, then she accepted that uselessness. She gave her life, her work, even her reputation, as one throws away a worthless trifle. It is impossible to read her seriously without loving her; at times her work brings her close to the spiritual writings of India, at others to St. Thérèse of Lisieux, so profound and so painful is the theology beneath the paper roses that people try to smother her in.

Yet Mme Guyon was a saintly woman, not a saint. Everything is in those words: she lived her whole life in innocence. Everything, and a formidable mystery.

When her stepmother, a harsh-tongued virago, asked her to pray for the success of a financial venture she was involved in, Mme Guyon replied *in all innocence*: "I don't know how to pray for things like that." Innocently, she was insulting sin. When her husband—a gouty old man who had married her when she was a child of sixteen, beautiful, witty, and noble— prevented her from praying because she was using her prayers as a way of evading him, she wept, she didn't understand; *in all innocence* she had insulted that corrupt, warped, distorted emotion men call love. And right up until the death of that crotchety, miserly, jealous old husband who nonetheless loved her, she continued to express amazement at the torments he inflicted on her, for, she wrote innocently, "I believe he loved me passionately."

When she found she was read and had a following, it was with pure joy, without pride and without modesty, modesty being too "private" an emotion for her to be much interested in it. She affected neither the language nor the dress of conventional piety: she was all impulse, all spontaneity. Unpleasant rumors began to circulate about her morals, about

her relationship with Fénelon, and most of all about her in-
timacy with a Barnabite, Père La Combe, whose spirit was as
much given to rapture as hers but was also, unfortunately, less
strong. After eleven years in prison, under pressure from those
who wished to use him to compromise Fénelon, this Barnabite
confessed everything that was asked of him: that he had been
Mme Guyon's lover "fifteen nights in succession," that he was
a heretic, and I don't know what else. No one dared to bring
them face to face; perhaps he would have been filled with
remorse in the presence of the woman he had so admired. But
they did triumphantly present Mme Guyon with the confession the unfortunate fellow had signed. "Oh, poor wretch!" she
said, not in the slightest put out. "It must be a forgery, or else
he has gone mad." Perhaps this was proof that she possessed
the gift of prophecy, for the ecstatic Père La Combe did in
fact go mad, and ended his days in Charenton. But this in-
vulnerability of innocence, this utterly unscathed self-assurance—Michelet affirms that she laughed, and though that is
not a historical fact, it does nevertheless correspond to the
psychological truth, to that monstrous ingenuousness that
makes Jeanne Guyon a heroine rather than a saint—is almost
frightening.

Even though she could answer for herself, could she answer
for him? Even if she could answer for all their actions and all
their words, could she answer for their thoughts, for his as
well as hers? And even supposing that through one of her
"inner communications" she was assured of the complete, im-
maculate purity of that poor priest's soul, could she have been
ignorant of the fact that fear and despair must have ravaged
that pure soul to reduce it to this denial of itself? No, a saint
would have wept, I think.

But she was innocent, which is to say blind to evil. There
is no other explanation for her imprudent folly, for her bold-
ness in the face of slander; there is an element of defiance, of
deliberate provocation in her behavior. She is determined to

ignore evil, to behave as though it did not exist. But evil is also man . . .

Though Fénelon was dear to her, and though he would have understood it, it was not to him that she confided her autobiography. No, it was to Bossuet, who had neither the wish nor the power to understand her, that she handed over that manuscript so full of generous impulses, dreams, premonitions, imprudences, in which her soul displayed itself naked, with all her wildest fantasies and phantasms, her most crazed visions and her most accurate intuitions. Sublime folly. She knew she would be scorned and jeered at. Perhaps she was seeking that supreme sacrifice. And at Bossuet's expense. He who accepts inevitable martyrdom is a saint; he who seeks martyrdom at the expense of an executioner who will be damned by it may be a hero, but nothing more. Hearing Bossuet's coarse raillery at her expense, a saint would have wept for him.

Innocence must weep, must be wounded before it can become purity. Yet we are inconsolable at losing it, and we never tire of admiring it.

I wrote two contradictory texts. One was called: *You can't sleep here*. The other: *We were made just to sing*.

You Can't Sleep Here (extract from my diary)

This morning I feel I'm going to work. Really work. I have managed to leave home with my brain more or less fresh, my nerves more or less intact. No one has clutched at me demanding five francs for a subscription or twenty francs' lunch money. Vincent hasn't lost his pen, Pauline hasn't mislaid her gym

shorts, and I have had less difficulty than usual keeping un-
wanted thoughts at bay: bills overdue, letters unanswered,
the dentist, having to take Alberte to the Conservatory, re-
questing a copy of Vincent's birth certificate, and am I eating
at home, and what had I better get for dinner, and above all,
mustn't forget to remember that magazine to which, in a
moment of aberration, of migraine, I promised an article on
Chopin, or was it Mount Everest . . .

For once, I have escaped. The octopus huddled in one
corner of the apartment with its innumerable tentacles, those
thousand little blood-sucking guilts that paralyze me with
angst, has slept on, and here I am outside, in the dark and
invigorating cold, and I bless seven o'clock in the morning,
my favorite time, my own time. Now I am stocking up with
cigarettes, I exchange a few words (with the furtive light-
heartedness of an escaped convict) with the newspaper seller,
and I am the first customer in the café; it is still being swept.
Sawdust hitting the floor, divine odor of eau de Javel. Morning.

Sometimes the sweeper is an old Arab in a beret, sometimes
a ruddy young lad from Normandy, but more often than not
it's an old, colorless woman, one of those old women who come
in with a basket piled up with bizarre packages wrapped in
newspaper, who wear grayish or brownish shawls and shapeless overcoats. They are shapeless too, always bent over, surrounded by buckets of dirty water, and doughy cleaning rags,
by the sickly scent of some detergent . . . A whole shapeless
and colorless mass of humanity rising like a mist from the
earth; and oughtn't we to think before all else of restoring
such people their dignity, their true forms, blurred as they
have become by a wan, dejected misery?

I muse. Some of those old women work only intermittently,
wear breastplates of paper under their cablestitch woollens,
sometimes sleep out of doors and drink iced beer in the morning. And then there are the others, the ones who maintain a
touching concern for respectability, sometimes even a tiny

remnant of girlish vanity: that old hat they are given, to which they add a satin bow that has lurked for years in the bottom of some cardboard box. I imagine the scene: the woman for whom they do a little housework after their cafés or their offices offers the hat, and they say to themselves "why not?" laughing inwardly, a little embarrassed at the sudden memory of the girl they once were, almost pretty, who sewed for herself on Sundays . . . And they "take a needle to it" (the act of hope, for women, represented by that little gesture: to take a needle to something, to take up a hem, sew on a bow, an absurd little panel somewhere) and they add the satin bow, relic of a dress long ago worn out, an old coat. But at the moment of seeing themselves in the mirror . . . they quickly push the hat on their heads, over last year's grown-out permanent, pick up their baskets, their maroon scarves, and they are on their way. In any case, who will see that bow? They leave their hat in the cloakroom. And besides, one never sees anything of them but their backs.

And their grandmotherly smile, when they do at last straighten up, when they push back that lock of hair and give a great sigh before packing up to go. It is still dark. But I have already lost a lot of time with my old woman. A great sigh, the hand rubbing automatically at the pain in the back, and she is off. An obscure feeling that we could have said something to one another, that there was perhaps something to be said, to be done, other than that impotent smile: a first breach in my morning gladness. But at last I begin. The bitter coffee, the persistent smell of the bleach . . . I work.

Yes, seven o'clock, eight o'clock, and all's well. A kindhearted waiter has put an out-of-order notice on the jukebox; he won't take it off until half past ten. After that, I just have to take my chances: perhaps a crowd will come in, perhaps no one— young people who will keep the machine on the verge of sonic disintegration, or a solitary tramp dropping off to sleep.

There are a great many sleepers among café customers. The

waiter comes and stands in front of them, hesitant. It's hard to disturb someone who's asleep, someone who has nowhere to go. When it's a young man dressed in a ragbag assortment of garments, then one tells oneself that he'll go and find friends, he'll be all right. But when it's an older man, dressed with that threadbare correctness that means the edge of the abyss, and he's sitting resting for a moment, his nose in the *Figaro* ad pages, it's more difficult. While the waiter hesitates, my pen hangs over the page. Then, with a gentleness that hurts: "Come on, you can't sleep here!" The eyes open with difficulty, a painful effort to fight back to consciousness, the gaze lowered toward the glass of coffee that will not be refilled, that cannot be refilled . . .

I want to say: "May I buy you a coffee?" I hesitate and then don't dare. Dolores wouldn't hesitate; and she'd know how to belabor him too, poor fellow, lash him with the metal of that beautiful voice if he ventured to speak out of turn. I don't dare, but my work suffers, loses its beautiful integrity, its fine porcelain finish, becomes painful, uncertain, like that out-of-work man's fitful sleep. "I told you you can't sleep here!" A little less gentle. The waiter wants you to see his position. "If I let you sit sleeping there, I'm the one who'll get it in the neck. It lowers the tone of the establishment, don't you see?" No, the sleeper with the veiled eyes doesn't see. Sometimes he finds shelter behind an abandoned newspaper, safe for a quarter of an hour, for half an hour. I breathe again. "I told you you can't sleep here!" He leaves, that brother I do not know, lurching as he goes, and it takes me a long time to get back to work, back to the old anguish of the words that may be meaningless, bring nothing, change nothing . . .

Even in the churches, there is usually an old, mistrustful, crabby sacristan sweeping the floor so he can bang his broom against the slouching tramp's legs and say: "You can't sleep here."

The anguish follows me even into my prayers, and the

prayer falters, loses its triumphant heavenward swing, becomes hesitant, painful. Even in joy, that wound, that open door, that voice: "You can't sleep here . . ."

We Were Made Just to Sing

Some years ago, as a way of celebrating Christmas at home with my parents, my parents-in-law, and my children, I had the idea of writing a little play, just the simplest little play that we could all be in together. It was to be, in a way, our present to each other.

I'm not sure that I like presents all that much any more. I used to be fond, very fond, of the traditional, mundane Christmas, those orgies of tinsel and neon, the shop windows, the color catalogues, the great conglomerations of food and bright packages, the bad taste of streets decorated with plastic Christmas trees and flashing stars. But it begins to wear off, the glamour of packing and ribbon. No matter what trouble you go to in choosing them, or making them really Christmassy, as we say, once those parcels have been given . . . "How sweet of you! Just what I wanted . . ." It has become rare for anything to happen at these moments that is really Christmas, the free gift of Christmas.

There are no feast days any more, just as there are no seasons. Advertising has now completely taken the place of that subtle chemistry of dreams that ought to surround the feast of Christmas, the Christmas gift. This new Father Christmas for Adults showers us with such a vast array of gifts all through our lives, from the illusion of becoming a femme fatale (with the aid of a tanning cream or a deodorant) to that of being whisked away to Florida or the Himalayas simply by buying a bath cap or a raincoat; this maelstrom of images and promises—as well as the "free gifts" that now accompany our packets of toast or washing powder—so successfully creates the illusion that life is one perpetual feast day, so cleverly dresses up daily life, "with its undemanding, tedious occupations," as a glittering masquerade, that the true meaning of a feast day has imperceptibly been buried under. There are too many feast days; and there aren't any feast days left. When a simple box of washing powder splashes a blinding carnival in Rio all over its posters and its packaging, with the White Power Knight and Fairy Enzyme dancing attendance, how can you expect a mere record or a pair of gloves for Christmas to mean anything today?

So I tried to think of something. It made me so sad, seeing the desire and then the letdown expressions of all who had neither a need nor an imperious desire for anything but who still hoped for . . . what? And when the parcel had been opened, there they stood, a little disappointed, a little deprived of who knows quite what . . .

Our little play was a deliberately simple attempt to give something that could not disappoint anyone, for the very reason that it would vanish as soon as it had been presented. It would naturally be a short play on a religious theme. At first we hoped to have Pauline, who had just been born, playing the part of the Christ child, but she proved so recalcitrant and screamed so much that we were reduced in the end to wrapping a log in felt. On the whole, however, it was a success: the children showed much more interest in this modest creation of ours than in complicated toys, which they generally destroy within a few weeks or use for quite different purposes that those they were pedagogically designed for. The first "mystery," as we rather grandly called it, was acted before the children's grandparents and godparents. I had written myself a small part in it as an ass.

The following year it seemed quite natural for everyone to wonder what we would do for Christmas this time. I was very glad that the idea of doing had taken over so naturally in my children's minds from the idea of giving and taking.

The subject we picked that year, St. Benedict and St. Scholastica, was a difficult one from my point of view because of the rhymes; but again it was a success. Then our "mystery" grew longer, to provide roles for my four little nieces, who gave us Hebrews (in our "Moses"), sailors (for our "Jonah"), harlequins, crocodiles, Pharaoh's fat cows . . . We became more and more ambitious; there was nothing we would not tackle: the crossing of the Red Sea, Jonah's whale, Solomon's harem . . . Friends began to join in. We felt it was essential that there be a musical contribution. The children wanted to sing. I learned the guitar sufficiently to accompany them. Vincent, who had been given a conjuror's outfit, wanted to do a few tricks. Each of the participants began to let me know what his or her preferences were in the way of parts—comic, dramatic, costume, etc. Our "mystery" became a hybrid, baroque, monstrous thing in which I had written every role specifically to fit its interpreter, using that person's particular aptitudes, dreams, tics. It was no longer just a game for the children; it was a return to childhood, that world of untrammeled choice, for all who took part in it.

It was—and it is. We still have our "mystery." We take great trouble over it. We make scenery and costumes, we hunt for and rehearse the music, we work on the text . . . And we know that it will all disappear after just an hour—on the afternoon of December 24—forever. I have deliberately avoided saying: Jacques paints the scenery, Alberte looks for songs, I write . . . That Christmas Eve afternoon it is truly "we" who do it all.

Last year an old friend was visiting us, and although she was unwell and preoccupied with a problem of quite a different nature, she agreed to don a paper miter, which did not detract one iota from her dignity, and play Pharaoh. In her "lotus" position, a fan in her hand, she sat in state on a little table. I looked at her lovingly: her gravity, her efforts of memory. Despite my simple and clumsy verses, I felt that her Pharaoh, the role she was playing, was indeed a present we were making to one another. Those friends suddenly chattering away about rehearsals and costumes with the seriousness of ten-year-olds, that hectic flush on our cheeks, the excitement that we ourselves laugh at, but without conviction —it's a game, just a game, isn't it? And yet there was something there all the same, passing between us, a simplicity, a giving . . . And the fact that not all our friends share our faith seemed at that moment, quite suddenly, not at all important. Overconfidence?

This year we have decided to enrich our "mystery" with a little choral singing. We are very seriously rehearsing the various parts of some Bach motets under Jacques's exacting supervision. On holidays and Sundays we remind one another: "Singing rehearsal at five!" We cluster around the piano, we argue. Who's flat? "I'm perfectly prepared to sing the alto parts to help out," Alberte says, "but it's not really my register." Pauline is acting the temperamental star, storming off into a corner because she's been told her A is not a true A. Then suddenly it all blows over. And really, every now and then, the effect is very good. It almost sounds like a real choir.

And someone suddenly bursts out: "Really, we were made just to sing!"

Pauline?

No. Me.

A Conversation about Happiness

Me: I can't finish my book because of the two pieces I've put at the end. They seem to contradict each other.

Vincent: I don't think so. It's not really a contradiction. People

are made to sing, to be happy, but because of the others
who aren't happy they can't be happy either. It's simple.

Alberte: People can't be happy and yet they're made for it?
It doesn't seem right.

Me: Maybe it's the word "happiness" that isn't right. Maybe
we should say joy instead, or . . .

Pauline: Gaiety! That's it! Gaiety!

Me: It isn't the same thing.

Alberte: Why not? The other day I saw the program about
Rubinstein, the pianist, and he said he was happy, but gay
too, he made funny faces all the time.

Me: I was thinking of that program too. Though I didn't see
it, I read a long article criticizing it, saying that the happiness he said he felt was a little affected, rather limited . . .
Did that strike you, when you were watching?

Alberte: I was glad for him. And, after all, music is meant to
console people . . .

Me: If you like. But even so, the fact remains that those people
are sad; otherwise there'd be no need to console them. And
there's always the chance that you'll fail.

Vincent: What does it matter if you do? It's still music.

Me: That's true in a sense. It's the same as with faith, or
beauty, or love. They exist anyway; but if you have a great
faith, a great love, if you see something very beautiful and
you think other people can't understand, can't share it, then
underneath your joy you do feel a sadness.

Alberte: You could have faith or play music on a desert
island . . .

Pauline (a little out of her depth till now): Yes, and then there'd
be a Negro or an Indian who'd come along, and you'd call
him Friday and you'd teach him do, re, mi, just like that!
Even I know enough music to teach a little Negro boy to
sing, and then we could play . . .

Me: I think what Alberte means is a deserted island. It's a
supposition, you see.

Pauline: I don't like suppositions.

Vincent (superior but kindly): That's because you're not big enough. She means, suppose you're on a desert island and you play some very beautiful music that no one can hear . . .

Pauline: If I were really on a desert island I wouldn't play music, I'd cry and cry until someone came to get me.

Alberte (irritated): Crying wouldn't do you any good. If there wasn't anyone to listen, you'd soon get tired of play-acting!

Pauline (bursting into tears): No, I wouldn't get tired! No, I wouldn't!

Alberte: Yes, you would . . .

Vincent: How stupid they are! Every time we start talking about something interesting . . .

Me: Now, Pauline, be sensible. It's just Alberte and Vincent who are making a supposition. It's an idea, but you're making it into a very nice story . . .

Pauline (unwilling to relinquish her dramatic despair, wailing): I don't want to go to a desert island without my mother!

Fortunately, this is all taking place during one of our "poetry evenings," so I am able to calm everyone down by distributing chocolate biscuits.

Me: Now, if I've understood what you are trying to say, it's that the beautiful is beautiful and the true true even if one's absolutely alone in recognizing the fact. One could be quite happy just knowing it. But isn't that very like a contemplative life, the life they live in monasteries and convents, just adoring God without telling other people about him the way missionaries do, and without doing good actively in the world, the way the Little Sisters of the Poor do, and couldn't one say . . .

Pauline: Do they want to keep God all for themselves in the convents, then?

Me: That expresses the problem very well. What I mean . . .

Pauline: I can express problems very well, can't I?

Me: Very well, yes. What I mean . . .

Pauline: I'm big enough for that, aren't I?

Me: Of course. What . . .

Pauline: It was a supposition too, wasn't it?

Me: Perhaps not quite, but . . .

Pauline (preparing to howl again): It wasn't a supposition?

Me (hurriedly): Yes, yes, it was a supposition.

Pauline (in triumph): Ha! Ha! Ha! Ha!

Me: We might *suppose* in fact that they want to keep God all to themselves, but we could also say that they want to demonstrate that they are so sure that God, or music, or anything you like, exists, that that alone is enough to fill a whole life, to justify a life. It's a little like what Alberte was trying to say with her desert island.

Pauline (chanting, not too soft, not too loud): I can make suppositions too, ah ah ah . . .

Vincent: You could say that it's rather selfish, though.

Me: Not insofar as other people can see you living like that, so that your life constitutes a sort of demonstration . . .

Pauline: A supposition.

Vincent (ignoring the interruption): Yes, but the others could say: they're all right in their convent, snug and happy, and if I'm unhappy they don't give a damn.

Me: Yes, exactly. The same as with Rubinstein. Is he right to be happy and gay and tell us all so, or is that selfish? Is it possible to have any happiness or joy that isn't selfish?

Alberte (without warning):

> *Life is a strange and agonized divorce.*
> *There is no happiness in love.*

Vincent: Are you just showing off how much you know?

Pauline: I know that too! I've heard it on the radio! It's by Georges Brassens! *[She begins singing too]* Life is a strange . . .

Alberte (calmly): It is by the poet Aragon. Brassens is just the singer.

Pauline: I like singers the best! Singers are much more fun! *[She begins jazzing up the song]* Life is a strange . . .

Alberte (indignant): It's not fun at all! It's a very sad poem! [*Very feelingly*] Life is a strange and agonized divorce . . . It's *sad*!

Pauline: Does it mean that if you're happy and love each other, then afterwards you always get divorced?

Vincent: Of course not! It's a manner of speaking, an image, you know, a . . .

Pauline (radiantly): A supposition!

[Vincent bursts out laughing. Alberte is rather put out that her favorite poet should be made the subject of jokes.]

Me: I think that what it means is just what we're talking about: that one is always divided between this need, this vocation of joy, and an awareness of other people's unhappiness . . .

Vincent (erudite): Torn apart. Like Ravaillac. [*Then to Pauline, who is opening her mouth*] Ravaillac tried to kill a king, so they tied him to two horses and he was torn apart. And it's history, not a supposition.

Me (gratefully): Yes, torn apart. That's it.

Alberte: And you're going to explain what to do about it, in your book?

Me: I'd certainly like to, but I haven't decided what to do about it myself yet.

Pauline: Then what will be the use of your book?

Me: You can never be very sure what use a book will be. Sometimes I've tried to write a book that I myself found very comforting, and then people have said to me: "How depressing your book is."

Pauline: It's not worth writing books just to depress people.

Vincent: I don't agree. It's not worth writing a book if it means writing lies.

Pauline: Enjoying yourself is not a lie.

Me: It's not a lie, but it's sometimes only one aspect of life. It would be a lie, too, never to talk about joy, of course.

Alberte: In other words, everything is always mixed up together?

Me: Yes, you could say that.

Vincent: The wheat and the tares.

Me: If you like.

Pauline: You oughtn't to worry about all that, Maman. You ought to write a detective story with a happy ending. Then everyone would be happy.

Alberte (deeply shocked at such cultural heresy): Oh, no!

Vincent: Not if she doesn't want to!

Me: But I would like to. I've thought about it sometimes. I used to think it would be a sort of rest for me. I wanted to have a woman detective, very nice and gay, with freckles, who kept on making awful mistakes and only hit upon the truth by chance. She would have just had a disappointment in love, and that's why she's become a detective. To forget.

Pauline: She's just had a disappointment in love and she's very gay?

Me: Yes, because she has a sunny disposition. Her fiancé left her for her best friend, so she investigates to find out exactly what happened, and she discovers she'd make a good detective.

Alberte: So then her fiancé comes back to her?

Me: No.

Alberte: Why not?

Me: Because then she'd be happy and she wouldn't start any more investigations.

Pauline: And if you were happy, wouldn't you write any more books?

[I am too taken aback to answer.]

Alberte (indignantly): She *is* happy.

Vincent: She's almost happy, but you can't be completely happy, so the bit that is missing is the bit that makes her write books.

Me (relieved): Brilliant. Though I'm not sure that you shouldn't say a bit extra, not a bit missing.

Vincent: Extra, on top of happiness?

Me: What I mean is, the idea that happiness isn't enough. Extra in that way.

Pauline (feeling these speculations have gone on long enough): You keep saying "I'm not sure if . . ." Don't you know anything, then?

Alberte (laughing): It's like her woman detective. The woman detective only finds out the truth by chance.

Me: But she does find it out.

Vincent: But she doesn't deserve to, does she?

Me: Must we always deserve things?

Vincent: But what if the chance didn't come?

Me: Oh, chance always comes.

Pauline: What's chance? Is it books?

Me: Absolutely. For me, chance happens to be books.